Wedding Preparation for Eternity:

A Woman's Search for True Love

Karen Masood

Wedding Preparation for Eternity:
A Woman's Search for True Love

Copyright © 2016, Karen Masood

Published by ITL-USA, Jesus to Muslims, Inc.,
P.O. Box 1555, Summerfield, FL 34492.
www.Jesustomuslims.org

ISBN: 978-1-5323-0750-8

While the author has made every effort to provide accurate Internet addresses at the time of publication, neither the publisher nor the author assumes any responsibility for errors or changes that occur after publication.

Cover design by David Lanham

Printed in the United States of America

To the Daughters of Eve
in search of love
I know how you feel

Contents

Contents

Contents

Prelude

Every movie that deeply touches our hearts ends with "and they lived happily ever after." This book is written to women who are looking for that one true love of your life that will love you for who you are forever, whether you believe it to be possible or not.

The Sound of Music is one of my favorite movies. So many love stories have been hits, and I am sure you have your own favorite love story. But with a divorce rate of over fifty percent in this nation, I gather that most women are looking for love in all the wrong places. They really want to know why the search seems to always leave one feeling so empty. I once felt that way myself.

Along my journey, I have discovered that the greatest love story ever told is God's love story written in the Bible of His divine love for His human creation. Following that example, out of a sincere love for all women, I felt led to reach out to all who would listen and are sincerely seeking truth about love. I would like to share what I found is required to find the love of your life and experience the peace and joy of your true destiny.

It is my heart's desire that through my story you will see how important it is to seek your Creator to discover why He has created you, and then to obey God, waiting upon Him for your own true love story. The joy, peace, and freedom I have in this everlasting love are not just a fairy tale; it is what I desire for you to have, as God wills it:

"The Lord hath appeared of old unto me, saying, Yea, I have loved thee with an everlasting love: therefore with loving kindness have I drawn thee" (Jeremiah 31:3).

"Peace I leave with you; My peace I give to you; not as the world gives do I give to you. Let not your heart be troubled, neither let it be afraid" (John 14:27).

Sadly, like so many children in the past few generations in America, I have not been raised up in the way we should go according to the

Bible, as God had perfectly planned for His children. This sin of parents against God in American culture has grown rapidly since the rebellion of the sixties and quite possibly even earlier. The consequences have resulted in more divorces and unhealthy relationships in America since its Christian foundation and justified in being called "modern culture."

These results characterize the prophecies of the "end of the age" in Scripture being as "in the days of Noah." Rebellion is a generational curse that needs to be broken so healing can take place and true freedom be experienced.

As a woman, I know that in the deepest part of our souls we all truly desire to be loved: by family, friends, and by a wonderful man as well. In addition to having a purpose in life, God created us with the deep need to be loved. God is love (1 John 4:8) and we are created in His image. We are all looking for someone to understand us and be our closest intimate friend. That missing link is our greatest need and I submit to you that the perfect love we yearn for is God, first and foremost, for His love is perfect.

God wants us to be His friend, just as Abraham was known as a friend of God (Genesis 15:6; Romans 4:3; Isaiah 41:8; James 2:23). God is the only one who can love us in the way we yearn to be loved. God knows us so intimately; He knows what we need the most! We need Jesus, who is waiting for us to ask Him to come into our hearts and fill that emptiness with His perfect love! For perfect love casts out fear.

We, all like sheep have gone astray, each of us has gone our own way... (Isaiah 53:6). I wandered in the wilderness for 35 years before coming back to my Creator, willing to surrender my all to Him.

You probably keep your eyes peeled even now, looking for "the one" as I did most of my life. As a single woman desiring marriage, one tends to notice every good-looking man, stealing a glance at his left hand to see if he is married or not. In anticipation, one hopes that he (if single) will eventually ask for a date. Ladies, I have been through this agonizing process. Today I realize the truth was that I was desperate. Desperately seeking is also addicting and never truly satisfies. Most often when we are in this addiction we don't see it.

I have learned that the two most important decisions every person will make in this lifetime are accepting Jesus as our Savior and

Lord, and deciding who we will marry. In this matter I have learned the hard way how important it is to simply trust in God and follow His way instead of the world's way or culture!

This book will use my testimony of God directing my marriage to show you how God prepares His bride for Jesus, the Bridegroom. He draws us, wooing us to Himself ever so gently, being the gentleman He is. It is just like God to take the most "unlikely" candidates to become His pure unblemished Bride.

Our Father in heaven knows our beauty on the inside while man sees only beauty on the outside (1 Samuel 16:7). God provides the gown of beauty and righteousness, covered with jewels and majesty, to be worn by His Bride as He prepares her for the marriage supper in eternity. We must allow God to prepare us. He beckons us "Come, oh women of Jerusalem, come to the marriage supper prepared for you."

The condition of the church today weighs heavily on my heart, especially for its naivety. I have written this book especially for women who call themselves "Christians" and all women who are seeking to find TRUTH, no matter where that truth might lead them—even if it means they must live differently and change things that might be dear to them.

My deepest heart compassion is to set female captives free from the darkness and bondage of Satan's lies. I share my heart with you in the following pages and invite you to dare to come on a journey through my story so you too can find love everlasting.

Introduction

Almost every woman who has heard my husband's testimony or read his autobiography, *Into the Light: A Young Muslim Searching for the Truth*, asks me, "How did you meet this man?" They see God's miraculous intervention in my husband's life and notice something spectacular in our relationship that causes them to want to know "How can I get that too?" I so often hear "You two are perfect together!"

I realize that this question is not about me. There is nothing special in me that urged God to send me this man for marriage. My past life is full of disobedience, rebellion, and worldly ways that deserve nothing but punishment from a righteous God. However, I know that the day the Lord delivered me from the dysfunctional brokenness of my past was the same day that I became completely submissive to Him. It was only then that I wanted with every desire in my heart to only want God's way and not my way, Karen's way. It was only then that I chose to give up control and lay my life down for Jesus by dying to self.

My friend, out of sincere love for you, my greatest desire is to save you from needless heartache and pain that only the devil desires for you, through "the word of my testimony" in this book. Beloved, that defining moment for you, as it was for me, will be when Jesus is all you need for only He knows all you need. Only He truly knows who you are for He is your Creator and has known you since before the foundations of the earth.

Small Town American Gal Marries a Tribal Boy

This is the story of how God orchestrated a "true love story" bringing together two people, Steven and me, who lived over 8,000 miles apart! He did it all according to His marvelous plan. All we had to do was listen to Him and be obedient. A true love story can happen to you, too, if you listen to God's still small voice and choose to be obedient to His will and plan for your life instead of following your own will.

It sounds like a headline in a newspaper, doesn't it? As a matter of fact, this is the story of a small town (population 500) girl from the east, Maine, who married a tribal boy from the east, the northern frontier region of Pakistan near where Bin Laden was found. One thing they have in common is that Jesus is their Lord and Savior; they both worship the same God: the God of Abraham, Isaac, and Jacob, Almighty God of the Universe, the Jehovah God of Israel, the Creator of all! The other commonality is both were willing to ask why and seek truth wherever it led them.

In God's bigger picture, He was bringing Steven, His servant from the Eastern culture to the Western culture in order to equip others to understand Biblical Eastern culture. Today, the ministry *Jesus to Muslims*, in God's bigger picture, is here to equip Christians and reach Muslims with the Gospel. A great migration of Muslims to the West is taking place. Yes, they may have their agenda but God too has an agenda that they may know Jesus, the Savior (Acts 17:26). God is at work and He is allowing more and more Muslims reside in the USA for refuge, just as He sent Jews to America for refuge.

"For I know the plans I have for you," declares the Lord, "plans to prosper you and not to harm you, plans to give you hope and a future."- Jeremiah 29:11

Every day, as Steven and I open our eyes waking up to a new God-given day to be His ambassadors, we pray together and thank God once again for allowing us one more day together in His Name—to worship Him in our prayers and praise, and to live another day for His glory, serving Him in the plan He has for us.

We thank God for this free nation, the USA, which still allows us to live for Him without persecution as of yet. We thank God for our daily bread. God is so good and full of mercy! We pray that He uses us every day to be light in this dark world around us so that another lost soul may know Christ!

We want to encourage you, our sisters in Christ, to walk closer in fellowship with Jesus, so to know the glorious plan He has for you! I promise you His plan for you is divine and beyond your human

15

understanding. We thank the Lord for uniting us in marriage. Together, we seek to honor Christ alone in all we do!

The Lord has ordained marriage between one man and one woman as a picture of His bride preparing for the pure and righteous bridegroom, Jesus! He is coming soon to take his purified bride, who is the remnant body of Christ, home! God is preparing and refining us by fire day by day to be ready for our soon coming King and Savior!

When I married the man who has been my husband for over ten years, I asked myself, "Why me? Why has God sent this incredible man into my life for 'such a time as this'?" (Esther 4:14) I believe that the reason is tied to my surrendering my life entirely to the Lord to use any way He wants to. After I had totally died to my flesh and my worldly ideas of what I thought my life should be like, God blessed me beyond my own human understanding!

God's waiting with open arms to take us on the journey that He alone knows is perfect for each one of us! I want to share with you my testimony to give you hope! I testify to you the truth; that all things are possible through Christ who strengthens you. If you are in a broken situation, I've been where you are now, but God saved me from my hopeless situations, the pains of my past, my sins, my mistakes, and all my failed relationships! God took this broken clay pot and molded it to become a treasure.

The Hiding Place by Corrie Ten Boom illustrates how God's love knows no bounds. Corrie Ten Boom's sister, Betsey, coined the phrase, "There is no pit deeper that God is not deeper still" when they were in a concentration camp in Germany for hiding Jews from the Nazis.

In my testimony, some of the names have been changed out of respect for the mentioned people's privacy and in a few cases, for their security. The law of apostasy in Islam has been taken into consideration to protect all those it may affect.

1

Childhood

Crying to a God I Didn't yet Personally Know

I was born in a small rural town of five-hundred people, with one small gas station, in the state of Maine. I have come to learn it is the rural life that most new parents feel is best for children to grow up in so they can run and play freely with few restrictions as found in a city. I have grown to appreciate that in my older age after living in the city long enough.

I loved playing outdoors and playing with other children. I would play games with the neighborhood kids, like 'red light', 'Simon says', hopscotch, and tag. We would ride bikes, play house along the river and in the woods, fish, and run in the fields with the dog. (We always had dogs.) We played sports, like touch football and other competitive sports, with the neighbor kids. In the winter, we loved to slide down the hills in the fields and the snow banks created by bulldozers. I also loved to read, listen to music and dance in my room as I dreamed of beautiful things that would be. Using my fiery and boundless imagination, I could get carried away in my imaginary world.

As far back as I can remember, my brothers and I would fight and argue a lot, especially my oldest brother who was a year and four months younger than me. He used to get under my freckled skin like no one's business. So often he bullied me, picking at my scabs something terrible! My middle brother had the most love for me and listened to me compassionately. He tended to make light of things and joked a lot to divert me from the pain.

I remember changing my youngest brother's diapers and caring for him when he was a baby. My mother had promised me that he was going to be a girl. I wanted a sister so badly. I had this life sized walking doll called Susie Smart. Maybe my fashion sense began then when I saw how perfectly her dress would fit on my brother! And so it was! I love you, my baby brother, and I'm really sorry if I gave you a complex. Please forgive me for sharing this funny story!

As the oldest of four, I remember early in my childhood when many nights I would lay awake, hearing bitter fights between my parents downstairs. Most often my father was drunk, when yelling terrible, ugly words at my mother. I could hear sounds that duplicated throwing things or moving furniture, and maybe even hitting her, while Mom screamed and cried at the same time.

I believe this was why I was known by my parents, especially by my mother, as "a child who cried way too much" because of their unhealthy marriage. It must have been hard to focus on sorting out their fights while a baby cried around them. I have come to understand this was not God's intention but rather He desires for all of us to live in peace.

To be the best example for daughters, it is very important for fathers to truly love their wives, treating them with respect and kindness. As girls, we observe how adult men treat adult women, for this treatment is what we mimic in our own lives. It is important for us to see unconditional love and caring, modeled daily by our parents to each other, as well as to us. This is how a young girl learns God's best for her when she grows up. She deserves a man with Godly character who loves her so much he would be willing to lay his life down for her (Ephesians 5:25).

While hearing the fights, I would pray to God, a God I did not yet know, in fear for my mother's life. I always asked Him to help her and protect her from my dad. I now know that God heard my cries to Him, even then as a scared little girl as well as throughout my life. Somehow, I just knew that He was always there to talk to about anything. Yet, I really never got to know Him personally until much, much later in life. Being the talkative person I am, I talked to Him a lot but did not understand how to listen to God!

I felt more peace just knowing God was with me, whoever He was. After all, my mother told me that my first words were "See the light!" Considering where life would take me, I see that as prophetic. Somehow, I just had this childlike faith from the start. It was as if God saw me in "captivity" and hade His plan to rescue me.

Jesus said in Matthew 19:14: "Let the little children come to me and do not hinder them, for the kingdom of heaven belongs to such as these." Jesus came to set the captives free (Luke 4:18), including the little ones! How gentle the Father's love is as He comforts the little children, holding them in His loving arms to protect them in the midst of the chaotic sin that rebellious adults choose for themselves.

It saddens me even now as I think of the brokenness, the pain, and the bondage my parents must have suffered over the years. I have seen the results, even to this day, in my family; who isn't speaking to who and who is gossiping about whom. There are so many hidden thoughts toward each other and never truly knowing where you stand with each other. Please pray with me for healing and deliverance from the grip of Satan in my family.

The Human Need for Love

Every child is born with the deep need for love and the profound need for significance. Since God made us all in His image, and God is love, our greatest need is love. This most desperate need for love is for that "perfect love" that humans are incapable of giving, because this kind of love comes only from God, our Creator, who knows us and loves us unconditionally.

It is extremely important for the well-being and health of a child that he or she at the very least knows the love of God, our perfect Father in Heaven. Throughout our lives, we need to know that we are lovingly and gently held in His everlasting arms (Isaiah 40:11). God is our refuge and our fortress (Psalm 91:2). Yes, we must know to look outside our borders to find strength and courage beyond what is given to us on this earth. God, our Creator, is outside these earthly borders.

As human beings, we go on the "quest for love" from the time we are born until the time we die. We first seek this love in other humans. As babies, we hold on primarily to our parents. Children become rebellious if their relationships with their parents are broken, and will then lash out in different kinds of ways, as I experienced. Both lashing out and holding the pain inside are destructive.

As we grow, we hold on to our friends, our feelings, and our ways. We may even hold on to money or a career or fame. Eventually, and in many cases, a woman tries to hold on to a man. If we women have not yet truly learned that we are to hold on to Jesus first, then we will strive to hold on to any of the above as a replacement. If those people or feelings or ways of ours fail us (and they will), we naturally look to blame someone else or ourselves for the failure, rather than recognizing that true unconditional love and our worth come to us only from God. From the beginning, even Adam blamed Eve and Eve blamed the serpent.

If honest, every human being finds while searching deep inside ourselves, that we are all seeking to be truly loved for who we are. Not experiencing true love is naturally painful in our hearts. Sadly, so many people try to ignore the pain or push it aside, but it eventually comes out in our speech as we seek to hide that deep-rooted pain of offense and un-forgiveness. Many times we get angry at anyone who may expose that deep-rooted unresolved pain.

As adults, we will seek to find that love we so desperately need either in the world or we will seek to find it in God. When enough human beings disappoint us, we continue that quest in our work, in a hobby, in computers, in addictions: in anything that Satan can present that tempts us (to feed our lust of the flesh and keep us from God), as his quest is to destroy all humans along with him. Because of this, we need to honestly look inside ourselves to see where our priorities have been mixed up and then put them in order, with God being first.

We have an empty space in our hearts that can only be filled by our Perfect Loving Father in Heaven through Christ Jesus. He will lead us to what is good for us, so that we can live forever with Him. We need to hold on to Him! The words to the Twila Paris song "Hold On" inspire me and teach this important truth of how crucial it is to hold on to Jesus. In this song, she sings about how we try to hold on to fame, money, sorrow, pain and anger, but our only hope is to truly and unequivocally "Hold on to Jesus!" She expresses how every little baby comes into the world reaching for an anchor without knowing why and clinging to anything until the day we die.

Yes, we may even hold on to our broken unrepentant parents which comes naturally from the time we are born, even if they are an alcoholic, drug addict or a murderer. It is when we are young and vulnerable when a parent can even brainwash us with lies. That is how a Muslim child can grow up believing that killing for Allah is right and radical Islamic parents take advantage of teaching these wicked things to their young while believing it is the true way to please god.

A Place of Refuge and Comfort

My mother used to tell me that I cried more than any child she knew. Bringing me to Nana (her mom, my grandmother) seemed to calm me. Somehow, I always felt peace and joy around my Nana. I believe my parents' insecurity about their own love for each other in their marriage manifested itself in a very insecure love that I felt from both of them. Perhaps this caused me to cry excessively, because two angry arguing parents were not meeting my deep need for sincere love.

I was born in 1958 during an error of rebelliousness in this nation. Being popular with people who were all pressing toward rebellion couldn't have helped our family at all. As the eldest and only girl with three brothers, my parents relied on me to help around the house. I praise God for Nana, my loving grandmother, who prayed for us. She was always there for me when I just had to escape the chaos of conflict in our house with my brothers constantly fighting or tormenting me. As I see it, my Nana was the one God used to rescue me from the troubles at home, giving me His way out of my harmful and negative environment.

As I reminisce, pleasant memories come back to me: sweet, sweet memories of my Nana and me sitting out in the backyard of her little cottage on a little pond. I think of the two of us sitting there, looking out over the water and appreciating the beautiful blue *Morning Glories* crawling down the rounded banking that slid to the water. I loved that place more than anywhere else! I planted these flowers in my front garden last year to remember Nana again. Oh how beautiful their faces radiate in the sunlight daily yet by nightfall they wither. I see how this scenario simulates how we human faces glow in the light of Jesus but wither and die in the darkness of Satan.

While writing, I am sitting on a deck overlooking glistening water sparkling with joy! The creatures enjoy the bright new day and the lovely breeze. The dryness here due to no rain for about a month caused many forest fires this year. In God's mercy and as an answer to all of our prayers, He sent rain by the buckets the previous night. The smell of the smoke that had been lingering around for days in this area has now subsided. Although there seems to be a slight haze over the trees on the other shore across the water, the air smells fresh after the new rain! The frogs woke us up early in the morning, singing happily in celebration! One certain green frog even came to our window, calling loudly for us to get up. We both popped out of bed with such a startle, apparently thinking he was surely in our bed!

As I look out here, the size of the lake, the style of the houses across the lake, and the protruding docks all remind me of sitting with my Nana in those days of my childhood, just talking away the time. I learned to dive off their dock and swim in that pond by the time I was one year old. In those days, my grandfather would give us rides in his small fishing motorboat.

My grandparents had retired to this cottage from the big house in which they raised their four kids. It was a small cottage, a dark brown log cabin with red window trim, red flower boxes under the bay windows, and red doors in the front and back. My grandfather was "red paint happy." He had painted all the kitchen cupboard doors and counter top as well with shiny red paint! He even painted his worn out sneakers red!

I remember how Nana and I used to talk together there, admiring God's creation. I miss her so much right now. I can see her smiling face and her curly hair with the wisps of gray, though all the rest of her hair was brown. She never appeared old, except in the wrinkles that accumulated on her neck, face, and hands. She was always joyful and found the best in everything! She had a remarkable way of teaching me to see the good in everything." She spoke the truth in the most loving way.

Nana and I had a special connection. I just loved being with her! We would sit there talking, until we had to go in to "make

Grandpa's lunch" as she would say, though we all participated in the eating of it! Cooking was her daily duty that she seemed to enjoy the most. She taught me a lot about cooking; I still love cooking and entertaining today! There was just one thing I never seemed to be able to master: making piecrust for pies. Nana always made a fresh pie, almost every morning. By 7:30 in the morning, she had completed one or two pies (if she was making a pie for other people as well). She would tell me over and over how much housework she had finished as well as her breakfast and dishes by then, too! She would make for me my favorite pies: apple, pineapple cream and strawberry rhubarb.

I believe my Nana's prayers for me, the "prayers of the righteous," kept her living until she was one month short of 100 years old, just so she saw God had answered them before she left this earth to be with her Heavenly Father. As the Bible says, the prayers of the righteous "availeth much" (James 5:16). She spoke into my life regularly and I just know she prayed for me daily. She passed from this life very peacefully. She knew exactly where she was going, even though she sometimes questioned why God kept her here to such an old age.

I praise God for sending my husband at the time He did, so that my Nana got to meet and know Steven. When she passed on, Steven was able to comfort me in my loss of her. It was, by far, my most difficult loss I have ever experienced. But I am assured I will see her again in Heaven one day soon! I look forward to that day!

My Nana hardly ever missed church in her 74 year membership of her Congregational Church and was always involved with community outreach and ladies' church groups. She was a member of the Dorcas Society for 60 years, a benefit for churches and charities in her area. She was also a regular performer in the 'The old Peabody Pew' play inspired by Kate Douglas Wiggin's 1907 novel, the founder of the Dorcas Society.

I found it fascinating to learn that one of the books Wiggin's wrote is *Rebecca of Sunnybrook Farm*, a children's book, and Shirley Temple performed that story on stage in 1938. Wiggins was born in Maine and was known to my grandparents. Shirley Temple was one of my favorite shows as a kid, along with *I Love Lucy* and I still prefer both over most shows today.

23

Nana was the one person with whom I loved to spend time, as she would teach me how to sew, cook, and clean. I always felt her unconditional love in the way she talked to me and listened to me. She treated me with kindness and patience. As I think of Nana, I think of God's grace as I have come to know His grace. As I learned later in life, just as the Word of God teaches us, God's grace is sufficient (2 Corinthians 12:9).

Interestingly, the Hebrew meaning of Lillian, my Nana's name, is "my God is a vow." I thank God today that she not only prayed a lifetime for her grandchildren, but also managed to convince my parents to drop us off at church weekly, even though they didn't go. My mother told me that they saw that time of our absence from home as "time alone" for them.

Looking back, it seems that my parents used the church as a free childcare service. It is just so sad to me, as I think about it today, realizing how much more beneficial it would have been for the whole family if my parents also went to church. They needed Biblical guidance for their marriage as well as to learn how to bring up their children in the way they should go and have more Godly friends encouraging them toward God's ways.

My Childhood Environment and Temperament
Today, I understand that without God as the very foundation of a family, addictions, including alcoholism and the chaos around it, are all considered normal in today's American culture. Since alcohol was a regular part of life in our house and it can make one really moody, I now see and have experienced for myself that this was a cause for so many ups and downs and flying emotions in our home.

My perception is that my deep sensitivities, along with all of my insecurities, all the chaos, alcoholism, my parents' problems in their marriage, their yelling and the fears invoked in me, made my childhood dysfunctional. None of this is the love God intended for a child. My fears were manifested by a lack of security and very conditional love: "If you do this, then I will do that."
My parents disciplined with fear and intimidation in loud voices and threats to control us but rarely asked us to discuss why we did what we did. Whatever didn't line up with their agenda or their worldview

was not open for discussion. Hitting us was a regular part of that discipline. I remember thinking 'Why?' a lot but learned if I dare ask, the consequences would result in more anger. Rage and anger are one way to control people, including children. It is very unhealthy, leading to fear rather than freedom to be who God created us to be. It was evident that it would take no ordinary human being to be enough to help me heal from this kind of childhood trauma, especially being as sensitive as I am. Only Jesus could heal me and set me free from it all.

In my temperament studies, I have learned that as children, we all learn how to deal with our environments in different ways. Some learn to tip-toe around so as not to "upset the apple cart." Others learn to manipulate. Others just disappear, hiding in fear. Some try to smooth things out with a sense of humor. A few take all the blame and try to kill themselves or go into a deep depression. Still others run away or get into trouble outside the home in order to get attention, for someone to listen to them. We are all looking to be understood and it is extremely painful to feel we are not. Some lash out through crying and the gushing of emotion, in fear, anger, and frustration—like me.

I most often felt unloved by my parents as I grew up. Don't get me wrong. I do believe my parents tried to love all four of us children as well as they were humanly able. I know their hearts were sincere in their own right. However, I have learned since then that without God's help, none of us know how to face all the trials of life and truly love one another, especially those with a deeper need for more love than most.

I could always feel the tremendous amount of tension in attitudes and clearly read voice inflections. I learned to read body language so to try to keep myself safely out of the way when they were upset or angry. Because my parents didn't love God first and didn't even know how to love themselves before trying to love each other or others, there was certainly not enough love for me and my highly sensitive nature. I rarely felt like they understood me so most often I did not feel listened to or valued.

I felt so much like an orphan in my heart. I will give you an example about what I mean by feeling like an orphan. So often after being reprimanded by my parents, I felt alone and so misunderstood, with no audience to plead my case. I used to go crying while running all the way to my room to be alone. There I would start talking to myself or to a God that I did not know at all. I would cry out, reasoning in my heart and mind, "I was just telling the truth! Why do they continue to accuse me of lying when it is them, my brothers mostly, who are lying? Please help me! God help me! Why am I the one who is the problem? What did I do? I only told the truth so why am I the one being yelled at and blamed for what I didn't do? How can I stand against them? They are all so mean to me. I can't take this! I can't take this anymore! What is wrong with me? Help me God!"

My parents did not understand the personality type that I was created with: Sanguine. A Sanguine (in the areas of affection, inclusion, and control) is a person with a profound need for unconditional love and deep, intense expression. That is how God made me to be. God has known us since before the foundation of the earth and assures us in Psalm 139 that we are fearfully and wonderfully made. As the perfect God and Creator, He has a purpose for every one of our unique temperaments.

I believe all babies are born with qualities designed to teach their parents lessons to grow and become all God intends them to be. Yes, even if a child is born deformed or with a disease, all babies are intended by God to live for that lesson to be taught through them. I have come to understand that no man has a right to decide life or death of a child for any reason whatsoever, for only God, our Creator, has the authority over life and death. I will discuss this life and death issue later. We all have a choice: to learn from all we are given to become better or to not learn and resent these lessons, becoming bitter.

This Sanguine temperament combination is the most unique in the world and is also the most misunderstood. Yet, it mirrors the light and love of Jesus, because a Sanguine also has much love to give out to people as well and sensitive to other's needs. This I began to learn in my late forties, in Temperament Counseling training. I actually gain more energy to love by being around lots of people! I am also highly sensitive to people's moods in sensing when there is a problem in their life. I can usually tell when someone does not like or understand me.

Now I realize that in a Sanguine, this great need for love and the ability to love must first be found in our Perfect Father, God, in order to benefit the world and to be healed of the pain of the past. My need for love was so deep that only God and His true followers could possibly fulfill my profound need for attention and acceptance. Yet, without the protection of this deep love, Satan can easily tempt a Sanguine with a counterfeit love for a long period of time. Being addicted to and reckless over Jesus protects our love from being exploited by Satan.

Passionate love is immensely valuable for the Bride. God is love and men need this love to help mold them for God's purpose of leadership. Passionate love is God's greatest requirement in order to love His people into the body of Christ, for perfect love casts out all fear (1 John 4:18). How else can we also love our enemies?

The Voice of the Lord

As a creative, visual person, by the time I was eight years old, I began thinking about creating outfits for myself. I had the natural ability to see the big picture beforehand. My mom gave me old sheets on which to practice. One day, I sat on the floor of my room and used my own nightgown as a pattern, and began creating my own style of a nightdress out of a sheet. I used a needle and thread and sewed it by hand. Sewing became a very favorite skill that I learned. I enjoyed seeing it through to its finished product.

It was on one of those days of designing, while sitting on my bedroom floor, that I remember clearly hearing the voice of the Lord speaking to me, telling me, "You are chosen." I remember feeling a very special feeling of warmth and presence. Just knowing that God was always there to hear me as I talked to Him constantly was such a comfort.

This is when, in my "visionary gifting," I began seeing clothing creations in my mind. I was able to see this entire garment in advance. I cut it out and just knew how to sew it together by hand, including pink trim in the design. I loved sewing and creating new fashion styles. That kept me focused and I enjoyed every minute of it. My Nana's love and encouragement in this design and sewing talent also encouraged me to pursue it.

Remember, I was still being dropped off at the local church most every weekend. I remember finding great joy there in learning and knowing that Jesus loved me and all the little children of the world, causing me to feel more validated. For this reason, I wanted to go to church regularly and learn more about Jesus' love for me. I even earned pins for perfect attendance.

Family Life

Being the eldest child and the only girl gave me the privilege of having my own room. I loved to sing and dance and look in the mirror, "performing." My mother often commented that I should become an actress someday. I think there was something about her desire for me that was truly a desire for herself to have been an actress. She still seems to idolize actors/actresses today. She watched a lot of soap operas and read a lot of "love stories" and still does. As children, we would sometimes find her crying over them when we got home from school.

If only she realized that Satan was leading her into his own road of temptation to just another addiction, seeking to find true love in their 'love' stories so to fulfill her deep need for real true love. Satan's goal was only to keep her engrossed and far away from getting to know God's true love for her. She could only find and know the truth about His perfect love through studying His Word.

My favorite times with my mom were when she would play the piano and I would sing with her. That was a time I could feel and see her joy. We usually sang church hymns like "The Old Rugged Cross" and "The Saints Go Marching In." Music is such a beautiful gift and what a great way to feel joy and find peace with God. I just love music and singing as well. For years I wondered why Mom knew these songs by heart, yet she never went to church with her kids. It was just recently I discovered how my father lured her away with the idea that church time would become "alone time" for them.

Her justification she verbalized to me many years later was that I could not know how hard it was to raise four children. If only she could see that without Christ nothing is possible and that only Christ could give her that strength to raise up her children in the way they should go. Only Christ could give her the fruits of the Spirit to help her with love, joy, peace, long suffering, gentleness, goodness, faith, meekness & patience. (Gal 5:22-23)

Although she so angrily tells me she is 'saved already and is a good enough person to get to heaven', I rarely see the joy of the Lord in her face or eyes. It reminds me of the parable of the sower in

28

Matthew 13:3-7. Sadly, what my mother had learned in Sunday school was not enough to make her hunger and thirst after righteousness, especially when it came to her love life. Her man became much more important to please than Jesus. I would eventually carry on that generational sin for years myself.

I remember playing with Barbie and Ken dolls for most of my childhood and dreaming about what it would be like to be married. Imagining how I would dress and how my husband would dress was intriguing to me. I liked spending my allowance on doll clothes and creating a home-like environment for them in my room, as well as out in the woods and on the banks of a frog pond near our home.

Sometimes I would play dolls with girlfriends from school or church. However, I don't really remember my mom playing dolls with me. I was mostly left to play dolls on my own or with my girlfriend in the neighborhood, who was my mom's best friend's daughter.

My parents enjoyed sports and outdoor activities; their children followed in their footsteps. We were always busy and anytime we could be dropped off, it was usually welcomed by my parents. We played baseball, softball, basketball, and various other sports. Our parents never missed going to our games. My mom coached the girls' softball team on which I played shortstop. She chauffeured me to other activities, such as baton lessons, 4-H, Girl Scouts, as well as youth cheerleading for the basketball team. I am still so grateful to her for being there in them as I so enjoyed them all.

I was taught how to do chores around the house and expected to do them every Saturday as part of being responsible. In addition to our Saturday chores, on weekends we participated in family events. My parents were very proud of the "family life" they organized, which included the whole family spending time together on the weekends doing activities such as snowmobiling, waterskiing, camping, beach picnics, as well as playing pool, ping pong, and board games. I clearly recollect our family time being important to me. While I have fond memories of loving sports, it always included booze for my parents, as did every activity we did as a family, especially when other friends or Dad's relatives were included.

The Trouble with Alcohol

We were told that alcohol was for adults only. The adults' drinking alcohol meant there was always a lot of high competition and it could get brutal, with arguments, jealousy, and accusations of cheating. Peace and respect for one another was rare, but sadly most American families consider this as typical.

As my brothers and I learned through the example of our parents, it always seemed to be the booze that adults turned to in order to "ease the stress" caused by life's difficulties and the troubles at work. I believe many people try to mask problems in life with alcohol. It was later in my own life that I realized this is a worldly remedy that today's society promotes. In my early adult years, I learned that although it tends to subdue pain until sober again, it does not make the problems go away. Maturity in confronting and overcoming problems and learning how to communicate, even if two people disagree, was never learned but sadly evaded over and over.

My parents had many alcohol-induced fights. The effects of the alcohol tended to peak in the evening. Many times, my brothers and I also experienced our Dad's drunken anger. The older I grew, becoming more aware of my surroundings and observing more of what went on around me, I noticed that the more my father drank, the angrier he got at us kids. The more he yelled, the less he tried to understand us. Communication was broken and rage seemed to be the way to resolve problems as the final authority of intimidation was, "Because I said so!"

I gradually began to recognize that my Nana didn't drink. She was much more peaceful than anyone else on both sides of our family. I looked to be with my Nana as much as possible because I felt her peace and unconditional love toward me. I felt more loved by Nana than anyone else in my own immediate family. Love, time and attention were what I specifically seemed to need and she so willingly gave it!

Reflections on Parenthood

While my parents might have meant well in their hearts and tried to raise their children "better" than they thought their own parents did, the Bible actually teaches that we, in our own efforts, can do nothing without God's help. It is actually impossible for parents to raise their children well in their own strength and with their own fleshly efforts, ideas, and human rationale. Parents need God's intervention! God's thoughts and ways are higher than our thoughts (Isaiah 55:8-9).

Jesus loves the little children and calls them to Him (Matthew 19:14)! God has entrusted parents with their children to "raise them up in the way they should go" (Proverbs 22:6) —according to the Word of God. God Himself will hold every parent accountable for this crucial responsibility. Clear Bible teaching is vital and our church leaders will also be held accountable for that.

Parents are to know the Word of God and model Jesus' teachings in their lives. If a parent is commanding a child to do things that are directly against the Word of God and the child has learned right from wrong according to God's Word, then the child's pastor should be involved in helping the innocent child to stand for truth. This includes helping the parents learn the Bible and the importance of obeying God. Discipleship, as the Bible teaches us, is to "go and make disciples" (Matthew 28:19).

Parents with bad boundaries produce children with bad boundaries. My parents did not understand that. If only my parents would have been willing to go to church and read their Bible (that was in the house and sometimes in the hands of their own children) to learn what God had for them, that would have given them a fulfilling life and helped them raise their kids well and be good parents.

I recently learned from my mother what she claims to have turned her away from the church. My Baptist preacher where I went told her, "Only Baptists are going to Heaven."

Well, while we as Christians make mistakes, we still need to keep our eyes on Jesus Christ! The unconditional love of God does not force anyone to love Him and choose His way. He gives us all free choice. God is the "perfect gentleman" and truly desires that we willingly choose Him and love Him of our own free will. It pleases God when we choose Him. His Spirit draws us to Him. The choices my parents made to seek their own ways included rejecting having a relationship with God through Jesus at that time. Relationships are definitely a two-way street between two people and relationship with God is no different!

Now, as an adult who has chosen in my later years to follow after God's ways rather than my own, I have learned that when my husband and I follow Christ's ways, we are blessed. I have seen other people's families, who chose to follow God's ways, have wonderful, healthy, and loving relationships with their children and grandchildren, long after their upbringing. They followed the Bible instead of their own ways. I have seen that having a strong relationship with God brings love for the whole family. The Word of God brings them closer together and their communication with one another is transparent, peaceful and respectful.

Although I never experienced this kind of communication in my family growing up, I am so thankful for God's mercy in His healing me day by day and giving me this kind of communication with others today. There is hope in the Lord and His ways. Every answer to life's dilemmas is in the Bible if we choose to seek there.

To become the Bride of Christ, God is calling His believers out of the old lifestyle and into a new lifestyle that includes reading His Word daily to learn how to handle the troubles of this world. Jesus tells us:

> "I have told you these things, so that in Me you may have [perfect] peace and confidence. In the world you have tribulation and trials and distress and frustration; but be of good cheer [take courage; be confident, certain, undaunted]! For I have overcome the world. [I have deprived it of power to harm you and have conquered it for you.]" - John 16:33 (AMP).

32

2

Teenage Years

Don't Believe the Lies

My best friend had physically developed as a young lady by the age of 8 or 9 while I didn't until I was about 15 years old. As you can imagine, the boys swarmed around her and not me, except to tease me. There were times I wished I was blonde like her, and developed, so that they would be interested in me, too. I was a redhead and got teased a lot about that. Kids at school would call me "Red" and "Carrot top."

I was also mocked for being "flat as a board and never been laid!" –boys would say. Little did I realize back then that this was God's protection over me! With all these feelings of being unloved by family and schoolmates, I deeply yearned to be loved, accepted and valued by someone. Maybe you can relate?

In looking back now, it's all so clear to me. I want to help you see it clearer. Do you believe lies about yourself because of what others from your past have said to you to demean you and elevate themselves? Lies like:

"I'm not *pretty* enough."
cool
good
smart
wanted
_____

"Alpha" (snooty – mean or bully) girls who do not love Jesus often put other girls down by transmitting these lies. Alpha girls don't rise to authority and lording over others without permission by others who don't want to get stung. To be Christ-like, we need to stand up to these pack leaders and teach them how their dominating, demeaning ways are wrong and teach them to become "other-centered" rather than "me- centered." You are better than that.

Do not fall into the trap of gossip and slander, or putting others down instead of encouraging them. Grow to be a leader with a kind heart, loving others with Jesus' love. Follow the Golden Rule (Luke 6:31). Love them even when they're mean. Eventually they will get tired of picking on you and you'll come out smelling like a rose.

How have the mean girls of the world been hurt so they in turn hurt others? I would wager a bet there is something deep rooted in them that cause them to lash out at others – especially those they deem as weaker vessels. Their meanness can make their victims feel invisible.

You are NOT invisible. When you believe the lies of those who put you down, you are letting the liars do the talking instead of receiving what God your Creator says about you. He thinks the world of you (Psalm 139:1-17).

Shoplifting

At age 13, my friend encouraged me to steal an ID bracelet at the beach wharf kiosks. I so desired to please people, especially my friend; I wanted to prove my love as well as receive her love and acceptance. We both knew that our parents would never spend that much money for one of these bracelets for us, and we didn't have boyfriends who might buy them for us.

After stealing the bracelet, I could not sleep for nights because of the conviction in my heart of doing wrong. I just tossed and turned all night long. I cried out to God for relief and tried to figure out what to do. I felt I couldn't return it, as I would have to tell my parents to take me there. I just knew that if I told my parents, they would "kill" me. Of course, not literally, but these were words passed down to me through the generations to mean that it would be really, really bad for me. I wonder if such desensitization is the reason that the literal words used by ISIS (*Da'ish*) are not being taken seriously today by the majority of Americans.

Salvation

When I went to the youth basketball game a few days later, the youth pastor shared a message of hope at the end: anyone could be forgiven of any sin by coming up front to repent and giving their heart to Jesus. The Pastor told us that Jesus would throw those sins as far as the east is from the west, and remember them no more! (Psalms 103:12) This I knew I needed. This was the answer to my guilt! This was where my help came from: Jesus! What a sweet name. I prayed to receive Jesus into my heart as my Savior that evening!

After returning home, I got that bracelet out of its hiding place. I opened my bedroom window facing the woods and threw the bracelet as far as my softball arm could throw it. I felt free of the guilt and shame from then on. I began to go to more youth events after that. Roller-skating, basketball games, and social events at the youth pastor's house or in the recreation hall over the garage and had great fun. My favorite time was going to a summer youth camp and bunking with a few girls in the dorm rooms. We did arts and crafts and went swimming and diving in the lake. This was at the Word of Life Camp on Schroon Lake in upstate NY. We learned Bible lessons during the day and memorized some verses. We sat around campfires at night, singing songs to Jesus. I really loved that!

It was at camp that I learned the song, *"What a Friend We Have in Jesus."* Deep in my soul I knew I really needed a true friend. To this day, it gets me all choked up, bringing back these precious memories. I just loved to sing and praise the Lord and talk about His love for me. I felt His love and truly felt empowered that Someone Special loved me just the way I was.

I remember feeling like I never wanted to leave there. I felt really good about being with other Christian friends, too. I remember a couple of families I enjoyed hanging out with in my youth group activities. The more I attended youth group activities and sports and developed these new friendships, the more I felt loved, and the more I wanted to spend time with those friends.

The more I learned about God, the more I noticed the way my parents were living at home behind closed doors. They associated with others who approved of their way of living: use of profanity, alcohol abuse, smoking, hostile rage toward each other, harshness in the way they disciplined their kids, gambling, and having secrets they would laugh about but not share. So often I had burning questions. Whenever I asked about these things, I was told it was none of my business. They were adults and one day we would be adults. Then, we could do what wasn't allowed for us as teens.

I remember feeling resentful about the hypocrisy I saw among the old, expecting one thing from us and doing the opposite in their own lives. We weren't allowed to lie to them, but were told to lie on the phone and tell someone they didn't want to talk to that they were not home. They could be screaming at us for no reason, yet when company arrived, their tone would immediately change, and they would treat the guests so nicely. My parents used the law to discipline their children in word but not deed.

Unless parents demonstrate the law themselves by leading by example, the children are bound to rebel against the law their parents command. If not defiantly in their face, then they will rebel behind their backs. Don't get me wrong, I really love my parents but I felt lonely, unloved, misunderstood and never really felt free to talk honestly about my feelings. I had resentment building up inside. I knew something was wrong but didn't really understand the devil was leading them down a destructive path. It would be many years before I realized they knew not what they did and learned to forgive them as Jesus taught me.

My Relationship with My Father

My father worked on submarines for the government as an air-conditioning/refrigeration mechanic. He drove 50 miles to work five days a week, driving a van of men. Many times he would come home drunk, demanding that the meal be on the table by 5:30 sharp, or else! God forbid if we went to the beach with Mom and got home later than expected.

Dad frequently expressed his desire to have received more than just a sixth grade education. Perhaps this feeling of inadequacy caused him to use words like "Are you stupid or something?" so often while yelling at us children. I remember he used it most often to my brother born after me. Sadly, these kinds of words serve only to destroy a person's value rather than build them up. I know now that

God grieves over this kind of talk and it only causes a child to seek love and value elsewhere. The truth in the Word of God speaking to fathers, says: "Do not provoke your children to anger." (Ephesians 6:4). God desires to protect the relationship between fathers and their children. His plan is for fathers to lead by example. Children yearn to imitate their parents.

I believe that America is suffering from this very problem. Men are either dominating over their family or wimping out from taking the responsibility to lead as God teaches them in His Word. Parents are not taking the time to understand each of their children and their uniqueness. Most are focusing on themselves, their careers and materialism as their gods, neglecting the family responsibilities.

Children are crying out inside to be heard, understood and valued. Over 60% of families are fatherless today and mothers are doubly burdened to do it all. Therefore, children are feeling like orphans and so look for significance in all kinds of ways.

No wonder, ISIS is taking advantage of the anger insides these teens to use it for *Jihad*. This gives the teens maturing into adulthood significance in the role to fight for a cause greater than themselves. War video games have programmed them for it. I saw this firsthand just recently when a fifteen year old boy was taken by his 'Christian' mother to a meeting that opened up with an Islam bashing video. The boy got so angry that he rose in fury screaming *'Allah Akbar'* and many more incriminating words in Arabic with perfect pronunciation. ISIS or sympathizers had clearly indoctrinated him for long hours in the past three years, as we discovered later. His parents, who never went to church nor read the Bible yet claimed to be Christians, were certainly shocked at their son's response.

In my family, we always heard about how poor we were though I never felt poor as I see poor out there today. One thing that motivated me to eventually pursue work that I enjoyed was my father telling us how much he hated his job and how he hoped we would enjoy whatever we did for a living someday.

My dad did not understand women. His parents were two peas in a pod; his mom seemed just as "manly" as his dad. They all sat around drinking booze, talking and swearing for entertainment. My cousins on dad's side drank as teens with their parents. That's just how they were with no desire to change, believing this was how to have fun in life. In their hearts, they didn't mean any harm. I remember feeling love from them, but not in the profound way I needed. I understood from my dad, their home was open and the kids could run around and do whatever they wanted both inside and outside. That's how my dad grew up. He did not know any other way. He did not know how to raise me, a girl. My father, his brothers, and my brothers were known as "manly" men.

I remember vividly at age 13, during an argument, how my dad "washed his hands of me" as he motioned with his hands while screaming those cutting words at me and looking at my mother. Then he said to her, "You discipline her and I will discipline the boys." These words put a knife through my childlike heart and caused a lifetime wound. To this day, I remember it just as clearly as if it were yesterday. I felt rejected by him and my heart was broken. From then on my dad became emotionally unavailable to me, his only daughter.

I felt like an orphan – fatherless, emotionally separated from my dad. His words brought me to my knees in bereavement. I've been left behind, fired, dumped, snubbed, and removed. My sensitivity – hopelessness – multiplied after this. So often my tender heart felt as if it had been grazed by a bullet. The pain was excruciating. As a teen, in seeing the hypocrisy in my parents, I was driven to seek love outside of my family, since I didn't trust their love for me.

After that devastating day when I was thirteen, the most personal attention I really got from my dad was when he was drunk, coming home late after going out with Mom. Normally I stayed up babysitting the boys while they were out, watching late night shows and falling asleep when the TV went off the air. The TV helped me with my fears of being alone.

My dad would come home drunk those nights and that was the only time he would tell me he loved me, while holding me and dancing with me, slurring those "empty" words in my ear. I felt disgusted in my gut, but my fear of him was so great I couldn't tell him to "lay off" as my heart wanted to say. Instead, I just thought, "Yeah, sure you do. You only say it when you're drunk. I know you don't mean it, since you yell, put me down, hit me all the time, and say you don't want anything to do with me." Today I realize, like the majority of the world does, he used alcohol to cope with life's problems. (Luke 8:17; John 16:33) He had no power to overcome it because he did not know God and His Holy Spirit power to overcome.

I also got Dad's attention when we played a highly competitive game together, as competition was a common thread in our family. As God knows, I relished those times! My neediness for love from a man stemmed from the need for my own earthly father to love me and accept me for who God created me to be, a girl, even if he didn't understand me. I yearned to be close to my dad. I found myself asking if I could go to the professional baseball games with him and my brothers, but was denied. I would go to the free local baseball games with my mom, but I was never invited to go to Boston to the Red Sox games with Dad and the boys.

In the past 12 years of my counseling women with the use of the Bible, I have learned that every girl needs her daddy to treat her as his "princess." The father/daughter relationship should be safe, loving, and nurturing. This healthy relationship with a male will help her recognize in the future "the one" that God has chosen for her, her lifetime marriage partner. God's unconditional love desires the very best for us. It is man's imperfection that messes it up by our own choices.

The culture and the world have lied to people to believe we can have happy homes by picking our spouse based on chemistry. This is 'lust' at first sight. Other worldly traits are having something in common, good looks or wealth or fame and many others. Through my own experiences in doing it that way, I am asking you to consider that the prince of this world is Satan and he wants you to believe these lies so to destroy you. God, your Creator, is asking you to seek first the Kingdom of God and all these things (desires of your heart) will be added unto you. God is not a liar but only speaks the truth. He has even given us His instruction manual; the Bible for life.

We are fallen and sinful people who do not know what is best for us. When we buy a product, we must read the instruction manual to use it properly. In the same way, we must go to our Creator in order to have a blessed and happy life. Only our Creator knows who else He created that would work together best with us. I have learned this the hard way. It saddens me that my mother did not choose to go to her

Creator, who would bless her and harmonize together with her best, but instead went her own way.

When we do not know God or know who we are as a Christ follower, we are easily led and even rationalize the devil's ways in our sinful nature instead of trusting God to lead us. We so often trust in what we see the majority of the people in the world doing rather than being set apart by listening to that still small voice inside who is the Holy Spirit. He promises to guide us into all truth. The Devil is a liar and a deceiver and desires to destroy us and lead us down the road of destruction along with him.

God's perfect intention, according to the Bible, is that a parent would bring up a child in the way he/she should go. (Proverb 22:6) God's perfect intention for every parent is that they would choose to follow the Bible's perfect instruction: "*Fathers, do not provoke your children to anger but bring them up in the discipline and instructions of the Lord*" (Ephesians 6:4, Colossians 3:21).

Falling Away and Focusing on Boys

That evangelizing youth pastor at our church, there temporarily, very soon left our town. He was the positive male role model in my life. After that, I remember feeling like there wasn't anything left in the church youth group for me. I never really felt comfortable sharing my teenage burdens or problems with anyone at home.

Talking about sex at church was "forbidden." Instead of personally explaining "the birds and the bees" to me, and discussing with me what I was going through in my teen years, my mom merely handed me a book to read. It just never felt safe to ask questions about what I was feeling as a developing teenage girl, so I began hiding my thoughts. There was so much wrath at home that I knew if I asked anything, I would probably face further condemnation. I trusted my promiscuous girlfriend for information more than my mom.

My parents were not interested in leading me by example in many areas of life but preferred the doctorial method of discipline. As I often would do with my own son, it just felt like you were in control even though deep inside you knew you were not. Instead they clung to the areas of sin they loved too much to give up. I certainly noticed and resented this. All this did was cause rebelliousness to grow inside of me toward them. I eventually found other friends outside of the church group. The devil was certainly willing to find worldly friends to get my "sexual questions" answered. I began to keep secrets from my parents about where I was and with whom I socialized.

As a teen, I struggled with the issue of boys. Somehow, my mom had given me the notion that a girl's value is only found in a relationship with a man. She watched and cried through love stories displayed in soap operas. The way she obsessed about John F. Kennedy (she made all of us kids sit and watch every detail of his death so as to remember it forever) caused me to surmise that she valued "good-looking" rich and famous men. As I have learned and concluded, Kennedy was killed because he actually stood behind Martin Luther King and rights for the blacks. Knowing my parents had a racial problem, I can only conclude she was ignorant to the facts.

In addition, by this time she had shared with me that she wanted to have an affair. Can you imagine telling your only daughter such a thing? I certainly knew she struggled with Dad's treatment of her, since their fights at night woke me from a very young age. I struggled with understanding why it had to be that way for her. In my imagination, I looked forward to creating a better home life with my own "Prince Charming" one day. I truly related to Cinderella and dreamed of how it would be. I believe these thoughts were the beginning of knowing that I never wanted a relationship like my mom's relationship with my dad. I dreamed I would marry a man who would truly love me and I him. I dreamed of a world that could be for its possibilities and chose not to believe that it would be as troublesome as this.

It turned out that the first boy interested in me was a basketball player from the church youth group. There certainly was no discipleship going on for the teens at this youth group at that time. He made a bet with his guy friends that he could "get me laid" (a term they used for "having sex"). By the time I discovered this little secret, I had already suntanned his initials on my back and had his high school ring. Oh how easily I was lured! I was just so innocent and naive to the games boys play to act on the lust in their hearts.

One day when we were at the house without parents chaperoning us, he got me drunk for the first time, in order to win that bet.

Well, God fixed this guy! After all his perseverance, all that happened was, when he drove me down the road into the woods to be alone, I ended up throwing up all over his red hot Camaro. It was red hot all right; he had gotten me drunk on Sangria! It makes me chuckle today but that day I was so sick I didn't have any laughter in me, only agony. God protected me that time, and that young man lost the bet. *For thou hast been a shelter for me, and a strong tower from the enemy.* (Psalm 61:3, also Ps 91:2-4)

Lustful Men

I had saved some money so I could go on the Junior High School class trip to Spain. To show how much I loved and related to my Nana, I invited her to be one of the chaperones on the trip. I am so glad she was.

At the restaurant/discotheque where we were all hanging out one night, some French guy, during a dance with me, tried to persuade me to go away from there with him. My Nana protected me and told him, "Absolutely not. You will not take my granddaughter anywhere!" Nana was always so proud, the way she claimed me as her granddaughter to others. I loved that! It always made me feel so loved.

At one point, I decided to go to my hotel room to get something. When I went up the stairs and into the hallway toward my hotel room, all of a sudden some guy grabbed me and was trying to maul me, making sexual remarks. I was so scared. I screamed and he put his hand over my mouth. Just in time, one of the school football players, nicknamed "Pizza", came around the corner and yelled "Hey!" The man fled. Thank You, God, for using Pizza to rescue me again!

Between these incidents and the men jeering at me while walking on the sidewalks, I did not feel very safe there. Needless to say, I came home with a bad impression of Spain, though I had great memories of being with my Nana and of the sightseeing we did. I took lots of pictures of the sights, especially of the beautiful churches and cathedrals. I still cherish the time with Nana and the pictures. This event happened in 1975.

Church: The Body of Christ, Not Just Buildings

In light of the condition of the worldwide church today, I realize now, though oblivious then, that the church building was never meant to become a tourist attraction. As I reflect upon my experience of the churches in Spain, it seems like such a contradiction: people outside the church following their lustful flesh (men jeering at me, a 16 year old girl) while the beautiful church buildings are not really being used for the work God intended.

Much later I realized that it is the believers that are the church. If only the beauty people would admire about church would be the believers, built up inside with a real heart to reach the lost outside in the streets. That beauty can only be achieved through loving God with all our heart, soul and mind, and loving our neighbors as ourselves, as God says to do in the Bible (Matthew 22:37-40).

These true disciples created with the help of the Holy Spirit would, in turn, reflect this beauty through their purity, and produce the fruit of the Spirit: *love, joy, peace, forbearance, kindness, goodness, faithfulness, gentleness, and self-control* (Galatians 5:22-23). The Bride of Christ needs to be reaching out to the communities with the fruit of the Spirit and the Light of Christ: to live out the Great Commission and use the church buildings to commune together, and disciple new and growing believers while reaching out into the community with the gospel message.

My First Boyfriend and Giving in to Temptation

My teenage years became more and more chaotic, as there were always arguments, yelling and uneasiness at home. The broken relationship between my dad and me and the constant fights with my mom damaged my perceptions of life. Once I went walking down the road to get away, and along came some guy from another town. I said "yes" to a ride with him, kind of knowing he had a thing for me. He drove me straight to the woods, "just to be alone," as he expressed.

In fear, I found myself jumping out of the car and running without even knowing where to go. I believe God turned the guy's heart around for he did end up driving me out of there and where I wanted to go. I praise God for rescuing me from a possible rape that day! I knew though, to stay away from that guy from then on. Because of my innocence, vulnerability and lack of boundaries, combined with my desire to talk with and trust everyone, I could easily find myself in trouble. I have come to understand that it was God who rescued me each time and not the way the world calls it 'luck'.

At age 17, my mom let me go to my girlfriend's high school dance. It was there I met a boy who did not go to the church's youth events. I guessed that it didn't seem to make a real difference, as far as I could see. I also really liked his mother because she seemed a lot more understanding of me than my own mother. She seemed to be sweet to all four of her children and to me. The father was a Merchant Marine and was usually not around. The boy had long hair. I later discovered he drank and smoked pot. My parents only knew about the long hair and his loud Camaro car, and didn't like him.

His sister, who was being abused by her husband, became my friend, too. I seemed to have that "gift" even then for being compassionate and listening to "woe stories" of women friends. Most of our activities were based around alcohol, but it was the same scene with my parents and their friends as well. I was just doing it rebelliously, without my parents knowing it. However, every time I went to see her, I would end up alone with her brother.

I remember talking to God about contemplating having sex with my fiancé, especially since he put pressure on me by telling me when it would happen. He told me that I should go get protection from a local doctor, one his sister knew was "pretty cool" because he did not inform the parents of minors of this prescription. I hid the decision to get birth control from my parents.

I was so scared about the whole thing. I now know this was the "'righteous fear of God" to help me discern between right and wrong, which He had given me on the day of my salvation. I remember arguing with God that I really loved my fiancé. We had already engaged in necking, kissing and lots of touching just as I had seen on my mother's soap operas and they said they loved each other. We were engaged now and after all, I was going to marry him, for sure! God said "No." I fought God right up to the very last moment. My fiancé was kind and gentle in persuasion, but God was there with me saying "No Karen, don't do it."

The next thing I know, my desire to feel loved through being touched by a man stopped my conversation with God. My flesh just gave in. I dove into what felt good. From that moment on, I lost something I had with God, as my life went into a downward spiral of trouble after trouble. If only I knew it was His protection when He said

'No' in my spirit. That was conviction of truth and God's love, knowing what was best for me. If only I had God's Word in my heart as my "sword" (Ephesians 6:17) to fight off this temptation. If only I understood God's love was greater than the love of this man.

I remember feeling "cheap'" after that first time and wishing I hadn't done it, but every time after that, when my fiancé arranged the times, I just couldn't stop myself. I was afraid he would break up with me if I said no or he would think I didn't really love him. I did think I loved him and I really thought he was "the one." In my unhealthy perception, I thought sex meant love. I craved the attention and touch of a man who expressed this "love" to me. Later in life I would learn that one of my love languages is touch. How the devil plays on our weaknesses! Somehow, I knew God didn't approve of my lifestyle but I just couldn't give him up. I didn't understand the difference between the lust of the flesh and the need for love that drove me.

Years later, a pastor taught me a Scripture that applies here and is essential for the bride in becoming prepared for her bridegroom for eternity: *"A person who is full refuses honey, but even bitter food tastes sweet to the hungry"* (Proverbs 27:7). In other words, when one is full with the Word of God, even honey cannot tempt them, but void of the Word, even what is bad for you seems right to you. *"For man does not live by bread alone but by every word from God"* (Deuteronomy 8:3). If only my Sunday school time had prepared me for real life encounters and how to handle them according to Scripture. Remember, sex was not discussed in my church.

Later Teen Years

Now that I was seeing my fiancé more, using the excuse of going to see his sister, alcohol was becoming even more a part of the equation. Alcohol eventually became "my competition" in getting attention from my fiancé. The more he drank, especially with his sister's husband, the more arrogant and selfish he became with me. Drinking gave him a boldness contrary to his shy nature I had known.

I felt more distanced from him emotionally and felt taken for granted and disrespected. As I struggled with verbally expressing my feelings, he clammed up. Our two temperaments were opposite in that way. The less we communicated, the more empty and used I felt. As I began to feel more and more taken for granted, it fueled my desire to attend college far away from home so to run from the pain.

The next year was my senior year of high school. Besides fighting with my raging hormones, I fought with my mom a lot about my fiancé, college, my parents' hypocrisy, and more. I was very rebellious, but of course I was also trying to hide what I was doing.

By the time I turned 18 in March 1976, I moved out of my parents' house and into an apartment with a couple of girlfriends near high school. I graduated high school with honors. I worked three jobs that summer in order to pay my own way to college. I wanted to go far away from home. My parents wanted me to go to the local college but I fought that. I got a student loan and received some scholarships. My parents paid a little over $1000 and I paid the rest with what I earned from those summer jobs. I got a student loan for the rest, which would take me the next 10 years to pay off. The most important thing to me was; I was "free at last" from the rules and control at home or so I thought.

The Dysfunctional Growing up Years of Steven

Meanwhile, back in the North Frontier region of Pakistan, Masood Ahmad Kahn, later known as Steven Masood, had a different kind of dysfunctional upbringing than I did. That compelled him to search for God and to question the religion he had been raised to believe: Islam. As he tried to please his family members by doing things for them in order to receive the love he so desperately needed, he was rejected and used. Masood's father did not provide adequately for all of his family's many needs. Masood would do homework for others to earn money, as well as work in the vegetable market to pay for his school fees and food for the family. He indirectly sought love and approval by working hard and caring for his family.

Masood was raised with 14 other brothers and sisters. They had the same father who had a few concubines and had married four wives, one of whom was Masood's mother. In the light of the Qur'an and what Muhammad said and did, the Islamic law (*Shari'ah*) allows such a custom. In fact a wife is considered to be her husband's property: his tilth (i.e. cultivated land) (Sura 2:223). This is an ancient yet accepted tradition in Islam even today, as the men are considered superior to women. A Muslim woman is equal to half the value of a man in Islamic law (Sura 4:11 and 2:282).

From his childhood, Masood was challenged by other Muslims as not being a good Muslim belonging to a heretic denomination. Unsatisfied, Masood although a teen, focused on searching for the truth. He struggled to find assurance that he would make it to Paradise. In the years to come as a young man, he found that after performing all the works required to be a Muslim, like praying in a specific way five times a day, fasting, giving alms (giving to poor), performing *hajj* (Pilgrimage to Mecca) and obeying all the rules, his only true guarantee to Paradise was martyrdom as a Jihadist. That wasn't even 100% certain. Who is to decide that a particular battle taking place is for Allah (the name of God in Islam) and not a geo-political issue?

Masood's family life always included religion. However, in his father's electric business, his father taught him it was acceptable to be corrupt. His dad did this by punishing him for helping a customer understand that the only problem with a radio was the misplacement of the batteries. As a teen, Masood turned to Islamic studies for answers. It bothered him, too, that most other Muslims did not consider the sect to which his family adhered to be "true Muslims." He set out to become a true and good Muslim.

Comparing Our Teen Years

At the age of 13, after reading the Gospel of John in his language, Steven's compelling question to his Muslim teacher was, "Is God our Father?" His own father was unavailable to him both physically and emotionally. His dad condemned him for being different from his other children. In comparison to my situation at age 13, when my father washed his hands of me, I was an emotional young girl desperately in need of the love of my father. I needed to learn what the man in my future should be like through my dad's example. Steven and I understand that the way our fathers treated us during childhood was a critical factor in our lives, because childhood is a crucial time for learning about the characteristics of a good father. Obviously, I felt like I wasn't good enough for my father and felt devalued, just like Steven did. I now see how brokenness met brokenness here. This emotional understanding formed a common bond. Like me, Steven would raise

47

an issue with, "But why?" he would get slapped and told, "Because I said so!"

As for me, the harsh tone of voice, as well as the false accusations and misunderstandings, were just unbearable. I just wanted to understand why . . . why should I or shouldn't I do the things I was commanded to do? I would never tell my kids, "Because I said so." That was just not a good enough answer for me. My heart's desire was to truly understand why.

In Pakistan, Steven dared ask "why" to his Muslim family members as well as to the imams and scholars. Under the bondage of both Islam and his parents, he was constantly told that he wasn't allowed to ask questions about their ideology. He was reprimanded and told he shouldn't question Allah, Muhammad or the Qur'an. Yet, in his deep desire to sincerely know why and to know the truth, he was compelled to continue to ask questions. He learned to seek understanding in a humble way that often gained him favor.

At age 13, Masood discovered the Gospel of John in his friend's library at home. Reading it motivated him to ask his Islamic teacher, "Is God our father?" This question was dear to his heart because of his unsuccessful attempt at gaining love from his own father, who was incapable of providing the kind of love he needed.

Masood would discover later in his life with me that he was also a Sanguine in the area of affection. Sanguine means pleasure-seeking and sociable according to Wikipedia.[1] In affection[2] it simply means a person has a great need for affability. I believe his male capability to compartmentalize emotions helped him put his need for love

---

[1] One of five temperaments similar to personality types. There is a clinical diagnostic tool through the Arno Profile system (APS) test to determine temperament type. See www.apsreport.com/History.html Counselors are certified by the NCCA www.ncca.org

[2] See YouTube video http://www.youtube.com/watch?v=okC0yc-TPUg explaining area of affection relating to the need for love and affection and need to establish and maintain deep personal relationships supported by the NCCA and the Arno Temperament system

and affection aside. I learned that he also has a high capacity for discipline in his temperament.

I would like to divert a minute to explain what counseling method determines temperaments. It is the Arno Profile System which "does not measure a person's behavior; it identifies a person's inborn, God-given temperament. Who God created us to be (temperament) and who we become (through learned behavior) can be entirely different. We need to find out who we really are, and find ways to become the person God wants us to be (the true self) instead of the person we have learned to be (the masked self)." I believe this with all my heart. I know God directed me to the NCCA certification program and Mr. and Mrs. Arno through my Pro-life director and friend to help me understand who I really am and who He is teaching me to be. I will talk more about the Pro-life issue and how it relates to me later.

In his studies, Masood found a way to disprove the founders of the *Ahmadiyya* movement (the Muslim sect in which he grew up). Being quite proud of his discoveries, he proceeded to share them in the mosque. This stunt almost got him killed by his own father, forcing him to run away from home at 17 years old. Needless to say, his parents' relationship with him was not a loving one.

While my life was not in danger, when I was 18, all of the fights I had with my mother made things increasingly worse between us. She didn't give me the answers I needed about boys or about how to live as a woman nor did she really understand who God made me. My father did not give me answers either. Instead, I got my "answers" from the secular world and set off for college and adventure! Now, I have learned to forgive them for they know not what they do without God's guidance.

Peace with My Dad

Looking back today, I do not blame my parents for the 30-35 years I wasted in the desert without God, looking for Love in all the wrong places. I have forgiven them and know that I am responsible for the choices I made. When my dad was diagnosed with Parkinson's disease and became unsteady on a ladder, I began to help him put his Christmas lights on his house. In the summer of 2009, God, in His mercy, gave me good times with dad. We lived fairly close to each other, and I cherish being with him in his final couple of years. The disease had caused him to slow down and he became easy to get along with. He was just like a teddy bear. Amazingly, even with Parkinson's, we still played tennis, golf, and board games. I will never forget that special time! In his final week with me in Florida, we played ping pong for two hours until he gave up, frustrated that he kept losing!

When my father was at the end of his life, my younger brother made sure I was able to go see him since they had moved him back to Maine. I thank God for that! When the nurse whispered in his ear that his daughter was here, he lifted his head for the first time in a week and tears rolled down his cheek. I knew he was happy I was there. I spent three days at the nursing home a few days before he passed, just doting over him. I read him the Bible, sang songs about Jesus to him, and shared the Gospel. When I asked him to confirm that he understood the message I shared with him, he opened one eye and looked at me and closed his fingers on my hand. That was the confirmation he gave me that he accepted Jesus as his Savior three days before he passed.

God gave me such complete peace that even when the nurse called to tell me he had passed, I had peace knowing he was now free of all pain and was in the arms of Jesus! I look forward to seeing my dad in Heaven when Jesus returns to take us home, or when God chooses to take me home. I praise my Lord and Savior for the incredible closure I got with my dad and the peace I have about his salvation! It reminds me of the thief on the cross who was saved at the last minute before his death when Jesus said, "Truly I tell you, today you will be with me in paradise." (Luke 23:43)

Pain Concerning My Mom and Others in My Family

The wonderful relationships I experience with my husband and church family are so beautiful, and I grieve over the absence of this kind of relationship with my mother and brothers. I pray for them all daily and trust in God, my Heavenly Father, who loves me and who loves them, too. God knows I have made every effort I possibly can at this point, yet most have chosen, so far, to rebel against the truth of the Gospel simply through rejecting my sharing with them.

Rejection - yes Jesus has mentioned it (Matthew 13:57-58). He certainly experienced it in a much more extreme way than I do. At least my family haven't thrown physical stones at me and persecuted me physically. Part of picking up our cross daily is the pain we must experience in walking with the Lord. It prepares us by building our perseverance and character for much harder times to come. God has called us, as His Bride, to be overcomers. In Philippians 1:29, Paul says, "For it has been granted to you on behalf of Christ not only to believe in him, but also to suffer for him."

In Matthew 10:34-37 we find Jesus saying, "Whoever loves father or mother more than me is not worthy of me, and whoever loves son or daughter more than me is not worthy of me." Laying our whole life down for Jesus, is one way the Bride (the church) is purified for her soon coming Bridegroom, Jesus.

3

Young Adulthood

Running Away to College

Part of my desire to run away to college was to rid myself of the guilt, shame, and disrespect I felt from the relationship with my fiancé. The other part of that desire was to get away from the two-faced rules of my parents. Living in Florida by the beach was an added enticement. Ultimately it all amounted to my running from God. Sometimes we think running from our guilt and shame will make it go away, but actually the solution is the opposite: it is to confront the guilt and shame with the light of God's Word. God can heal us and take away our guilt and shame. Remember, Adam and Eve hid in the garden yet God knew where they were and what they had done.

Another reason I really wanted to go to college was because of my love for learning. I had always gotten top grades in school. I loved a challenge and it just felt like there was something better out there in the world. I never seemed to give up hope for a better destiny. I was excited to explore it, especially now, with this new disappointment in my relationship with my fiancé. But all the while, I in some way felt there was something out there bigger than myself.

Somehow, I seemed to know that I was gifted for something better, something bigger than what I experienced here in this little town. Then and still now, I feel God when I drive on the road. I had a sense of adventure somewhere out there. I wanted to spread my wings and fly like a bird. Since then, I have had many adventures and look forward to what else God has for the future.

My mother flew with me to college and we stopped first in Orlando. We went to Disney World for the first time. I loved it; it was like a visual fantasy for me. I loved the Cinderella Castle, the colors, animation, and all the lights! It felt like my dream came true and I would live happily ever after with my true love. Even then, there was a shadow shaped like a man in my future that I did not know but God knew very well.

When I got to the college, an all-girls fashion college in Miami, I was well on my way to pursuing my dream of being a famous fashion designer. The college brochures had filled me with excitement, showing the beautiful surroundings. When I arrived however, I found it to be on the most polluted river in Miami. How's that for a smack in the face? The brochure that alluded to the college being on the water obviously deceived me; I had assumed it was on the beach. This would be just the beginning of much deception to come. For how could I know without calling upon the power of the Holy Spirit to lead me into all truth?

Breaking up and Dating Around

I had to work my own way through college and one of the ways I earned money for that was bartending. While bartending in Miami, I met many famous baseball players who took an interest in me. These men would often express how beautiful I was. I was really never told that by my fiancé or my dad; neither one complimented me very much. I didn't think about the fact that these men were telling me these things while they were drunk.

I think I was a little awestruck by their fame and fortune. What a fool I was, trusting their words of "I love you and I think you're beautiful" just because these men were rich and famous. Apparently, because I was a small town girl, I had this idea that men outside of my own town would lead me to a better "forever after"—like in the Hollywood movies and on TV. The soap operas my mother watched and the romance novels she read gave me this impression as well. It wasn't long after I discovered that all men, with or without money and fame, can break your heart the same way.

At the time, in a brand new place, deep inside I had this huge desire to be noticed. The very thought of dating someone famous really intrigued me. I believed some things that Americans so often say, my mother included, "There are plenty of fish in the sea" and "you can marry a rich man just as well as a poor one." I think I had dreams of grandeur: to be rich and famous with future possibilities. This gave me the inkling that I could escape the disrespect I felt from my fiancé. I broke it off with him over the phone. He didn't handle it very well.

Later, on one of my vacation trips to Maine to see my family, I was persuaded to visit him near Boston. He had my pictures plastered over his walls. He hopelessly tried to convince me to go back to him and move to Boston after I left college. However, something inside of me yearned for more in life. I couldn't bear to listen to empty words. Once again, much like my family's love, this verbal expression of love for me never really felt like love. I still felt betrayed in my broken state of heart and mind.

I won't name names, but one famous baseball player pursued me and I felt flattered. He easily enticed me into a relationship arranged around his demanding schedule. As you might conclude, I didn't see him often but that was alright with me. In my inexperience, I felt some kind of higher value in dating a famous athlete.

I eventually worked two jobs, as a bartender and a cashier, and continued to excel in my schoolwork. I don't know how I still managed to go out after the bar closed to dance, drink, and meet people at nightclubs. I had no real fear of meeting new people—I fed on it. It actually energized me. Later on in life, while studying temperaments, I realized that this social trait is part of my Sanguine temperament. It is also the exact reason why it is so important for a person of my temperament to be grounded in the Word of God: to stay focused on the right reasons for this "relational gifting." For it was inevitable that the wrong people could easily influence me, and so they did.

While attending college, I never really went to church, because, "I did not have time." (Haven't we all heard this excuse?) Going to church would have at least surrounded me with more people who were at least searching for the things of God. I now know that using the excuse "no time" means I freely chose not to make it one of my top priorities.

Regardless, I continued in my schooling and continued to be pursued by many men; not surprisingly, many were much older than I. In my desperate unconscious search for a father, I ended up with a big age gap between the men I dated and me. One of these men was a magician from Venezuela. He was very charming and witty. I could say that he pretty much entertained me, but again was always distant.

One man I dated was an African American security officer at my cashier job. The long and short of it was that indirectly, or directly, at age nineteen, I wanted to rub this interracial relationship into my prejudiced parents' face out of rebelliousness. This was in 1979.

I recently saw a movie called *Deep in My Heart* (1999) on YouTube. It was a true story from 1963, when the white culture of America was predominantly racist against black people. It was a sad story of a white woman who was raped by a black man. Society in 1963 compelled her, in order to save face with her neighbors, relatives and environment, to give the baby up for adoption. She gave her up to a black family who raised the little girl with sincere love. All was wonderful for the black family.

When the little girl was about ten years old, knowing no other mother although fatherless, DCF[1] came along and against the will of both child and mother, removed the child from this happy home. DCF, clearly with financial gain, pulled the child from a loving home and placed her with new white parents with money, who were barren. The child was so devastated that she lost her joy and became a recluse. The father left, even leaving this home to be fatherless but DCF never cared about this case of fatherlessness. The child grew up with a deep desire to find out why her birth mother left her.

Her difficult experience shows me that I was a woman before my time according to society, yet a woman after God's heart according to the Bible, since God loves all people equally (Galatians 3:28; Revelation 7:9) – no matter their skin color – and is the Father to the fatherless (Psalm 68:5). It is a sad situation in the world in these days when companies are formed by our government, like DCF, to supposedly help people when the only intention is to exploit people just to make money. To top it off, the government makes it a law people must follow it or be arrested.

---

[1] Department of Children and Family Services

Whirlwind Romance

I was never really fully committed to anyone until one night when I was in a disco club dancing as usual. I loved to dance. A good-looking dark-haired, delightful guy with a huge beautiful smile, incredible dancing skills, and a witty personality that never ceased to make me laugh, asked me to dance. He swept me off my feet, just like in my Cinderella dream! As we danced the "Hustle" (Remember the John Travolta dance?), the people moved off the dance floor, staring and clapping.

From that first night I met him until I moved in with him, he consistently drove up from the Florida Keys to Miami to dance with me on the weekends or I drove down to the Keys. I not only loved dancing; I loved all the attention we got from the people who would watch us dance.

One night, "Prince Charming" went to his knees and asked me to marry him in front of everybody. When he proposed to me on the dance floor in public and in front of all our beach bum and waiter friends, I felt like the center of attention, which is what my temperament loves. Well, he had now really won my heart! I said a profound "Yes! I will marry you!" It was like a romantic movie, but did I mention to you, we were all drunk?

It was just a fantasy, but I saw it as real, and a dream come true. He not only danced me off my feet, but also out of my mind. I lost all my sense of right and wrong. When you are "in love" or, as I have come to realize, "in lust," something inside your brain short circuits. You tend to lose all ability to think rationally. Instead our hearts cave in and we call it "romance."

Our culture casts romance and excitement as our savior and rescuer, like we will be healed, complete and delivered if only we find our soul mate. Yes, one might enjoy being at one of New York's exclusive restaurants, wining and dining, daintily savoring filet mignon, and dancing cheek to cheek on Valentine's Day. However, that is just a temporary high.

We often miss our True Love by expecting a fairy tale or fantasies of some knockout gorgeous rich body builder who doesn't stand up to reality. It's all a lie that keeps woman from having the voice of our loving relational Creator edging us closer and closer to the beautifully molded and freed piece of pottery designed perfectly just for you.

During the weeks that followed, I planned out my dream wedding. I used all my creative skills to design and make all the dresses, the wedding cake, the decorations, and the entire schedule. The wedding was to take place near my hometown in Maine with all of my family, in the fall, after my college graduation. My parents were happy for me.

The guy was from Massachusetts and his very well-to-do family was quite well known there. He was a very handsome, witty man who could charm anybody into anything. He went to my graduation and saw me graduate as the second highest student in my class. This was in May of 1978.

Since we were both passionate people in our temperaments, he convinced me that because I had worked so hard, I deserved to take a year off before going to New York City to pursue my career. He persuaded me not to take the position I already had lined up in New York City. He wanted me to live with him in the Florida Keys before and after our wedding. He said that we would talk later about when we would both go to New York and pursue our careers together.

While living in the Keys, we worked together as a team in a tourist lodge. I worked as a cocktail waitress while he served food and entertained customers with his witty jokes and outstanding personality. We made big bucks together and he managed the money. At that time it felt like a dream come true. I really believed that the Cinderella story was happening to me.

But, there was trouble in paradise. We worked at night and beached by day, drinking and partying. He occasionally even persuaded me to join him in his weekend cocaine habit, which I soon discovered was his addiction. He tried to convince me that cocaine is not addictive. There are many lies out there, which convince people that they are in control when they really are not at all.

A Wedding Day to Die for

As one can understand, the living together before marriage situation resulted in my getting pregnant. My Prince Charming coerced me to get an abortion with his concern about the cocaine he had used. In addition he felt, "We aren't ready for a child and what about our careers?" So, my fiancé insisted that the only choice we both had was to abort this baby.

As if having an abortion wasn't enough torture for my heart, he insisted that I get the abortion at a clinic in Maine on the day of our wedding, while my family was busy preparing food and decorating! In his brilliant manipulative mind, he managed to hide the pregnancy from both his and my families. Absolutely brilliant, don't you think? Only God knows what his reasoning was but somehow I felt trapped without any voice in the decision. I can only imagine feeling intimidated by his coerciveness.

What a wedding "to die for!" Horribly, the victims for this wedding were the poor innocent child, my nurturing soul, broken heart, and my dead mind. Can you imagine trying to act like this was the happiest day of my life, while the life inside my spirit had completely died on that day, along with my dreams? All the while I was smiling on the outside for a supposed lifetime photo album. When I think about it now, I just can't believe how controlled I was by a mere man!

God actually gave my mother and me a visual warning that morning when we all woke up to the stench of the chicken cacciatore gone bad. (Cacciatore is a meal prepared with cream and butter. My mom had made it the day before.) If only my mother and I had spiritual discernment! If only I had listened to God warning me that this "dream wedding" had a stench to it and would definitely go bad. If only I cried out to God for His help to give me the boldness and strength to walk away that day.

I don't remember if I really realized God was giving me this visual to warn me against going through with aborting my baby, but I do remember running off with "Prince Charming" to the clinic and leaving my mother to bury the chicken cacciatore in the woods. When I look back, I see it was a visual sign from God that this was not a day of joy, but a day of revelation that something was horribly wrong.

When my fiancé secretly took me to the abortion clinic, I faced the worst nightmare of any woman's dream gone wrong. I remember how scared I became at the clinic; I begged for drugs to knock me out. The doctor said that since I was only a couple of months along, what was inside of my womb, was not technically a baby, but rather just tissue. He would take care of it after giving me a drug so I could sleep. I would wake up and it would be over. His words "You can just go on with your life," still ring in my ears to this day. At that time, I told myself that's all I needed to focus on, moving on with my life.

While waiting to get the abortion, I felt just devastated inside. So many thoughts went through my head. Why does this feel so wrong? Why doesn't my soon-to-be husband want this baby? Why do I feel like I have no choice? Why doesn't he understand my perspective? I actually felt that having a baby would be a wonderful thing and make me feel as if he loved me enough to have this baby with me. Right then, the thought occurred to me, "Having a baby is a terrible inconvenience, at least in the eyes of my new husband that I will marry today."

It was just so confusing. Before I knew it, I was waking up from the effects of the drug. Instantly, I began vomiting. It seems I was there longer than the other women around me because of the sickness that I had. I had pain. I also had to keep this secret. This was supposed to be the happiest day of my life. The only way I knew how to keep this a secret and look happy was to get drunk. Gee, I wonder where I learned that ...?

And so I got married and tried to forget about my feelings, including the pain. We both acted as if it never happened. We danced and entertained people as we had so often done. We were married in October of 1978. If only I had read the sign God gave me that day, hearing His voice, and had not gone through with that wedding!

I Corinthians 10:13 reads, "No temptation has overtaken you but such as is common to man; and God is faithful, who will not allow you to be tempted beyond what you are able, but with the temptation will provide the way of escape also, so that you will be able to endure it." So as you see, God does not tempt man. He always gives us a way out. He gave me a sign of 'Cacciatore gone bad' before the abortion and before the wedding. I did not listen to God but to a mere man.

Abortion is murder according to one of the Ten Commandments in Exodus 20:13: "Thou shall not murder." What part of murder do we not understand? The bridegrooms that God chooses for His daughters would never tempt us with premarital sex, nor convince us that we should murder our babies. I should have run for both of our lives! Psalm 139:13-16 says, "For you created my inmost being; you knit me together in my mother's womb. I praise you because I am fearfully and wonderfully made; your works are wonderful, I know that full well. My frame was not hidden from you when I was made in the secret place, when I was woven together in the depths of the earth. Your eyes saw my unformed body; all the days ordained for me were written in your book before one of them came to be."

Therefore, God knows each child, making each one a viable life. God promises in His Word, in Luke 8:17 to be exact, that every hidden thing will be revealed.

Trouble in 'Paradise'

Our marriage lasted for five months before the fights grew in intensity. Many of those battles were over my pain that he refused to feel or understand. As a result of my anger building up inside of me toward him, his selfishness, and his lack of consideration of my feelings, everything exploded like a bomb.

About three months after the wedding, I finally persuaded him to agree to leave Florida and go to New York City together to pursue our careers. His career was teaching and mine was fashion design. Getting ready for the move, we sold our van and ended our apartment lease. Interestingly, our apartment was located right next to a church. As I look back, I can clearly see how God was continually offering me His love and way out; I was just too, blindly "in love" with this ungodly man to see it.

The week before we were scheduled to leave for "The Big Apple," he left on a one-week drug and alcohol binge, with no notice and no contact. Upon his return, drunk and high on cocaine, he picked an argument about not going and ended up physically beating me up. He tried to convince me that the only way we could stay together would be to stay in Florida.

Escape to My Parents' House

God provided escape for me through a loving Christian neighbor that I met the week my husband was gone. It was her house I ran to that day to escape the abuse; he did not know where I was. God used this woman to remind me of when I was saved at the tender age of 13 and its purpose. I felt love in her presence and that she really truly cared for me. I never felt condemned by her. She talked with me about re-dedicating my life to Christ. She gave me a Bible that I could under-stand, called a Student's Bible. She also helped me change my plane ticket from New York to my parents' house in Maine.

For the first time, I saw my father rise up and protect me after I poured out my woes about my husband beating me up. I never told my family about the abortion. I began the process of a Pro Se divorce (which means being my own lawyer) and learned that according to the law, if this was an uncontested divorce, I could actually get an an-nulment.

Later, when my husband called my parents' house to find me, my father threatened to use his gun on him if he showed up to contest the divorce. He believed my dad and never showed up. I got a quick annulment. My father had a couple of guns in the house, as he was a hunter. For the first time, I actually felt protected by my dad and it felt rather good!

Oh how I wish that I had gone back to church, but the church in Maine had left a bad taste in my mouth. The only thing I could think of, without consulting God, was to go back to work as a cocktail waitress, where I knew how to make a lot of money fast. My personal-ity and "good looks" seemed to really help me achieve this.

While I had rededicated my life to Jesus there in the Florida Keys, without any follow-up accountability and discipleship, I did not grow. I just rationalized in my mind that my problem was choosing the wrong person. So, I blamed my ex-husband for what he had done to me and for my decisions.

Although I started to believe that there was something wrong with me, I thought I would figure it out. I tend to get over bad situa-tions rather quickly, due to my Sanguine temperament. Meeting new people and embarking on new adventures helped me feel better. I gravitated toward people who would help me suppress my inner feel-ings of turmoil. I had no idea of what I would be up against in sup-pressing the pain, feelings and my secret.

Getting Out of My Parents' House Again

Living at my parents became a challenge once again. My mom and I fought as my dad stayed distant emotionally. Through my acquaintances at work, I found a living situation with other people and went there for the rest of the summer. A college friend and I began plans to move to New York City and share a studio with three other girls.

One day my mother sent her girlfriend to talk with me over lunch. She tried to convince me to improve my relationship with my mom. I vented to her that my mother just didn't understand me and wasn't happy unless I was living the way she wanted. I complained that I knew Mom's way of living sure wasn't making her happy, so why should I listen to her? I always felt I knew all about her marriage; it wasn't the kind of marriage I wanted.

My mom's friend also tried to comfort me over my failed marriage. She encouraged me by saying all wasn't lost. Her good news that she had met my cousin and was going to marry him comforted me. I was happy for her, but continued to feel the rift between my mother and me.

Meanwhile, whenever I wasn't being responsible in making money to save for my move to New York, I would just go to a bar. Or, I would drink at my own workplace after work to numb the pain of rejection and the pain of losing "the love of my Prince Charming." At that time, I had no idea that I was also naturally grieving the loss of my child that had been ripped out of my womb. That was a pain that I would suppress for many years to come.

Much later, I would discover that it was the cause of my anger that I so often inflicted on others. I had great difficulty in handling conflict calmly and often lost friends this way. Without seeing this challenge lived out in my family or going to church for discipleship, how could I learn this? After all, most of the people I hung out with related to the same kind of conflict resolution.

This difficult time would have been a perfect time to really seek God's answers for my life. After all, it is He who is my Rescuer, my Security, and my Savior. Why couldn't I see it? I had no Christian accountability. My rebellion, my pain, and all these feelings should have driven me to God for His perfect answers, but instead I just sought to pursue my career. I just changed my focus.

Instead of listening to God, I was listening to Satan's lies. We all know that "misery loves company." Satan tempts us to follow his ways; he fools us into thinking they are our ways and are the best for us. He knows that all those who ultimately follow his ways will go to hell with him. While there is nothing wrong with pursuing one's career, I followed Satan's lies by substituting seeking and obeying God with the idol of putting myself first.

Jesus says, "Whoever does not bear his own cross and come after me cannot be my disciple." (Luke 14:27). Although at that time I blew my chance to seek God with all my heart, soul and mind, it is my prayer that if you have experienced anything like I just described, you will do what's best for you and seek God and ask for His forgiveness. Your Father in Heaven only wants the best for you.

When you confess your sins and turn to Jesus, abiding in Him through studying and obeying His precious Word, you can be His disciple and experience His healing. If I could have done this over, I would have sought God so to mature and be purified in Christ back then. I cannot change my past, but I can help you to not make the same mistakes I did. After all, Christ can transform you and make you a new Creation, like He did with me and continues!

God wants people to bless and help each other. Going to a Bible believing church to find Godly counsel and mentors will help your growth in your relationship with God. When you seek Him wholeheartedly, He will find you and prepare you as His Bride for eternity.

Do you have any secret sins? There is no time like the present to purify your heart, your thoughts and be free from Satan's bondage of lies. Confess them to God and repent of them. That means to turn around and sin no more in those areas of sin. Let the blood of Jesus wash you white as snow so you can truly be free to be all that God intends for you. As you obey Him, be accountable to a more mature believer. God will truly bless you beyond your wildest dreams! Living a life of purity in your heart and thoughts, and keeping your eyes on Christ, your soon coming Bridegroom, prepares you for the Marriage Supper of the Lamb in eternity.

4

Getting into More Trouble

Off to New York City to Become a Fashion Designer

Off I went to NYC, the Big Apple! I remember thinking when I got there, "Wow! Look at all the people!" How excited I was to meet new people and at least have the chance to make it big, hopefully as a famous fashion designer. That was my dream. I decided I would just focus loving my career and forget about the love of men.

That love thing didn't work for me anyway, so I decided to become task oriented; that will make me worthy, I thought. People will notice my worth as a fashion designer. After all, I had worked hard for the money to attend college and I wanted to make it work for me. No one knew anything about me here so I didn't need to worry about feeling or receiving condemnation for abortion or divorce. It was so easy to get lost in such a crowd of people.

The first night I was in my apartment, on the 6th floor or so, I hung out on the balcony, looking out on the city, just taking it all in. I began thinking about changing my name to Elaine Karen instead of Karen Elaine Johnson, which was so plain. I needed flair to sound like a designer. I had been floating around the apartment, dreaming about which designer I really wanted to work for and looking for jobs in the newspaper. I was really excited about the prospect of my career ahead of me.

Suddenly, I heard a commotion across the street. As I looked to see what was going on, I saw a man who appeared to have been thrown out the front door of a bar. He landed on the sidewalk. Very shortly, another man came out raging. He grabbed the first man and started beating his head against the cement sidewalk. Then, he just walked away down the street. Within about five minutes I heard the sirens of police cars and an ambulance. I think I had just literally watched a man being killed by another.

The paramedics went to the man on the sidewalk. In no time at all, they put a blanket over the man's body, including his face and head. All of a sudden, panic came over me. I remembered *Bonanza* on TV and thought, "Oh my God, this stuff doesn't just happen on TV! I just saw it happen in real life!" Only in my present understanding of how God speaks to us do I realize why God could have allowed me to see this. The other girls didn't seem to be too concerned, so I called my mother. I thought I would let her know that I arrived safely, and then slip in what I had just seen to gauge her reaction. My mother reacted with, "Don't be silly, Karen, those are things that just don't happen in real life. That's just on TV."

Was she calling me a liar? I just discounted it as one more time I wasn't listened to and felt devalued by my family's remarks. Nothing was new under the sun in my family relationship.

After all, what I saw was a lot like those soap operas and dramas she watched. Today this is a reminder of my own desperate need to come to God in true repentance for my secret sins. I had taken life and death in my own hands, just like the murder I saw, by choosing to abort my own baby. God doesn't see either one of these two murders as worse than any other. Watching it caused me to curse another man for murder. As a "seer" of God like the prophets He has sent in the past 2,000 years, may the word of my testimony warn God's children in America today. Do not curse the darkness lest you be cursed by unbelievers who know not what they do. This dishonors God and hurts the reputation of Christ's followers.

Sexual Harassment in the Fashion Industry

The next day, with my resume and portfolio of dress designs in hand, I began pounding the pavement, visiting companies in the garment district in search of a job. Most companies told me that my degree from Miami was not accredited in the Northeast, so I would have to go to FIT (Fashion Institute of Technology) there in New York City to retake most of the courses before I would qualify for a position. This was very discouraging news and I wondered why no one would have told me this at the college. My parents never went to college so certainly would not know what to ask and I sure didn't know.

During my job search, the responses varied from, "No, you need to have experience" to "Let me take you to so and so," only to have one man take my portfolio out of sight. He came back to chat, asking questions about me and making small talk, as well as passes.

There were many allusions to my looks and to going out with him for a date or dinner, as well as the question, "What would you be willing to do to get a job here?" Within an hour he retrieved my portfolio, returning it to me with a promise to call. Years later while watching fashion shows, I saw designs that resembled mine, and I wondered if they might have stolen my ideas.

I suppose my deep need for attention, as well as my optimism, kept me looking for a job even though it seemed to be hopeless. However, my naivety made me vulnerable to the deception of these men's double-minded intentions in giving me their time. Their sexual remarks made me feel very uneasy but my passion to find a job in my career kept me searching regardless.

Other men in the fashion business actually made bold passes at me. When I rejected them, they said they were not interested in hiring me. I was sexually harassed by remarks and was even inappropriately touched. At one bridal manufacturer, I was sent home with a dress to sew, but the boss scared me so much that I never returned it, and they never called about it.

I was too naive to realize that I could have filed a lawsuit for sexual harassment. About five years later, women's libbers in that garment district began filing lawsuits and won large settlements from the harassers. I remember later thinking how God always gets His revenge, one way or another!

Missed Opportunity

As all my efforts to find a Fashion Design opportunity failed, I began to regret my year in the Florida Keys more than ever. I later realized God had actually provided a way for me to make a living in NYC the year after college, but I hadn't taken advantage of that opportunity. A man, who was a friend of our family from Maine, worked in the garment district for Universal Studios in New York City.

During my second year of college, he had given me an "in" by handing me a great project: to remake a silver jacket for Michael Jackson during the filming of *The Whiz*. This friend had given me this open door so that I could be known to the company and be offered a job with them after graduating. I did get to meet Michael Jackson. After trying on the jacket that I remade for him, he shook my hand, whispering, "Thank you," and gave me a signed photograph.

The friend from Maine had opened the door for me with his company in hopes that I would be offered a job at Universal Studios after graduating, and I blew it. While I was sidetracked with marrying and divorcing "Prince Charming," our friend retired. Now that I was in NYC, I no longer knew anyone at Universal, so I was never given an interview there.

I finally took a job with the designer Arnold Scaasi doing menial tasks, such as picking up pins and sewing the same small detail over and over in a factory. As I calculated the costs of living in NYC and going back to school, and considered my low salary, my discouragement grew. I felt defeated and deluded.

I decided to go back to restaurant work, which I had experience with since age 12. Because of this, I landed the first job I applied for in that field at the *Statler Hilton*. Do you remember the oldies song "Pennsylvania 6-5000" that is also in the movies? That's the same hotel.

It wasn't long before my Greek boss discovered my restaurant expertise and skills with people. He promoted me to bartender at the "lobby bar." This lobby bar was a new concept he had come up with: to display beautiful women in the middle of the entrance lobby. His strategy was to lure the businessmen who were waiting for their rooms or for meetings, to spend money drinking with the lobby girls.

I became good friends with all the young women who worked there. Life became exciting again, hanging out with my newfound friends. None of us were from Manhattan, so we all felt a certain security in being with one another, since we were "NYC newcomers." The money was pouring in and the hotel was doing great with the new lobby bar concept. Everyone was happy, or at least that was my perception of happiness then. Most of the girls were pursuing a career in another field: acting, modeling, fashion design, or movie directing.

We earned money at the hotel while waiting for our hoped-for lucky break to launch our "real careers." We talked about it many nights after work as we gathered at other bars and clubs to talk, dance and have fun.

Where Was God in my Life?

As long as I had friends and was making money while pursuing my career goals, I was mostly content, until men got involved in the picture. I think my friends and I talked about the existence of God, but none of us went to church or spent any time with Christian friends. We didn't read the Bible or go to Bible studies or Christian socials.

Maybe I just didn't want to spoil my new fun, but I do know that all these friends perceived life the same way—without God. For example, I toured St. Patrick's Cathedral on Fifth Avenue for the same reason that I went to see cathedrals in Spain on my junior high school trip. I saw it as a monument, as any tourist would, and admired the beauty of it.

I don't really remember seeking God for any direction during this time in my life, but I did talk to Him sometimes when I felt scared, confused, or needed help. I merely saw God as my security blanket. I never verbally denied His existence because I did believe in Him as my Creator. I believed in Jesus as my Savior. However, people were not able to see Jesus in me; I didn't really even know Him, nor did I know who I was in Him. Therefore, I never made Jesus Lord of my life. Knowing nothing about the Holy Spirit, I had no power to do that.

If only I had just sought out a church or spent time reading my Bible and got discipled, I might have found the strength to stand for truth and to see God's ways. But the world's ways—making the most money possible, having friends, and seeking a man—were so much more enticing to my flesh.

So-Called 'Christian' Girl Meets Worldly Muslim

Before long a new restaurant manager, Ali, was hired at the hotel. He was dark and handsome with a big beautiful smile, loads of charm, and was always impeccably dressed in designer clothes. His outward appearance made him seem rich. I began noticing that he favored me with the hours I wanted. Soon, he was asking me out on dates outside of work, wining and dining me at the best of NYC restaurants and nightclubs. As he grew more and more interested in me, he bought me designer clothes and was even willing to talk about God and sometimes about Jesus freely!

As a newly single American woman with small town innocence, I was completely unaware of the ride I was about to go on with this Palestinian from Tel Aviv. He rarely ever talked about his family back home. He had no real friends in the US except a middle-aged, wealthy American couple he knew in Tyson's Corner, Maryland. The husband owned a Toyota dealership.

I mentioned wanting to get a car and he took me to meet this friend who cut me a deal on a bright yellow Toyota. The color reminded me of my first car that my brother had taken out for a "test drive" and totaled. It had been the same color and I relished this new car with this sweet deal. Today I realize that he used the car as bait —lust of the flesh, lust of the eyes, and the pride of life (1 John 2:16) —to lure me into a relationship.

Within a few months, we had spent a lot of time together and it was intense. Of course, I loved the attention, and I especially loved the "finest taste of NYC", as he wined and dined me at the finest restaurants and clubs and bought me the finest clothes and jewelry.

We talked about marriage and children, God, fashion and a lot of things that kept my interest. The next thing I knew, he came with me to my parents' house to celebrate Christmas with us. He was quite the charmer and impressed my parents. My gifts to my family were a little more elaborate than usual that year, for he had contributed money to buy them nice presents. He seemed like such a 'nice guy' but of course. How else would he win me over? Today I hear this description often from people I meet who describe their own Muslim neighbor, boyfriend or relative as such a nice person!

When he gave me his Christmas gift, I was blown away! Opening the box revealed one of the desires of my heart. I couldn't believe it! There was a beautiful blue fox tail, the same color as the fox fur coat that I had tried on in Macy's once and loved. He said it represented the fur that was being made exclusively for me in a shop in Brooklyn.

What an impression this guy was making on my parents and me, and we weren't even engaged. Even though we had talked about marriage, I had expressed that I really wasn't ready yet. I just wanted to have fun for a while, and I was still recovering from my divorce.

Rich Arab Men Trying to Buy American Girls with Jewels

After a while, Ali left his position at the hotel where I worked and told me that he got a much better job elsewhere, although his new position was *the Maitre' D* for a posh restaurant, not a manager. He invited me many times to the upscale establishment. I met famous people there, though he was mostly introducing me to Arabian sheiks with more money than anyone I had ever known. After a while, he convinced me to introduce one of my friends to one of the sheiks so we could double date that weekend. So I did.

This gal, who was also a very social person like me, brought her cousin along that night, which prompted the sheik to call up and invite one of his rich friends to join us. The sheiks adorned my girl-friends with a lot of jewelry, and bought them the best of food and drinks. We danced and talked into the wee hours of the morning.

About this time, my two girlfriends were hinting that they needed to leave because of all they had to do the next day. However, the sheik and his friend tried persuading them to go back to their room with them, but they refused. The persuasion grew more intense with more jewelry and gifts given. Soon, the girls and I went to the bathroom together to have a conference.

My friends wanted to keep the jewelry and run out the back door. They had absolutely no intention of going into the fancy hotel with these men, as they put it, "not for all the tea in China!" They al-luded to the age, ugliness, and overweight bodies of the rich "givers." They wanted me to tell these men that they had an emergency and had to leave in a hurry. In other words, they wanted me to lie for them. While I understood their disgust, I did not want to lie.

I did not want to cause a problem with my boyfriend—as of then we hadn't had any —and therefore did not want to be privy to my friends' plot. By this point, I was used to receiving his plush royal treatment and I didn't want to be held responsible for my friends' de-parture. I begged them to go tell these men themselves, and to return the jewelry, but they refused. They took off out the back door, leaving me in a pickle.

I went back to the table and tried to stall, insisting I didn't know where they were. After a while, Ali convinced me to tell him the truth and did I ever see those men explode with uncontrollable tempers! If looks could kill, I would have been dead. From then on, my girlfriends hid out, not only from these two men but also from Ali and me.

Ali told me his rich friends were going to hunt down my fleeing friends and kill them if they did not return the jewelry. I tried to reason with him; technically those guys gave the jewelry to the girls. Nothing worked to convince Ali, nor could Ali convince these men, or so he told me. Finally, I did get some of the jewelry back from my friend at work, and returned the so-called gifts to Ali to give back to his friends. Either that appeased them, or they simply returned to their own country and or Ali hocked the jewelry himself..

This experience is one that God used as a lesson to prepare me for the future He had planned for me. You will see it later in my life journey. I have learned how important it is to seek God's wisdom in everything, for He knows the heart of every man. I thank God today that He protected us all from much worse consequences at that time. He promises to protect His own children as they seek Him and obey Him. Praying to God for wisdom and guidance and obeying it will prepare us for the right groom in our life and keep us from being deceived by our human reasoning.

Does America Owe Muslims Anything?

As a usual pastime, Ali and I would go to Macy's at Madison Square Garden to shop for new designer clothes. He almost always bought me something, so I was excited to go shopping with him. One day, we moseyed into the men's leather coat department. I began looking around for something I thought would look good on him. He was away from me and when I turned around to find him, I spotted him stuffing a leather jacket inside of leather jacket he was wearing! I caught him red-handed, stealing!

I shrieked, "What are you doing? Are you crazy or something?" He looked at me with a look that scared me, a look I had never seen on him before. His eyes were wide and evil looking and his face and mouth fierce with anger. I would classify it as demonic. He blurted out, "This country owes me!"

At that time, I had no idea what that statement meant, but one thing I did know was that the act of stealing was punishable with a jail sentence. I wanted nothing to do with being an accomplice. A huge red flag went up in my brain like an alarm as loud as any other. I ran from there and got onto the subway to go back to Brooklyn, where I had recently moved. There was God again, reminding me of my own conviction about stealing that bracelet a long time ago. I thought about how very wrong stealing is in God's eyes.

In almost a year's time of dating, I had never seen this side of him. He literally turned on a dime from loving and charitable to demonic, like a wild animal out to hunt down his prey, as you will soon see! As I thought this problem through, I realized it had only been a week or two before this that Ali had convinced me to let him move in with me while he was in between rental leases. What was I going to do about his possessions in my apartment?

When I got home, out of devastating fear, I told my landlords what happened. Ironically and God-ordained, they were Jewish and clearly understood high security tactics! Obviously, they had had enough experience with Muslims persecuting Jews and other people to know exactly what to do, as well as the speed necessary to do it!

They moved quickly, advising me to put all of his belongings on the curb. They immediately got a locksmith to come and change the locks. They also advised me not to answer my phone or let him in after the locks were changed. When he came back to where I lived, he started screaming and pounding on the door, cursing me out and threatening me when he saw his stuff on the curb. I was terrified!

I heard the landlord come out on the balcony and firmly, yet calmly, tell him to get off their property immediately or they would call the police. Later, they told me they had the phone ready in hand. It seemed to work. He stopped and left the premises. I felt safe and protected by my Jewish landlords. Praise God for using them to protect me.

Luke 6:45 says, "Out of the abundance of the heart, the mouth speaks." The Lord was now clearly revealing to me the character of the man I had been dating. For God will bring every deed into judgment, including every hidden thing, whether it is good or evil. (Ecclesiastes 12:14)

My First Encounter with Islam

Although I didn't identify it as such until later, this was my first encounter with Islam, just as my friends had encountered Islam with those Arab sheiks and their gifts of jewelry. In Islam, men own women (Qur'an, Sura 2:223, 4:3, 4:34). I could see in these men their ideology of ownership of women, the claiming of them as property and I sure felt it as chills in my bones.

Their hot tempers are disguised by sweet luring voices. Their "aim to please" is the trap to get women where they wanted them. I wish that was the end of it, but I learned the hard way that many Muslims are relentless in their pursuit of what they want. They are indoctrinated to believe that this Western country (the nation of infidels with whom God is angry, a "Christian nation") owes them much, according to jihad and the teachings of Islam.

Dangerous Stalker

As I went about my business, Ali stalked me. One day I went shopping in one of my usual places in Brooklyn. When I returned to my car I found him in the driver's seat. He must have duplicated my key secretly! Without thinking, I opened the passenger side, which was nearest me, and got in to confront him. As I did, he took off, driving the car forward with me half in and half out. I screamed at the top of my lungs for help. Just as I did, a police car with its loud siren roared across the next intersection. I was screaming, "He's stealing my car!" while still half in and half out. Ali got spooked, stopped the car, jumped out, and ran. To this day, I know that God rescued me from this man's evil grip by sending that police car.

I now realize this man thought he owned me. He was relentless in trying to get what he thought he deserved. I was reminded of that past Christmas in Maine with my family—how he had tried to woo my parents and woo me into marrying him when he gave me that fox tail as a Christmas gift, indicating he would be giving me a full fox fur. I wondered if it was even true. Once again, I had gotten sucked into a bad relationship, but this time with a thief and a liar.

Another day I returned to my parking spot only to find that my car was not there at all. It was obvious that Ali had succeeded in stealing it. I was making the loan payments on that car but somehow he thought he could take it from me. I brainstormed with my girl-

73

friend from college, who lived in the basement of this same two family house with me. Her boyfriend, who had spent enough time with Ali, knew how he thought. This guy was in the banking business. Little did I know it then, but he was also a thief. He eventually robbed an ATM account. I see now how God uses even the wicked to help His children.

This guy's mind worked like a thief's, and he knew Ali so well that he looked like the hero, especially to my friend who was his girlfriend, when he led me straight to my car. My car was perched on the 3rd or 4th floor of an elevated parking lot near the same shopping area where I had left it. When he drove us to the car, I was so excited.

Because I was being stalked, I figured I would get advice from a Subway cop with whom I had developed a friendship. He connected me with his lonely friend Anthony. Anthony came up with great ideas to help me stop this relentless Arab from bothering me. Through investigating, he found out that Ali lived right around the corner from him. Now, my "Knight in Shining Armor" helped me press charges against Ali. I filed a criminal report and an arrest warrant was issued for stalking and car theft. Anthony had enough on Ali to get him arrested and put in jail for a few days. It was obviously time for me to "get out of Dodge."

In the meantime at work, one of my patrons had given me his business card, telling me he knew people and could help me get another job if I needed it. I decided this was the right time, since Ali was only going to be detained for a short while. I was given a new job at LaGuardia Airport, as a Catering Manager at the Holiday Inn. They were desperate for help. I was able to move right away to an apartment in Queens.

I said goodbye to my kind Jewish landlords. It was a bittersweet farewell. They understood why I was moving, as well as why I made my phone unlisted and kept my address secret. In today's "Google information world," that would be quite impossible, so be aware ladies. Your enemy is prowling around in the form of a Muslim husband who wants to own and control you. You can run but you can't hide!

Sure enough, once I moved to Queens I never heard from Ali again. He did run into one of my friends years later and asked her about me. Thank God, she really didn't know where I was at that time. I had lost touch with her for a while before meeting up with her again in Florida twelve years ago.

When Good People Do Nothing

I only recently learned that Ali had called my parents when he couldn't find me. He threatened to throw acid in my face! When I asked my mother, "What did you do?", she said "Nothing!" I asked her what they were thinking at the time. She said, "Your father and I were scared to death for you! But what could we do? We didn't want to get involved."

It hurt me that they did nothing. I wanted to know why they didn't call the police about a man who was threatening such a horrific act against their own daughter. When I asked her this, she just shrugged her shoulders "I don't know." It's hard for me to believe, but that was my mother's response.

Many people simply ignore life-threatening issues, even when it is their children who are facing them. They just go on with their own lives without acting on behalf of those in danger. Edmund Burke once said, "All that is necessary for the triumph of evil is for good men to do nothing!"

For example, when prayer was removed from our nation's educational system because atheists demanded it, good men did nothing. My parents were from that very generation, but were too busy running from God and using alcohol in an effort to mask all their personal problems to notice what was happening in our country. Since my mother was unequally yoked with an unbeliever, she just ignored it all. Recently my mom expressed how difficult it was to raise four children for them so that seems to be her reason why she didn't notice this happening. Only God knows for sure.

Another way people ignore the problems of others is by simply going to the doctor to get drugs. If you sedate the pain and stress in life, the pain will go away temporarily while you are under sedation, but eventually reality hits. The problem that caused that pain will be greater than it was before. Your drugs will be taken away or you will be encountering God face to face one day, being held accountable for why you did nothing. Pretending there is no problem does not make it go away, as too many people so wrongly believe.

The hardest solution to problems is to face them head on and do whatever it takes to overcome them with God's help. Of course, even this proves we are truly helpless without God. *Abba,* Father draws us ever so gently at times and promises to always be with us.

If we don't run to God, then sometimes He just has to allow us to face the consequences of our continuous sin, in order to get our attention to come to Him. He will give us rest, as the Word tells us in Matthew 11:28. He wants to take us into His loving arms and just get us to be still and know He is God (Psalm 46:10). He has the perfect love that we so desperately desire.

Sister, don't do what I did. Go to your Father in Heaven, for His love is all you need. He knows who your perfect mate is. He is preparing him for you and will bring him at the perfect time and place. In the meantime, just listen and obey His voice for He is your strong tower, your refuge, and your strength. In your weakness, He is strong (Joel 3:10, Zechariah 4:6, 2 Corinthians 12:10). He wants to mold you and shape you into something beautiful – a lovely, radiant bride adorned for her worthy groom.

What Entices American Women to Hook up with Muslim Men?

After sharing with another lady my experience of dating Ali, she asked me, "What could possibly entice American women to get 'hooked up' with these Muslim men, here in America?" After all, we have freedom here in the USA! How could a self-respecting woman even date a Muslim man who, following the ideology of Islam, oppresses women? She said she had read a book called *Islam for Dummies.* Even in that book, it clearly shows that Islam teaches oppressing women (though most Muslims in America do not admit to that). Why would an American woman want that?

Sadly, many American women look for love in all the wrong places. In my case, I did not understand my value in the eyes of God nor did I understand anything about Islam. I was ignorant about Islam completely, as the majority of Americans are. I didn't know how to respect myself more than this because I never learned it from a role model.

76

God wanted to be my first love, for only He knows who is ⌐ best husband for me. Only He can lead me safely to His choice. God was simply waiting for me to take the first step toward Him: to believe and trust in Jesus as my only Lord and Savior.

I have learned that God is the ultimate gentleman and doesn't force His unconditional love on anyone. He desires that we choose His unconditional love over the world's conditional love. Satan preys on the weak, the innocent and the ignorant. A retired Lt. General from the army, William Boykin, says the first thing he did before going into battle was "to know his enemy." We need to understand that we are in a spiritual battle (with Satan) for the souls of men. We need to get equipped to know our enemy by seeking God's wisdom.

Most American women want to be married much more than they want to put God first in their life, and Satan knows it. My value was wrongly placed in finding a man to love me. I didn't know God wanted to be first. Now, if my dad had demonstrated how a man should treat a woman by truly loving and being kinder to my mom and me, then I might have known better. If my parents had allowed Jesus to be the center of their marriage, they would have learned how to demonstrate God's design for marriage. This in turn would have been my role model to follow so to also have more self-respect.

Tragically, American society has been corrupted with alcohol, drugs, abortion, lies, and so much more sin against God. Our freedom in Christ turned to "freedom to choose and do whatever we want." We have become a "me first society" which causes us to be enticed by Satan. The Word says, "All things are lawful, but not everything is beneficial." (1 Corinthians 10:23)

Satan is using domineering men, especially many Muslim men, to take down this Christian nation by marrying our women. Even Muslims understand they can dominate the world with Islam, their belief system, if they are "fruitful and multiply" by having lots of children. They even allow up to four marriages at one time and expect to increase the number of children they have this way. The average Muslim family has 8.1 children per family. Multiply that by four wives and you have a small army.

Most non-Muslim women do not know until it is too late that Muslim men expect to raise their children as Muslims, as true followers of Islam. In 2014, I discovered a very shocking statistic; over 500,000 American women have married Muslim men. Most identify themselves as Christians.

Wrongly, our American families have taught us women that our value is in being married and having a family, not in putting God first. I hear even Christian families nagging their daughters and young people in the church with the question, "Do you have a boyfriend yet?" Most youth are already fighting sexual urges. Being encouraged to get a boyfriend does not help. Yes, God created most women to want to be loved by a man. However, if we refuse to submit to God for His choice, we will submit to Satan for his choice.

Another reason American women are enticed to marry Muslim men is because many American men dominate in marriage or will not commit to marriage these days. Most couples live together with no long term commitment. They are pursuing worldly pleasures instead. Ladies, I assure you, you are much more valuable than this in God's eyes!

Muslim Men Deceiving American Christian Women
My current wonderful husband and I did a skit concerning a very serious matter that is happening around the United States today: some American Christian women (and others from different Western nations) are being easily deceived into marrying Muslim men. How does this happen? Either they are not strong in their faith and their walk with Jesus Christ, or they do not truly know Jesus as their Lord and Savior at all. Both come from not reading and applying the Word of God to their lives daily and never being discipled. Our relationship with God is a two way relationship not just a religion.

In the skit, I play the part of a naïve and weak Christian American woman, while my husband plays the part of a smooth-talking Muslim man who wants to marry me. The skit goes like this:

Scene: Christian woman reading the Bible at a university campus

Muslim man walking up to her: "Oh Hello!"

Christian woman: "Hi!"

Muslim man: "What is that you are reading?"

78

Christian woman: "That's the Bible."

Muslim man: "Really? You know that we Muslims also believe in the Bible."

Christian woman: "Really?"

Muslim man: "Yes we do. And by the way, we also believe that Jesus is also a prophet of God... So you are a Christian?

Christian woman: "Yes."

Muslim man: I just was wondering, you know that in my faith, we really have much in common. You believe in Jesus and we believe in Jesus, and we believe in the same God as you believe, the God of Abraham, Isaac and Jacob. You know that in my faith, we are allowed as Muslims to marry Christians. I'll be so honored. Actually I have been praying and asking God that I will find a wife who would be godly like you, and it would be an honor if you would accept."

Christian woman: "I'm so flattered."

Muslim man: "Just think about it. You don't have to even become a Muslim. You can remain a Christian no problem. You know that in my faith, we don't ask our wives to go and work—it is the man who works and provides, and the wife is the queen of the house."

Christian woman: "I agree with that!"

Muslim man: "I would like to meet your parents and ask them if I can marry you. You are such a noble woman. You believe in the Bible. I also believe in the Bible. You believe in Jesus, I also believe in Jesus."

Christian woman talking on the phone later with a female friend: "Do you know how I am always telling you how much I want to be married? Every time I see you and your husband together I so want to be married. I met this guy today—it must be from God—I mean, he believes in God. He believes in Jesus. He says he wants to marry me and he said that I didn't have to work and that I'd be the queen of the house.

Doesn't that sound like God to you? Isn't that amazing? I think God is speaking to me. Can you pray with me? "Father God, please let this be the man You have brought me to marry."

Meanwhile ...

Muslim man on the phone with another Muslim man: "Hello. The green card is on the way! What is that? Oh no it's not one of those terrible ones—she's a Christian. Oh she's a very beautiful woman. The Qur'an says marry beautiful women. Children explosion, yes, may Allah be praised."

Christian woman later talking to the Muslim man: "I was just reading here in the Bible, about how God is love, so I guess love is good huh?"

Muslim man: "It's the same thing in Islam. God is love, yes. And God is loving and kind and merciful and all this, yes certainly."

Christian woman: "Let me call my mom and see if we can come and see them."

They married. We usually have the saying: "They lived happily ever after" but, five years later. . .

Christian woman pacing until Muslim husband comes home: "Hi honey. The food . . ."

Muslim husband arrives and interrupts her: "I have told you don't call me honey. I am not your honeybee, okay? "

Christian woman: "I'm sorry."

Muslim man: "Why have these children not gone to the mosque? You spend too much time in the church. Don't take my children to the church. I've told you so many times—it is your duty to take them to the mosque."

I am writing this to warn you my friend, Christian women need to be on guard. Do not be unequally yoked (2 Corinthians 6:14). God's Scripture is written to protect us from harm. God is not a killjoy.

Christian Women: Before You Marry a Muslim, Beware!

Believe me, I know how desperate many American women, both Christian and non-Christian, are to marry. Steven and I revised and reprinted a wonderful leaflet that a friend of ours wrote, called *"Before You Marry a Muslim.¹"* which I believe every American woman needs to read this in order to understand how risky it is to marry a Muslim man.

It is such a deceptive proposition, that some Muslim men will actually try to convince Christian women that Islam and Christianity is one and the same. They claim that they worship the same God and believe in the same Jesus as Christians do. Recently I heard one woman tell me that her Muslim husband convinced her that Islam is just another denomination of Christianity. Ladies, I am telling you this is all a lie from the pit of hell! Beware! The devil is prowling around like a roaring lion looking to destroy (1 Peter 5:8).

If you fall for Satan's tricks, you will more than likely experience what many others and I have sadly experienced—hell on earth. Like those who get sucked in to the "Mob" have a hard time getting out, neither will you get out of a marriage with a Muslim man without big trouble. Satan is using Muslim men to seek out American women, especially Christian women, in his attempt to destroy their witness. Those who falsely believe that going to Heaven is achieved just by being a good person and that all religions follow a standard of right and wrong are easy targets.

If you are truly saved, you want to follow Jesus first, to please Him above your own fleshly desires. If you still have self on the throne of your heart rather than God on the throne of your life, then you will not agree with 1 Corinthians 6:14, which states how important it is to not be yoked with unbelievers (in this case, referring to marriage).

Christianity and Islam United?

I believe many of these problems with naïveté are coming from church leaders and pastors who are leading their sheep to the slaughter through unbiblical teaching and avoiding parts of the Bible as well, as by the way they live.

---

¹ Get a copy through the website www.jesustomuslims.org

There is a document called "A Common Word" which was produced by Muslim leaders to lure Christian leaders into signing a so-called peace initiative between Muslims and Christians. Many Christian leaders have joined with scholars and university leaders to agree with it in the "Yale Response" document. You can see our website for more information about it.[2]

The Muslim's agenda is to establish world peace by finding something in common between the two groups because Muslims and Christians make up 55% of the world population. This document deceptively lures Christians with the lie that we share a common belief, which is "loving God and loving our neighbor." Jesus Christ did indeed command His followers to love God and love their neighbors (Matthew 22:37-40). Muhammad however militarily fought against Pagan and Jewish neighbors who did not accept his claims of prophethood and growing political leadership. Is this loving your neighbor?

"It is mine to avenge. I will repay," says the Lord in both Deuteronomy 32:35 and Romans 12:19. While Jesus Christ also commanded His followers to love their enemies (Matthew 5:43-48; Luke 6:27-37), Muhammad fought against his enemies, eventually earning himself the political control of Arabia. The Qur'an includes verses that contradict Jesus Christ's commands and example to love enemies (Sura 5:33; 9:28-33, and many others).

After his death, Muhammad's political successor Abu Bakr fought apostates in Arabia, whereas Jesus Christ did not order his followers to kill or persecute apostates (John 6:63-69). Jesus even rebuked Peter for using the sword against one of those who came to arrest Him (Luke 22:49-52, Matthew 26:46-52; John 18:10-11).

Muhammad's later political successors conquered Syria, Palestine (including Jerusalem in 638 AD), Egypt and other African countries, Mesopotamia, the Byzantine Empire (changing Constantinople to Istanbul), the Persian Empire, Iberia, India, Romania, Hungary, and even attacking France and Austria.

---

[2] http://jesustomuslims.org/articles/whats-going-behind-church-doors

While most Muslims today are heavily influenced by modern Western ideals of tolerance, the example of Muhammad and his political successors clearly show the violent side of Islam. In contrast, Jesus Christ and His apostles did not lead military conflicts against the Romans who oppressed His people the Jews or the Jewish people who rejected Him. Rather, He loves all people.

Also, the Qur'an accuses those who believe Jesus Christ is God of blasphemy or denying the truth (Sura 5:17) and wants Allah to destroy those who believe Jesus is the Son of God (Sura 9:30), calling their minds perverted or deluded. This contradicts prophecies in the Bible concerning Jesus Christ being the Son of God (1 Chronicles 17:11-15, Psalm 2:6-8, Psalm 89:26-28, Isaiah 9:6-7). While some people do curse Christians, Jesus Christ commands His followers to bless those who curse you (Luke 6:28) and says that we are blessed when persecuted (Matthew 5:10-12).

While the Qur'an denies that God is our Father in Heaven (Sura 5:18), Jesus Christ taught us that God is our Father in Heaven (Matthew 23:9). It is vital to understand that Islam, which means submission to Allah (not peace), is not the way of Jesus Christ. Sadly, many people are ignorant of the Truth.

The point is that if our Christian leaders are uniting themselves unequally with unbelievers, where does that lead their sheep? The answer is to the slaughter, along with these leaders and false prophets, through deception and their teachings.

Remember, Jesus Christ warned us that false prophets would come and deceive many people, leading them astray (Matthew 24:11, 24). Trying to coexist with other faiths especially with Islam at the expense of accepting Jesus as any other prophet is impossible and simply shows pseudo "compassion" that offends God Almighty. True godly compassion cares more about a person's eternal soul than pleasing an earthly desire.

Islam is the mirror opposite of Christianity. Muslims and their books use a lot of similar words as Christians but have a different dictionary for their meaning. Satan is very subtle when he deceives us through Islam.

For example, a cashier at my local store helped me with my groceries and saw our ministry's *Jesus to Muslim* leaflets. He said to me, "Oh, a Muslim came to my church and taught us about his religion."

I asked, "You mean, a former Muslim who became a Christian?"

"No," he replied, "A Muslim Imam (leader)."

I told him that we teach Christians how to share the Gospel of Jesus with Muslims.

He protested, "All faiths are the same. They worship the same God as we do. They love Jesus more than we do and revere him."

This is a lie from the devil that many people are spoon-fed by leaders who do not obey the Great Commission and allow wolves in sheep's clothing to teach in their churches. All roads do not lead to God. These leaders just believe what the Muslims say instead of comparing the Qur'an with the Bible. They have not studied how the enemy deceives people.

The next week, I gave him a brochure comparing Islam and Christianity. When I asked him later if he read it, he replied, "It's a funny thing how they take all the bad things of Islam and compare them to the good things of Christianity." However, the brochure compares the truth about Islam with the truth about Christianity. He did not want to accept the differences however but rather is complacent believing a wolf in sheep's clothing (Matthew 7:15-20).

God help the innocent! Part of preparing for the bridegroom God has for you is keeping yourself holy and set apart from the world as the Bride of Christ. Jesus is the only way to God, for there is no other name by which souls may be saved (John 14:6, Acts 4:12).

Testimony of a Christian American Almost Marrying a Muslim
A friend I am mentoring nearly became a statistic—one of the many women who fall into the trap of marrying Muslim men. I will call her Kelly. While married to a Christian man who continually criticized her and made her feel unloved, she put her energies into being a witness to a very kind Muslim man, whom I will call Mahdi. Sadly, she was easily lured into an emotional affair with him. (It is so important for women to witness to women, and men to men, because it is so easy to inappropriately bond with a person of the opposite gender.)

Kelly let bitterness toward her husband grow in her heart, which paved the way for her to get closer to Mahdi, and inspired her to divorce her husband. Her relationship with Mahdi quickly developed into a budding romance. I interject a warning here that I have learned to be true; without spiritual and emotional intimacy as well as complete transparency in sorting out problems with our spouse, the devil will tempt you. The bait will entice you to look for validation from somewhere else.

Kelly rationalized her relationship with a Muslim by naively believing she would bring Mahdi and his whole family to Christ. She was temporarily blinded to the fact that disobedience to God hurt her witness to him instead of strengthening it. Moving into Mahdi's house and planning to marry him did not glorify Jesus Christ. It hurt her family and her reputation as well.

Looking back, Kelly strongly believes that God heard her family's fervent and daily prayers to wake her up to the Truth. (I am an advocate that prayer works to break strongholds so don't ever give up on praying for those whom you love.)

It was very difficult for her to pull away, due to the stronghold this Muslim man had over her. (If you or someone you love is trapped in a stronghold, I suggest also reading *Bondage Breaker* by Neil Anderson.) Several times she pulled away, only to return when he would again pledge his love for her and convince her to stay with him. I too experienced the taunt of the devil through a man's promised love and can certainly relate.

Kelly's dad, a man who loves and follows Jesus Christ patiently went many times at her request to bring her home, but she would always go back to Mahdi. Kelly's mom, friends and family prayed diligently for her. They encouraged her to refrain from an intimate relationship with Mahdi, but she refused to listen to them. Her mom shared her concern for Kelly with her women's prayer group. Together they offered pleas to God for this wayward Christian daughter. Lacking this from my own parents, my heart melts for such godly parents who stood in the gap for her.

The reason Kelly initially refused to listen to reason was because she was "in love." This powerful feeling of infatuation kept her from seeing the harm she was doing in pursuing this relationship.

Feelings so often lie to us and keep us from the real truth, but they certainly do not change truth.

The connection with Mahdi was holding her back from following Jesus Christ fully. Mahdi promised her that she was "free to practice her Christian faith." However, a real relationship with Christ is just that—a relationship. It is not a "practice."

An issue that made Kelly uneasy was Mahdi's desire to raise their would-be children as Muslims. Islam compels parents to raise their children as Muslims. Muslim men often do not tell their non-Muslim wife until after the children are born. Kelly was warned beforehand.

Free will to choose whether to follow Muhammad or not is discouraged in Islam. Muslims actually believe everyone is born a Muslim and if a person is not practicing Islam, it was their parents or society who caused them to follow a different path. Therefore, since they think every person was already a Muslim when they are born, when they become Muslim it is often considered to revert, instead of convert.

Muslims consider that it is their job to "revert" people back to Islam. The ultimate Islamic goal is to convert all people to Islam, dominate them, or kill them (Sura 9:29-33). Apostasy is also very heavily discouraged, with the threat of disownment and/or death looming over many of those who dare leave the faith (Sura 4:89). My husband Steven, as a former Muslim, has experienced that threat all his life, although he loves his neighbors and enemies and has never tried to kill or hurt anyone.

Kelly did not realize how difficult it is for a Muslim to renounce his faith or to not force that faith on his children. While Muslims can, of course, be kind, many do not react with kindness to their children who decide not to follow Muhammad or to people who invite them to follow Jesus Christ. If Kelly had married Mahdi and had children, it is most probable that the kindness he was exhibiting before marriage would have evaporated and been replaced by strict enforcement of Islam in his household, regardless of former promises to respect his wife's belief.

I have several friends today with testimonies about the sudden overnight change of attitudes by their Muslim husbands. Many have escaped, but not without tremendous consequences.

The kindness of Mahdi was thus part of the bait in the trap Satan was using to catch Kelly and render her ineffective by having her grow further away from Christ. Sadly, she had not felt kindness from the Christian man she had married and then divorced, so she was drawn, like a moth to a flame, to this kind Muslim man.

Although kindness is a component of love, the devil uses it as a lure for his prey. It is important to realize that people can be kind regardless of their belief, whether they are an atheist or a believer in God. We should always look to God instead of depending solely on the kindness of people. The devil so often comes as an angel of light, using kindness and other baits to lure people into darkness.

Little by little, God's gentle voice got through to Kelly's heart, exposing the folly blocking the truth. She still remembers one powerful moment as if it were yesterday. She was listening to Todd Agnew's song "Isaiah 6" and Mahdi walked into the room. He disliked the song and expressed that to her. She couldn't understand why he didn't like it; she loved it. It spoke to her spirit. She was enjoying praising the Creator as she sang along, heart outstretched to her Maker. Isaiah 6 is breathtaking and powerful in its description of God and His holiness. She reasoned at this moment that if he was going to get that angry over her worshipping Christ in song, it might be much worse later.

She called her dad to pick her up for the final time. I praise God for her parents' patience with her. As I see it, based on the teaching I have received from Steven, there is a strong possibility that Mahdi was rejecting her singing because singing is prohibited in Islam. He also may have been jealous of her praising God with such joy rather than praising him and his god.

Her Muslim lover couldn't understand the song or Isaiah 6 because he didn't belong to Jesus Christ. Even though she had fallen away from following Jesus through her actions, God never let her go. Ever so gently He had been calling her, seeking His little lost lamb that had wandered away from the fold. He always knew where she was; He knows everything. However, He wanted her to willingly, of her own accord, come back to Him.

Finally, Kelly realized that she was hopelessly lost and that her Shepherd was calling her. Isaiah 53:6 says we, like sheep, have gone astray and gone our own way. Understanding gripped her heart and enabled her to finally say goodbye to Mahdi. She at last comprehended, through the Holy Spirit's conviction, that 2 Corinthians 6:14 is applied to marriage today as well. Previously, she had rationalized this verse away when confronted by her sisters in Christ and her family, saying that it was only for those days. Kelly hurt Mahdi deeply. If she had not wandered away from Jesus, this would not have happened. Oh, the tangled web we weave by seeking love in the wrong place! It caused suffering to Mahdi and his family, and she genuinely regrets hurting him. Staying with him, however, was no longer an option, since her Shepherd, Jesus Christ, was calling her to follow Him. Because Mahdi was following Muhammad instead of Jesus Christ, they were obviously not on the same path. How could they walk together when going on different and opposite paths in life? They were not truly united in one Spirit.

Kelly still prays for Mahdi and his family. Although she no longer has any contact with him, she hopes that someday he and his family will come to Jesus Christ and follow Him instead of Muhammad.

Kelly also greatly hurt her ex-husband through her emotional adultery with Mahdi, which helped motivate her to divorce rather than work on her marriage. After she recognized her guilt, she asked her ex-husband for forgiveness and attempted reconciliation, but he had already moved on and later married another lady. Devastated at first, she earnestly sought counsel and learned that God had forgiven her when she repented. Because of God's great grace and mercy, she could marry again. She then trusted in God to bring her the man He had for her, who loves Him and follows Christ.

Kelly shares this story because she believes it could help a Christian woman who might be considering marriage to a Muslim man. Beloved sister, if that's you, please know that our Shepherd, Jesus Christ, wants us to follow him. Following him does not mean to marry people who don't follow him.

Muslims follow the teachings of Muhammad, not the teachings of Jesus Christ. Please do not allow yourself to fall in the trap Satan rigs with the bait of marriage. Please keep your eyes on Jesus Christ and allow Him to bring into your life the right man for you, a Christian man who truly loves Jesus Christ and truly follows Him.

As for my Christian friend, Kelly, she has now been married for four years to a wonderful Christian man who loves God with all his heart, and loves her, too. God, in His mercy, knitted their lives together as one; they worship and serve Him together. They are soul mates and are blessed with a very strong connection that is built on the Word of God. Their relationship is sealed with the unity of following Jesus Christ together. God is number one in their lives. They enjoy spiritual intimacy, as well as physical, sexual, emotional, and mental intimacy that is more than she ever imagined.

Kelly loves her husband and greatly appreciates his kindness to her, which she had not experienced before with her first husband. She is filled with gratitude that he reads the Bible and praises God in song with her, as well as prays daily to their Heavenly Father with her. They enjoy going to church together and being involved in helping the community. She is so thankful to God for rescuing her from marrying a person who was not following Jesus Christ. With Mahdi she could not have experienced these amazing blessings. God is so good!

Beloved Christian sister, let God write your love story. Please do not wander away from God's amazing plan for your life. God is good, and His plan for you is awesome! Even if it is not in God's plan for you to marry, God can greatly use your life as a blessing for the Kingdom of Heaven. For example, Corrie ten Boom, a follower of Jesus Christ, never got married but she blessed so many people by loving them and telling them about God's great love and forgiveness. Even though she suffered horrible injustice, (imprisoned in a Nazi jail then in a concentration camp) she trusted in God and has impacted thousands of lives by living for Christ. Many came to know Christ in that concentration camp when she and her sister shared God's love with them.

If you are lost and are not following Jesus Christ at this moment, please remember He is the Loving Shepherd who is calling you to follow Him. While following Muhammad is the way many people choose, Jesus is "the way, the truth, and the life" and the only way to God, our Heavenly Father (John 14:6).

Only the Bread of Life (John 6:35) can really make you full. A father's perfect Love – our very own Creator who knows us better than we know ourselves. Only our Heavenly Father's love can make you truly belong.

If you are considering marrying a Muslim, or have already married a Muslim, and if you need to talk with me or a Christian sister who understands what you are going through, please feel free to contact me and I will pray with you and help however I can.[3] You are already in my prayers and I would love to pray with you personally and offer you support. As sisters in Christ, we need to love, bless, and help each other.

Snares of the enemy are everywhere, so we need to keep our eyes on Jesus. Only He keeps us from falling and saves us when we do fall. When Peter fell while walking on the water after being distracted and having little faith, Jesus reached to pull him up and save him from drowning (Matthew 14:25-33). Like He rescued Peter, so He offers His hand of help and love to us!

Our Bridegroom is looking for a pure and holy Bride when He comes for her. All those who are true to Jesus will be the true Bride made ready for the marriage supper. Won't you allow Him to prepare you today not only for your earthly love but for the Marriage to your Bridegroom, Jesus for eternity?

---

[3] Karen@jesustomuslims.org

5

Second Marriage

After Escaping Ali

Now, let me take you back to my life story. You would think by now I would have given up on guys all together. I was only 23 years old and full of many more "brilliant" ideas, yet totally ignorant of how to change the destructive pattern of my life. I was blind to the generational curse of rebellion upon my family and me.

Totally engrossed in my new position as catering manager of a hotel, I was responsible for all the details of every catered function. They also relied on me during daily business hours to book events, run business meetings and deal with the attitudes of all the union employees.

Obviously, I had little time for dating, although Anthony, who was my hero, (since he rescued me from my evil stalker) still continued to pursue me for dates. He was willing to drive from Brooklyn to Queens to date me. On any given business day, the route could easily take up to two hours, packed as it is with traffic and traffic jams.

I had great responsibilities as the manager, so getting drunk on my time off could have jeopardized my "on call status". Now I had a purpose to distract me from my inner need to be loved. I began to feel heavy stress pushing upon me as I experienced the stubbornness and laziness of the union workers. The union protection actually gave them permission to refuse to do a thorough job and to treat me, their boss, like trash.

I recall one time I went into the kitchen to ask the dishwasher to wash the bread plates so we could use them for dessert, since supplies and finances were low. This union worker swore at me and refused my request, so I wrote him up. When the case went into arbitration, his union representative victoriously concluded the meeting, determining that because the worker spoke Spanish and his English was limited to those swear words he uttered, that his behavior should be forgiven.

The hotel was experiencing some financial difficulties. The CEOs asked the managers to take pay cuts, and to temporarily work for no pay until they could get ahead of the financial problems. So, my workload increased and now they wanted me to work for nothing.

A new hotel was being built across the highway. Just before it was due to open, it occurred to me that I had skills that would qualify me for the openings at this new hotel. I applied for the same position there as the one I currently had. The man interviewing me was thrilled and hired me on the spot. When I learned there was no union affiliated with this hotel, that my pay would be quite a bit higher, plus benefits, I grabbed it. I would now be the catering sales manager for this new hotel, the Marriot.

Now I felt much more important, working at a hotel with more prestige. I began to feel like I was making progress in my life. I had given up on my fashion design degree, but I was making $23,000 at age 23 in 1981. The work hours only slightly decreased, but I felt less used and more appreciated here. I still had no real social life.

Was This My Knight in Shining Armor?

This guy, Anthony, still continued to pursue me, getting me to see him here and there. He would offer to fix things in my apartment. Because of all he did for me, I trusted him and gave him a key to my place so he could do the repairs around his own schedule, mostly while I was at work. You see, without a role model to guide me as to what is right and wrong in the eyes of a perfect God, I had no reference except my feelings and human rationale, and the wrong crowd I hung out with.

He worked less than 40 hours a week; I worked normally around 80 to sometimes 100 hours a week. I was impressed with the little things Anthony would do at my apartment to make my life more convenient, but didn't really think much about him, except he seemed kind when I did see him. He was always trying to please me. I eventually realized it was not out of the goodness of his heart, but because he wanted a sexual relationship with me.

Now almost 25 years old, I felt like I wanted to settle down again with just one guy. I began to think about having a family, but because I had no social life, there really were no prospects in sight. I did have fun with the personnel director at work. He was from Texas. I loved that accent and Texan mannerisms. He was so respectful and obliging, but he didn't really seem interested in anything but a work friendship with me. It began to hit me that this guy, Anthony, was really the only guy pursuing me at the time.

Even though I didn't really feel anything for him romantically, I somehow felt an obligation to him for all he had done for me. I reasoned myself into giving him a chance with me. Of course, as soon as I gave him the green light to date me and not just be a nice guy, he pursued me alright. One of the first things he convinced me to do was to take a week off from work and go to the Bahamas with him.

I tend to be enthusiastic and spontaneous, so I got excited about going on a vacation—to the beach, no less. I certainly didn't feel like Anthony was a stranger. We also had been intimate some, so why not go away with him; he rescued me from Ali and was a police officer—surely he must be someone I could trust! That was my human rationale.

So, I went to the Bahamas with Anthony. From my memory and the pictures I still have, I could see that I was drunk most of the time. Being inebriated numbed the pain deep inside of me. I seemed to feel this pain inside somewhere whenever I got intimate with a guy. The amazing thing about this trip being taken on a whim was, as I later found out, I was the only one who enjoyed spontaneity. Anthony did not; this trip was the last spontaneous thing we did together.

By the time I got back from this trip, I had spilled my guts too much to this man. The sense of obligation I felt toward him propelled me to want to give in to him, just for the sake of getting attention and touch. My imagination dreamed up the way it would be, to find my true love in him, even though I didn't see that potential in him. Whenever we were drinking, he was affectionate with me. When we weren't, he was very hard to read. He acted nice and lured me to where he wanted me. My deep need for love and touch once again caused me to submit until I eventually felt like I was in love.

Pregnant Again, Second Marriage

One day I felt a familiar feeling and went to the doctor to verify it. Sure enough, I was pregnant. Most birth control methods had not worked for me because of sensitivities so I had to use caution, which obviously was not reliable. I was almost 25 years old. I could only hide my pregnancy from my work for so long. Sadly, they had a stigma against women being pregnant, especially in management positions, making it just one more reason why women weren't as readily promoted in those days.

Already traumatized due to my experience with my first husband and the abortion at age 21, I was doubly devastated when Anthony said he was too old for kids and I should abort this child! He also didn't like the idea of marrying me for the sake of a child. However, I finally convinced him through begging and crying, as I was convinced it was all for the sake of our child: to have a father. Believe it or not, it was then that I actually prayed continually to God for Him to help me convince Anthony to marry me. Be careful of what you pray for, because you just might get it!

When we married, I was five months pregnant. It was a private wedding inside his apartment with the Justice of the Peace. By the way, he lived with his mother. She lived on the first floor and he lived on the second. His cousin, a single mother, lived in the basement with her daughter. Attending the wedding were his mother and her boyfriend, my parents, two couples who were his friends (later the wives became my friends as well), and my friend KD and her boyfriend.

I was the only one who didn't drink that day, out of consideration for the health of my baby. I soon regretted the marriage when the Justice of the Peace showed up with a divorce agreement (between Anthony and another woman) for him to sign that same day. In addition to not knowing about that previous marriage, I found out through our marriage certificate that Anthony was 15 years older than I. He had told me that he was only 7 years older.

I wished I could drink to numb the pain of betrayal that I once again felt. I felt my only choice was to go through with it and hope for the best. I remember feeling fortunate that at least this child will live and have a father. Keep in mind; I felt I was doing a good thing for my child. I didn't feel worthy of true love from a man; and I didn't experience true love from Anthony either. I soon learned he did not know how to love anyone, being bound by anger and resentment toward others. He always blamed others for his life's failures and blamed God for the death of his father and more, of which I was then unaware.

The Birth of Christopher

When my baby boy was born, I named him after Christ because I gave Him the credit for saving my baby from abortion, by changing Anthony's mind. Now, my gratitude for this miraculous birth had caused me to seek God again. When I held my baby, looking down at those tiny little hands and beautiful face, I just knew that no man made this child, but only a perfect God. I could see God's face in him.

I felt so undone before such a holy God who could create such beauty and life. With tears in my eyes I prayed, "For the sake of this child I need to change my life. God, please forgive me for not listening to You in the past. Help me change so I can be a good mother for this precious child. I need your help desperately Father God!" Every tiny baby comes into the world looking for something to hold on to. These words only now come to me, as a song goes, and how could he hold on to me when I was so unstable on my own feet in the life I had chosen for myself?

Being in Another Abusive Marriage

Living with Anthony was an emotional roller coaster of constant fighting. Out of desperation, I realized that I needed to go back to church. If not for me, because I had really messed up my life again, then I needed to go for the sake of my child. I just did not want him to have to endure a life of abuse, lies, and misery like I did. I wanted him to have a better life than I did.

While Anthony had originally stated that his motive for joining the police force was to help people, he was fed up with many of the people he met. It was clear to me, through living with him and seeing how he really operated in his home life, that he was not living up to his calling to help others. If he couldn't treat his wife with honor, respect, and kindness, how could he help people in the public in a kind, respectful, and honoring way?

For instance, he justified his prejudice against blacks because they were mostly the ones he arrested. I told him that I felt people who broke the law, regardless of their skin color, needed love because they hadn't gotten it at home. They were desperately grasping for attention, even for negative attention, through breaking the law. I explained to him they had no self-worth because they did not know they are valued creations of our loving God. They needed counsel—not condemnation.

As I sit today on a lawn chair at one of my favorite beaches and watch people, I realize that God gave me such incredible foresight about His love for all people. In 1979, without realizing it was God's heart, I had the foresight and clear understanding of God and His perfect love: God's love sees no color or race and values no one person over another. My relationship with an African American man flew in the face of my parents' wrong perceptions, ignorance and prejudices. While I had great love and respect for him, his desire to protect me stopped the possibility of marriage.

Back to Anthony, his inner hatred for people became clear to me after the marriage, but not before. I began to learn a lot about Anthony after our wedding. Even on the day I delivered our baby, Anthony didn't come into the delivery room to support me. When he heard my screams, he left the hospital. I felt so alone. I was married, yet I felt so alone all the time. Anthony's mother didn't help much; she panicked at every problem I faced with my baby.

Anthony manipulated and controlled me with his perfectionism. I questioned his controlling ways, his temper, and his unwillingness to kindly communicate openly with me. His stubbornness, outright refusal to listen to me, and constant demanding to have control over what I could say and not say, and what I could do and not do, was most definitely hurtful. I actually developed ulcers from having to hold in all my communication, as God created me a verbal person. Anthony ended up hating and resenting me all his life because ultimately I refused to submit to his control.

I did try to lead him to God and get him to church. So did my pastors, but to no avail. Anthony was not the slightest bit interested in

God, nor in finding the answer to living a happy and contented life of joy in Christ. Many of our arguments were over "his way" as opposed to God's ways that I tried to suggest, which he called foolishness. I was unaware at the time that he could not see God's way without the Holy Spirit Who Christians receive by believing in and obeying Jesus (John 14-16; Acts 2).

Anthony was extremely jealous of anyone who looked at me and blamed me for it, yet he insisted I dress promiscuously when going out with him. He was one person on the streets and another person at home.

My parents didn't encourage me or give me emotional support, but instead hurt me emotionally with more condemnation. When my mother came to visit, I felt she loved Anthony more than she did me. She would side with him even as he became increasingly mean to me. I lived only around 300 miles away from my parents, but our already strained relationship began to wane due to my complaining about Anthony's abuse. My mom blamed me and actually said, "You made your bed; you lie in it."

It wasn't long after Chris's birth that I became pregnant again. The doctor said it is common because of being so fertile. I knew this child didn't have a chance. Just as I expected, I was demanded by Anthony to abort the baby. Honestly, I couldn't stand the thought of bringing another child into this abusive marriage. The prospect of ending up a single mom and trying to make it with two kids rather than one scared me incredibly.

I am sad to say that I did not seek any counsel. Consequently, I never even thought of the idea of giving the baby to another couple for adoption, nor was this option brought up by anyone I knew, including the Doctor. My emotions and pain from abuse, including fear of what would happen to me if I did not abort the baby, were my determining factors over the life of this child. I hate that an innocent child was the victim in this whole abusive situation. Today, I know I was wrong to rationalize this way and should have gone to my Pastors.

Anthony's resentment at having to spend his money on our living child caused him to insist I sell my car so we would have no car payment. This took away my independence. He also attempted to curtail my freedom in other ways. He tried to restrict me from seeing any of my girlfriends, especially KD who lived in town. Defiantly, I cried many times on her shoulder about the abuse while we bashed men together. We "drank away" our woes together, since her boyfriend had now left her after our wedding.

I also found out that Anthony had not only been married to the woman he divorced on the day of our marriage, but also to another young woman who had left him years earlier, after having two baby boys with him. She fled to Mexico to get a divorce without his knowledge or consent. He never saw those kids or her again. Obviously, she feared him; I wasn't his only abused wife. He also blamed God for that.

Since birth, Anthony had lived at home with his mom. The house had been left to his mother after the death of his father. His mom was such a kind person; she would do just about anything for anyone and especially for her son and eventually our son, her grandson. Unfortunately, a person can be so tenderhearted that they can actually cripple the growth of the people they allow to grow dependent upon them, especially their adult children.

Anthony's mom became his enabler; he never really had to take on so much of his own life's responsibilities. She cooked for him and did errands for him and continued to do all the hard things in life for him, just to help make his life easier. This resulted in Anthony's efforts being minimized in life, causing a very lazy character. His mother was basically carrying his "backpack" for him. Whenever this happens, as is the case so often with some men and their mothers, that person's character is not built to develop a healthy, mature, well-rounded individual.

Unfortunately for Anthony, all that her enabling did was, cause him to become more and more arrogant and selfish. This alienated people from him and after our divorce, he never married again. He inherited half the house with his only sister and just became an increasingly bitter person.

Anthony's father had died when he was just 17 years old. Because of this, he held a great resentment against God and others. He sought "healing" in drinking alcohol and in smoking. Many nights he would drink a bottle of gin in his own living room bar. He smoked cigarettes in secret and lied that he didn't.

Drinking alcohol makes us feel as if it is numbing the pain deep inside. In a way, it does... temporarily. Killing brain cells and being numb causes us to forget our troubles at that time. When we come back to our senses without the high or numbness, the reality of our problems still remains. So, in essence, all we've done is delay the pain and problems. They don't go away, but can even become worse. Killing brain cells can inevitably affect us in old age as well.

My dysfunctional upbringing obviously caused me to be attracted to the wrong kind of men. Because I had become accustomed to my father's rage and fears and drunkard ways, I had learned to sneak around them. As an adult, I drifted toward men just like my father, men who had the same problems with alcohol, rage, and fears.

I have since learned the hard way that the only way to get rid of pain and problems is to face them head on and deal with them truthfully, as God directs us to do in the Bible. The Bible is the only real standard for Truth, and so exposes the lies. Through prayer and submission to His ways, we are set free from slavery to the pain in our lives. Jesus is our healer. His teachings of forgiveness set us free from the pain that holds us with contempt causing us to hold grudges toward those who have hurt us. We must learn to lay it down at the foot of the cross. Anyone who stubbornly chooses to refuse to deal with pain and problems honestly, but instead keeps stuffing them like Anthony chose to do, will eventually self-destruct emotionally and physically.

Our marriage was most definitely far from being a healthy one. Once again I felt betrayed in so many ways. His anger at who I really was, which was not who he wanted me to be, became the daily fight. I was seeking truth and he wanted to simply hide behind his lies. The kindness and romance he had feigned before the wedding disintegrated quickly after the marriage, with two people seeking opposite paths in life.

He stopped taking me dancing and out to eat; he expected me to cook every day. He wanted me to clean like his mother and fold his clothes in perfect squares—military style. His perfectionism included his demands on me to alphabetize and keep his videos in order. His expectations of perfection were verbally demanded. Punishment was the silent treatment or worse. For example, one day he threw an entire plate of food that I made him against the wall. His temper was mostly out of control.

His motto seemed to be: "It's my way or the highway!" Looking back now, I understand that when people are out of control inside themselves, they then obsess with controlling someone or something else. Married life to Anthony reminded me of my childhood, listening to my father cursing my mother and throwing things late at night, as well as screaming when dinner was not on the table at 5:30 sharp, and so much more.

Why Do People Endure Abusive Relationships?

Enduring abuse in an intimate relationship is just one of the ways Satan holds us in bondage and keeps us from fulfilling our God-given life's purpose. My heart grieves for the women (and men) all around the world who are held captive to lives of misery in unhealthy relationships. Under Islamic ideology, many women are completely under men's authority and control. This bondage causes psychological damage, where the woman thinks it is her place in life to receive the abuse. She most likely feels valueless. Or, she actually thinks it is God's will for her submission to her husband to include being a door mat for him. Often, her husband will easily convince her that she is disobedient even to God.

Bondage in an intimate relationship can be a generational curse as well; even my mother believed that she was under my father's control. However, Jesus came to set the captives free. God's intention for marriage is not for a man to hold a woman in bondage to him. The Scripture says that husbands and wives should submit to one another (Ephesians 5:21). The ideal marriage is used by God as an example of a union of purity and transparency.

Women are not slaves to men. Rather, God wants to use the woman's gifts and the man's gifts together as one flesh, to create a perfect union and relationship, which is a marriage covenant, symbolizing our covenant with God. Marriage is the earthly example of our covenant with God. There is neither male nor female for those united with Christ (Galatians 3:26-28), meaning we are equal in God's eyes, with different roles. This is what the devil tries to destroy; he targets marriages, as well as all the relationships in the family.

Sadly, many couples strive to make their marriages be all they can be without God. When a person is isolated from the truth of God, that person is like a single strand rope. When two people strive to make marriage work without God, they only have a double strand rope, which is not very strong. However, when marriage is built with God at the center, you have a triple strand rope that is the strongest by far.

I have subsequently learned that unless a person is complete in Jesus first before having an intimate relationship with another, the demand will be on the partner in the relationship to complete the other. Two incomplete people will never find completeness but two complete people will complement each other. The movie *Jerry McGuire* uses the terminology "You complete me" as an indication of a perfect love or indirectly alluding to being one flesh. Two imperfect people without God to glue them together with the power of the Holy Spirit can never truly become one flesh.

Only today can I look back and see how God could turn this evil abuse around for His glory. He has given me the compassion to understand the position women are in when they face abuse by their spouse or another relationship. I believe all this prepared me for the calling He would eventually put on my life, as well as build my character and perseverance for the future.

Escaping Abuse

For escape and help, I went to church. The more topics about God I would bring up with Anthony to discuss, the angrier he would get toward me. He would argue constantly, demanding that I shut up because he didn't want to discuss these "irrelevant" subjects. So, his hatred toward God came viciously at me for bringing up God's name.

All I knew was that I saw a lot more love and kindness in the people at church than I saw in him and in my own family. So many nights, especially when he was working, I would just cry myself to sleep. I felt like I was in jail with no way out. I was married, yet in my lifetime, I never felt so alone as I did with Anthony.

The pastor and his wife at the Presbyterian Church I attended began to take an interest in me, seeing that I was coming to church with my baby and no husband. After I spilled my guts to them, they agreed to counsel us. Getting him to agree was like pulling teeth.

We tried his choice of counselor first and when that man didn't say what Anthony wanted to hear, he finally agreed to go to the church, especially because the counseling there was free. This however, was also short lived, as Anthony didn't want to change anything. Without the willingness of both of us, it was hopeless.

Anthony's idea of marriage did not include romance, as was made evident in our lives and our counseling sessions. As the Presbyterian pastor and his wife sat down to counsel Anthony and me, they once asked Anthony if he had taken me out dancing and on dates before we got married. When he answered yes, they asked why he no longer was interested in doing so. Anthony only replied, "Well, isn't that what you have to do to get a girl?"

Both pastors in this lovely husband and wife team could see that Anthony was stubborn and hard of heart. They recognized my desire to grow in Christ and change to improve myself by becoming more like Jesus, while they noticed he wanted literally nothing to do with God, nor desired to change anything. They eventually told me privately that there was little hope in making our marriage work, which I could also see. They soberly informed me that separation and possibly divorce was the only solution, but stressed the need for me to continue growing in Christ.

My Second Divorce

Well, remember that when I got pregnant, Anthony didn't want to marry me? You would think he would be fine with divorcing me. However, Anthony told me that if I divorced him, he would kill me and then probably kill himself. His threat was so real, I got scared and worried. I began to pray, crying out to God for help.

One day, we were driving somewhere. I was in the passenger seat of his car. Somehow, per usual we got into a terrible argument. Suddenly, Anthony pulled a gun out from under his driver's seat and threw it in my lap. He screamed at me, "Go ahead; kill me. Do it. Do it!" I was terrified. Without a second thought, I rolled down my window in order to throw the gun out the window before one of us could get hurt. He grabbed the gun from me and stopped the car. He began to choke my neck, screaming, "If you throw my gun out, I will kill you!" This was the last straw. I could not be another day with this man. I feared for not only my own life, but also Chris' innocent life too. I had to do something.

I was still playing racquetball once in a while and had begun developing a friendship with a gal, Francine. I went to see her the day of Anthony's threat, leaving Chris with my mother-in law. Chris was barely 17 months at the time. Francine noticed that I was troubled and playing terribly, so she got me to open up and tell her everything. As God would have it, as He always provides a way out for His children, she offered for me to move in with her and her two boys. Her parents had given her one of their houses, since her husband had left her for drugs.

One night, while Anthony was at work and Chris was asleep, God showed me the plan for my escape: I would wait for a day when Anthony was working day shift. Then, I would arrange for a moving company to move my furniture into storage. I would take my necessities with a rented car and drive to Francine's house. I planned the date and took money from our account. I got out that day, although Anthony's cousin, who lived in the basement slashed the tires of the car I used. I divorced Anthony in 1985, one and a half years after my son's birth.

Struggling As a Single Mom

My father previously warned me that if I ever divorced Anthony, he and my mom would disown me. For three years after I left Anthony, my parents did not speak to me. They did not help me at all. My Heavenly Father provided safety and love for me; He provided my way out of this abuse into a safe place for Chris and me. This reminds me of Psalm 27:10.

After I left, for six months Chris and I stayed with Francine and her two boys. Fran was a dear close friend for many years. Her whole family became our family. She was Italian like most of my friends from the area were. I loved the hospitality of the Italians and that everything centered around food. I learned a lot of Italian cooking from Fran, as I did from Chris' grandmother. Making 'gravy' as they would call pasta sauce was an art and going to the bakeries for Italian pastries was the best! I also loved the bread and the bagels in metro

NY. The pizza was the best far and wide as well! Years later I would be missing all this when moving elsewhere. I could always strike up a conversation with most anyone there but I especially learned talking with my hands from the Italians. I do get teased about that a lot these days.

I soon found a job in Manhattan at an Italian restaurant/bar. Bartending again, I soon made enough money for an apartment for my son and me to live on our own. It was in the same community of Brooklyn near the water where Anthony lived. Chris called our new apartment "the castle" because the architecture reminded us of a castle. That was perfectly fine with me. He was just 2 years old then.

Anthony's friend, the judge who saw to it that I could not move any further than 50 miles away, had manipulated our divorce agreement. I never read the fine print and was too intimidated without an attorney to question anything. My goal was to just end the marriage as cheaply as possible. Anthony got to see Chris every weekend and half of every holiday. In those days, this was unusual. He only had to pay $100 a week for child support for the rest of Chris's childhood, while he himself continued to conveniently live pretty much rent free at his mom's house.

Unfortunately, because of my desire to be loved and my desire to find a new and better male role model for my son and believing that was up to me, I ended up living with one guy after another. I failed over and over again in both of these desires.

Additionally, the stress of working a couple of jobs as a single mother, including late night bar hours, often meant not getting home before 3:00 am. This also did not help me in raising my son. Rather, it caused me to be very moody at times. I made about a $1,500 a week so I rationalized that the money was worth it. I didn't know how to trust in God to provide. My moods from failed relationships, being tired, and doing things I regretted, like abortion, weighed me down emotionally. Eventually, chronic bronchitis that resulted from the smoky environment caused me to leave bartending. The doctor told me that because my lungs were black, if I didn't quit, it was going to kill me.

I began to explore working in real estate to get some independence, have better hours and work closer to home. I particularly enjoyed showing the Brownstones in Brooklyn. I was hired at a real estate firm where the owner confessed his Christianity. Since I had been to church, I confessed to being a "Christian" also. I did well enough quickly, which allowed me to stop bartending. This helped me to have more time with Chris by making more money in a shorter period of time.

God was drawing me one step at a time to be holy and set apart for Him in order to prepare me for my soon coming Bridegroom, Jesus. I needed to choose to walk in His path even when I didn't see what's ahead but to simply trust Him. God gave me grace here at this real estate firm but will I have faith and choose rightly? Let us see.

6

Dating after Divorce

Deceived yet again?

Still seeking love from a man, as well as a good male role model for Chris, and still not understanding that I needed to seek God with all my heart, I began dating again. I "fell in love" with Ted and bought a house with him in Brooklyn, NY through the firm for which I worked.

I had met Ted at my real estate job when he came to invest in a home in Brooklyn. I made Chris tolerate this guy since I made the decision for us to live with him by buying this house. I had also reasoned that it would be better for Chris if I owned a house rather than rent. I did not want to get married again; I did not want to make another marriage mistake. Besides, Ted did not want to get married either.

I reasoned all this from my past experiences and my parents' example, for I knew nothing else. I never sought God for His best; I did not have faith in His ways for love nor trusted mine in marriage. By default, I was trusting in my ways by getting involved intimately but without full commitment. I was playing house but didn't trust the relationship enough to marry that man. Therefore, I had one foot in and one foot out of this relationship; just as in the Hokey Pokey dance I would be shaking my foot all about.

Declining real estate sales forced me to pick up a few more bartending shifts at a local bar. For this reason I was fired from the real estate company. They told me that as Christians, they did not allow an employee of theirs to work at a bar. Losing that job devastated me because I needed the income to pay my bills and this new house, which they knew I had purchased with this man. Today, I understand this reasoning but then I was really put off by it. If only I had seen that this was God talking to me through this Christian realtor about what was best for my life and Chris.

If only I decided to seek God's answers, I might have learned that God was my Provider. Maybe not taking the bar job and staying with the real estate firm would have taught me that. If I had more dependence on prayer to God and finding answers in His Word rather than trusting people who were ungodly, I would have been blessed. I needed that accountability the Christian realtor was trying to teach me but I couldn't hear God's caring voice in it because my un-repented sin still seemed more like love to me.

Eventually God took me out of this bar environment when I found out I was highly allergic to cigarette smoke. I listened to the doctor's advice and quit for the sake of my health. I realized then I cared more about being available to my son as a mother than sacrificing my health for money.

The next job I was blessed to get for a time was working as a freelance seamstress, making samples for Bob Mackie in Manhattan. This time I was able to do the work from home. I was quite impressed with myself to be now working for Cher's dress designer. Do you remember Sonny and Cher Bono? "I Got You Babe" was their hit song.[1]

Ted had a pretty laid back personality and drank a lot on the weekdays after work, as well as the weekends. He worked for the NYC tax office and had a high opinion of himself in his position there. He was also a real estate investor. We broke up in about a year because of my inability to tolerate his constant drinking and careless state of mind at home, as well as a shady deal in which he stabbed me in the back.

I built up resentment and anger toward him. At that time I believed these feelings were due to his taking advantage of me in this real estate deal. However, later you will see there was a much deeper issue here for my strong, resentful feelings. I lost money, whereas he and his sister gained money by manipulating words in the contract, persuading the real estate lawyer to go along with it. (I have since for-

---

[1] www.biography.com/people/sonny-bono-9542076

given them, for without Christ they know not what they do.) As I look back on this situation where Ted and his sister took advantage of me, I realize that this real estate deal was a gift to me from God, to keep me from getting involved with this guy and possibly future destructive male relationships.

If I had only just moved into the condo in question with Chris, I would have at least had some security. I had gotten a sweet deal on the condo from a friend. I could have had a chance to do well financially by living in it and eventually selling it myself. But there I was, trusting a guy again, without seeking God's ways first. This kind of love is blind. I had counted on having the bigger house with Ted and so agreed to sell the condo to his sister. God had once again provided me a way out but I allowed greed and lust to lead me astray.

As I have since learned, I pray that my readers will learn from my bad experiences. Living by feelings and emotions is very unstable and bound to fall apart eventually. God's best for us never looks immoral like a man and woman living together without marriage. God's best is an honorable man who respects and honors God's created daughter enough to marry her because of his reverence for Him.

Living together is blessed in a covenant marriage for eternity. There is a better way that is stable so we all do have a better choice. In it, there is hope. I was also struggling with greed and covetousness here to want bigger and better without contentment, only seeing with my eyes but blindsided by a relationship. I was paying the consequences of my sin.

Deceived Yet Again

Soon, I was easily lured into the arms of another man who listened to my sob story of being shafted by Ted. This new guy, Sam, was introduced to me by one of my lobby bar girlfriends. He was an entertainment-booking agent, which enticed me to be interested in him. He so easily lured me to move in with him and work for him by promising me connections and encouraging me in my desire to be a famous fashion designer.

Now, because someone else was waiting "in the wings," I easily walked away from Ted. Chris and I then moved to New Jersey with Sam. Soon after, I sold my half of the Brooklyn house back to him and took the money. I soon bought another house with him in NJ using my money from the Brooklyn house.   As I am writing this, it all sounds so foolish now, trusting one guy after another with my living arrangements and my finances. I know now that God was waiting patiently for me to run to Him so He could protect me from all of this chaos and those who would take advantage of my trusting nature and my desperate need for love.

This move to New Jersey had to be within fifty miles of Chris's father but he didn't fight me when I moved four miles further. By this time, age 31, my irritation with NYC traffic, parking, and people had caused resentment to build up inside of me, though God knew it was a deeper issue. Rather than face this anger inside and get to the root of it, I just blamed the circumstances. I tried changing my surroundings, which made me feel better for the time being. I was actually running from God; I did not want to face Him with my feelings of guilt. Oh what a tangled web we weave!

I worked for Sam in his booking agency as his office manager. He booked entertainment all over the world. I met many famous people including Little Richie, Jerry Lee Lewis, Helen Ready, and many oldies groups. I even stayed in Elvis Presley's house during my travels to Palm Springs, California. I came close to doing a line of jeans for Sonny Bono called "I got you Babe" jeans but Sonny bought a restaurant and spent the money he planned for the line, or so he told me. He was the mayor of Palm Springs then. We would hang out in his restaurant with him.

With my credit, Sam and I bought a condo on the beach in NJ and lived "high on the hog," as they say. I was engaged and thought life was great then. After over a year of escalating troubles with helping Sam in his shady business transactions, raising his two daughters, and dealing with his controlling mother, it was apparent that our relationship was declining. We argued and fought over truth and lies and ended up in a physical battle that caused me great grief.

I went to the local church to find relief and love. God was answering my need for rescue without my knowing it then. I met a woman, Kathy, at a ladies meeting who demonstrated a Mary Kay makeover on a lady there. I was so impressed with the "before and after" that I accepted her invitation to do a free makeover on me. I fell in love with the way I looked in the mirror as a result and bought the whole set of makeup. In feeling better about myself, my age, and looking beautiful, I got excited about the prospect of being my own business owner also.

I figured if my fiancé could run his own business by being corrupt, I could do better by being honest. I know for sure being a Mary Kay consultant was from God. I became successful and excited about it. Kathy became a good friend. She encouraged me that I could do this: run my own business. The group of woman I learned from highly encouraged me too, but the prospect of my success became a threat to Sam and my role in his life as he had planned it. Our relationship was strained further as I also began talking about putting God first.

One day I came home from a Mary Kay appointment only to find that he had moved out and taken all his possessions. He left me holding the bag or more specifically, holding the debt to the tune of a half a million dollars of credit cards and two properties. Out of pity, I was foolish enough to allow him to use my credit for everything we accumulated after he convinced me his ex-wife had ruined his credit. Oh the things we do for "love." But, is this truly love?

It had only been a year and a half of living together and no attorney would take the case to go after him because it had not been seven years. In New Jersey, living together for seven years is known as "common law marriage." He had moved to an unknown address. Although I personally tracked him down, he simply denied everything in my face. I ran out crying like a puppy with its tail between its legs, realizing it was his word against mine. He was so good at lying, especially to protect his own skin.

As a result, my heart was broken. I lost my confidence in my Mary Kay business and ended up going bankrupt. I couldn't fake joy when I felt so broken and defeated. I experienced great depression and became anorexic until all I could do was look up. The creditors scared me to death with their threats so much that I moved out of my house and took an apartment with a girl and her cat for a year. The good that came out of this was that the girl gave my son her cat, *Bangles*. When our lease was up, she went and married a military man. Chris loved the cat. I moved back to my house for a while before the bank finally took it.

The Harm to My Son

When I think of it now, I feel so badly for my son and all he had to deal with because of my desperate search for love. Chris' view of love was in peril since he had no positive male role model living with us and my model of love was skewed. I did apologize and asked his forgiveness later on, in his adult years, but the repercussions from what I put him through are still felt to this day.

Just as my parents' lifestyle had a negative effect on me, my bad decisions have negatively impacted my son. I ask that since the prayers of the righteous are heard in Heaven, that all of you who love Jesus would pray for Chris to come back to God and know His unconditional love through Jesus. I do know that God, his Creator and mine, wants all to be saved. He loves Chris more than I possibly ever could.

My mind is exhausted from remembering the details of what I went through with Sam. I regret that this man was not the last one, though how I wish he were. As you can see, I made many mistakes and poor choices during the raising of my son. I don't blame him for having anger toward me. Although I had his best interest at heart, I sadly did not go to the best source to find my true love and the ideal father figure for my son, which is God. My best interest never came close to God's best for Chris. My best was so limited by my past imperfect experiences. God's best was, is and always will be perfect and has no human limits.

God is where I should have sought refuge and help, by following His way, not my way. God has the only perfect standard of right and wrong. All people are broken and do not have that perfect standard within their own human understanding (Romans 6:23).

Instead of seeking God, I just went from being manipulated by one guy to another. My resentment toward men grew more intense. My deep-rooted pain became worse and worse. God was the only Healer for my soul, but I did not seek His healing and give Him my all. I did not change my lifestyle yet, nor seek Him with all my heart. Instead, unbeknownst to me at that time, I was seeking perfect love and healing from a man rather than God. That would be a never-ending, impossible journey.

The Grace of God

After losing my house to bankruptcy in New Jersey and getting over my heartbreak for another lost love, we were still allowed to live in the house a while. It was during the late 80s, when the whole real estate market fell and the banks had too many houses on their hands. I found an additional job as a waitress in a little Italian café while re-building my Mary Kay business.

I had an encounter with God when I lost all my material possessions in the bankruptcy. My obsession over money and not having enough was a form of worshipping it as an idol. I now know I had worshipped fame and fortune, too.

God allowed me to lose my possessions in order to gain Him and worship Him only. For what good is it for someone to gain the whole world and forfeit their soul? (Matthew 16:26, Mark 8:36) Idols being removed from our lives are another way God uses to get us to set our eyes on Him only. This incredible trial of losing earthly possessions helped me to reorder my priorities and seek after my Father God, who would continue to prepare me for my heavenly Bridegroom for eternity. He was truly refining me by fire.

Mary Kay's philosophy for life was to put God first, family second and career last. In that order, all things would work together for our good. Out of that order, we would experience chaos. I certainly could attest to the chaos to be true! So now I was considering these priorities in my life to also be fully true.

I went back to the Congregational church in town. The pastor at the time, also from Maine, had compassion for me. He helped me a bit financially and sent me to a supposedly Christian counselor at another Congregational church. I remember that this counselor never opened a Bible or prayed with me.

Somehow being back in church caused me to question myself. What have I done wrong to get myself into these predicaments with men? Like a revelation, having sex before marriage came to me, so I asked the counselor about it. He told me that it was no big deal that I had sex before marriage since I was engaged, and that I should not concern myself with this matter. What a lie that was.

Don't believe everything you read or hear, unless it comes straight from the Bible. I got no help from that counselor that was lasting. I began questioning: If there was nothing wrong with sex before marriage, why did all those relationships fall apart so abruptly? The Word of God says, *"Let us reason together"* (Isaiah 1:18).

As I began to pick up the pieces of my life by returning to church and getting my self-esteem back, my ability to earn a living grew again. In my restaurant work, many people tipped me well and also believed in me enough that they helped me get my Mary Kay business off to a great start again. Mary Kay women began to encourage me, saying that I was capable. I didn't even believe in myself for guilt had weighed me down. How could I, except for God intervening?

During my Mary Kay career, I learned another important lesson about myself, as well as how to achieve success God's way. I was 32 years old at the time. My belief in myself was so low from being brought up by a woman who also had little belief in herself, as well as from all those failures in my relationships with men.

My Mary Kay Director, Joan Brooks, was very successful in her career and in her family life, as far as I could see. I confided in her one day about my inabilities to achieve the next level in Mary Kay. I was just not like all those who had achieved higher levels than I had. She asked me a question that prompted me to change:

First, she asked who told me that I could not accomplish what others had achieved. I answered, "My mother."

She then asked me, "How old are you?"

"Thirty-two," I said.

"Do you need a mother at age thirty-two?"

As I thought about the answer to that question, I realized I did not and replied, "No. I guess not."

Then she asked, "Do you want to be like your mother?"

Out of my heart, my mouth spoke out adamantly, "No! Definitely not!"

She proceeded to explain that we should only seek to learn from people that we would like to emulate. That made so much sense to me. Like the bumblebee, the symbol of Mary Kay, I flew to success.

Aerodynamically a bumblebee with such a large heavy body and tiny wings should not be able to fly, though it doesn't know any better. Without knowing any better, I went on to be a very successful Pink Cadillac Mary Kay Sr. Sales Director.

Boy, did I prove my mother wrong and surprise myself at the same time. Don't misunderstand; I sure give God all the glory. As I sought Him, He led me, giving me His strength and wisdom throughout the whole process. I could not have done it without Him as my leader. The peace and joy I had in my career by going God's way proved to be a much better way to achieve success.

As I gained confidence, I began developing friendships and strong relationships with women through Mary Kay. This was really the first time in my life that I developed friendships with stable women. Many of them had long happy marriages, strong families, and had experienced financial success. I enjoyed associating with these women who were building successful lives and families.

God would use much of what I learned in Mary Kay, like having faith, the importance of helping others, and how God provides to prepare me for my lifetime partner, as well as for my eternal Bridegroom, Jesus.

Other Relationships Don't Heal Hurt
Somewhere during the course of my growing a successful career in Mary Kay, I met another guy, who I'll call Tom. He began pursuing me at the restaurant. I remember what a smooth talker he was. Somehow he persuaded me, with his sophistication and education, to go to his house, sometimes with his daughter there and other times, alone. He was a single parent who juggled his successful career over his family.

I really can't tell you how he seduced me but I had little resistance to him. I had trouble with physical boundaries because my flesh was so weak. As a Sanguine, my deep need for love, connected with physical touch and attention, always seemed to win out, even over moral issues. I had great difficulty resisting him and ended up feeling manipulated and used. He reminded me of today's politicians.

Eventually, I terminated the relationship after I had enough of his games and the order of priority he put our relationship with no full commitment. The old anger inside me resurfaced because of where my involvement with him led me again. He lured me at unexpected times, leading me to another immoral situation and decision. This time I remember being so angry with him that I accepted my last invitation to lunch and told him off!

Sometime after that, I met Fred, another guy who kept coming to the restaurant. He was by far the one who treated me with the most respect and kindness. We fell for each other hard. He got along great with Chris. He was most humble; he never did anything manipulative or cruel to me. He was very communicative and had a joyful personality, which made him fun to be around. He was the most considerate of my feelings than any other guy before. He was actually looking for a commitment from me.

Fred had three kids: a 13 year old boy with a learning disability, a 16 year old girl who smoked pot, and a 22 year old boy who was too lazy to get a job. Fred was an enabler and continued to provide for his adult child. As long as his kids weren't around, we got along great. I just couldn't deal with his kids. Fred was also financially challenged, which affected us in a moral decision at one point.

Since I really wasn't healed, I couldn't help anyone else heal from deep issues. I broke it off after about a year, feeling overwhelmed. Sadly, I know I really broke his heart, but for the first time I felt that I did what was best for all of us, based on seeking God's guidance. Although Fred was not offended or afraid to talk about God, we had determined that we did disagree about who God is. This was the first man that my search for the truth about God was met with some approval or at least an open willing conversation.

Eventually, the time arrived when Chris and I had to leave our house because the bank was taking it. An ad in the paper led us to move in with another single mom, who I'll call Sandra, and her two younger kids in another school district. Going to another school and having to make new friends did not sit well with Chris by this age.

I remember feeling very pleased to find out that Sandra was a Christian. She introduced me to my first non-denominational church. I instantly knew that this was the kind of church God wanted me to join. I had been singing songs I made up since I was young. The contemporary music at this church reminded me of those songs God brought to my heart as a child.

I began learning more about what a Christian is supposed to be like, according to God's ways, which are revealed in the Bible. Recently, I heard a wonderful teaching by a British lady who described what she has observed concerning what we in the West think of God: "We think of Him as a concept or an idea in which we shape according to our own ideas. But God is the opposite. He is reality who actually shapes us."

This British lady went on to say that in thinking culturally, I just wanted a Jesus that wouldn't cost me anything because He doesn't change us like so many Christians here in America want today. The Jesus preached today fits our Western values that we have received from our ungodly parents. This Jesus does not rearrange our life. We are weightier than this God instead of Him being weightier than us. Instead of taking up our cross daily and following Jesus, we want Him to be our genie to fulfill our wishes.

The Bible is clear that God is the Potter who shapes us, as we are the clay that He is molding into a beautiful pot. That reshaping can be very hard for us at times, like being fired in the kiln. It can really get hot for us as God refines us by fire.

My eyes opened to the sin in which I had been involved. Before, I had continuously justified my fleshly desires to fit my life's conveniences. My secret sins began to plague my soul and I felt convicted. My spirit began to be repentant, but I still couldn't seem to give it all to God and trust Him completely with it. My past was all far too painful even to think about.

Larry

It didn't take too long before a particular man, I'll call him Larry, became interested in me. I could tell by the way he looked at me that he wanted to know me more intimately. We would hang out together at church and he seemed to show up at some of the same events I did. It just took longer than I had experienced before, for him to approach me for a physical relationship. Although I struggled at times when he got more persistent, it was much easier, without the influence of alcohol, to verbally discourage him from physical intimacy with me.

This was the first time I had been approached inappropriately by a man from church. I somehow expected something different from church people, but while he seemed to know what the Bible says, he did not apply it to himself. Once again I was being lured into intimacy, but this time with someone calling himself a "Christian." Now I felt I might be on a right path.

However, the teachings in the church were contrary to this. Ironically, he would give the right answers in Sunday school, but just not disclose what he was actually doing in his private life. I learned that a book doesn't always match its cover. I hadn't quite learned how to apply that to myself. Only now do I realize I was as much of a hypocrite as he was, although I was oblivious to it then. I do believe he was very conscious of his own hypocrisy and enjoyed the power he felt in it.

Somewhere along the way, while we were at a church function, I realized this guy was Sandra's estranged husband—they were in the midst of a nasty divorce. I don't know for sure his motive for becoming involved with me—maybe to antagonize her—but this was a clear example of another "Christian" divorce statistic.

After this shocking revelation, Sandra immediately evicted my son and me from her house without notice. I am sure she was in pain due to her soon-to-be ex-husband's betrayal and didn't understand that I did not know who he was.

God did rescue us through the parents of a friend of Chris from school. I became friends with the boy's mom, Silvia. She and her husband allowed us to live in their basement apartment for the rest of the school year.

Silvia was a very outspoken Cuban Christian woman with lots of influence in the community. Her husband was a very successful but humble businessman. This couple was very good to Chris and me. They encouraged me during this tough period of my life and I was intrigued with the honor and respect he gave his wife. I went to their church a few times and attended some social events, but preferred the nondenominational style of church.

I did encounter a new kind of relationship with another man at one point or another. He was an entrepreneurial financial planner and his company followed the principles of God first also. He treated me like a lady and honored my request for no intimate relationships in my life. I saw the fear of God in him. He sent me customers and went to many of my Mary Kay events as support, which I really appreciated.

Eventually, I realized that he was falling for me. While I believe God used this friendship to help me curb my hate and disgust for men, I learned that it really is pretty impossible for a man and a woman to be just friends without one falling emotionally for the other. I felt bad that he was hurt by my rejection, so I decided not to pursue a friendship only with a man again. This was an entirely new relationship and I believe the Lord used it to break my bondage to lies I had believed, and maybe even bondage to generational sins.

Growing As a "Baby" Christian

At a Christian concert, a woman from a smaller church persuaded me to go to her church after having a Mary Kay class for me. I discovered so much love there from couples and families; I felt right at home. There really weren't too many single men at this church, and I actually felt glad about that for the first time.

I did eventually meet my next boyfriend, Antonio, somewhere else. He claimed to be a "Christian" and was very outgoing, conversational, and seemed to be more open about his emotions than even I at times. He was going through a tough divorce situation, and eventually ended up having to go bankrupt. He did introduce me to Twila Paris' music. Learning and listening to her music helped me to grow in Christ more. The words to her music ministered to my heart.

I had such compassion for this man. This brought us together in a mutual validation of the flesh for a short while, a sort of victim loves victim scenario. I do remember feeling guilt and persuading him to go to my church with me. Eventually, his personal financial fall scared me. I never wanted to be in that position again. I decided that I especially didn't want to knowingly walk into that situation.

How is it that the weak-minded are always attracted to other weak-minded individuals? I have learned it is such a dangerous combination and it never lasts. The devil knows that and is clearly prowling around, looking for someone to devour. He wants to destroy lives and break hearts. Misery loves company.

The more I began to learn through reading the Bible, the more my eyes were opened to the fact that Antonio and I were together for all the wrong reasons. I broke it off with him and broke his heart. He eventually attached himself to another woman and I moved on to try to just be alone for a while.

Based on what I was reading and learning in the Bible, I now began to truly see the hypocrisy of being a Christian yet conducting one's love life just like the world does. Now, I wanted to truly follow Jesus Christ, not just in name but also in action. I learned that being a Christian is a two way street: Jesus Christ laid His life down for us and asks us to be willing to lay our lives down for Him. This reminds me of the following quote:

> "A theoretical Jesus who exists on the level of ideas, religious traditions, institutional trappings, and history does not disturb most people. But Jesus, who died for the world's sins, rose from the dead, and presently lives in his followers, calling for real change in the way all people live – that Jesus cannot be ignored. That Jesus makes people mad." (Larry Richards, *The Bible Made Easy*, p. 287.)

In my personal conviction of wanting to live according to Scripture, I wanted to change, turn around and sin no more in the area in which I was convicted. Today, the Holy Spirit revealed to me an important lesson I learned from reflecting on my life.

Ladies, if a man you are interested in is also being drawn to God, he will like that about you. However, if he does not want to repent of his sins and live for God; your desire to live for God will repel him. People who are running from God love their sin more than anything else in life and do not appreciate being convicted, since they don't want to change.

The men I chose with my flesh appeared to be people they were not. Many times, I was deceived by outward appearances and fell into the arms of men from the world. Finally I cried out to my Lord

119

and Savior to save me, to rescue me from the world and from myself. Hearing me, Jesus reached out and took me into His heavenly and holy arms! He comforted me, holding me tight in His embrace, loving me unconditionally, no matter what mistakes I had made. This God, my Father, was still willing to forgive me regardless of all my sins.

David, after committing adultery with Bathsheba and murdering her husband, was broken. He humbly pleaded to God for His mercy in Psalm 51. He said: *"Then I will teach transgressors your ways, so that sinners will turn back to you... My sacrifice, O God, is a broken spirit; a broken and contrite heart you, God, will not despise."* Remember it's not the sinner God hates, but the sin. Study Psalm 51, for it is a plea to God, asking Him for forgiveness and for Him to create in us a clean heart, cleansing us of our guilt and shame. Jesus fulfills this by taking the horrendous punishment for us that we deserved, though He was completely innocent. All God asks from us is that we sincerely repent of our sins with a broken spirit and contrite heart, then believe with all our heart, soul and mind in what Jesus did for us and accept God's gift of grace to us through Christ.

Jesus was crucified for you and me and for all those who confess with their mouth that He is Lord, believing in their heart what He has done for us: that He died, was buried, and rose again to pay for our sins. Jesus was victorious over death so He could offer us eternal life! He was bruised for our sins (Isaiah 53) and took the excruciating pain in the piercing of His hands and feet for our transgressions. He took a flogging for every sinful choice we made in disobedience to Him (and I made plenty). His blood was shed to wash us clean and as white as snow (Isaiah 1:18). The song, "Wash me and I Shall be Whiter than Snow" beautifully illustrates this Truth.

Jesus is the "Bread of Life" (John 6:35). His body was broken for our transgressions, as the bread is broken to eat. He rose from the dead, however, and will come back again, the triumphant King on the throne of David forever (Psalm 2, Luke 1:31-33, John 14:1-3). Paradise with God guaranteed for eternity!

I thank and praise God for forgiving me for my fears and unbelief, as well as all my iniquities. I thank God that He sent Jesus to pay that price for me. We humans cannot pay the price ourselves. Thank You Jesus for taking the punishment I deserved. Thank You for not only forgiving me, but also for giving me the free gift of eternal life! Thank You God for saving me from eternal separation from You: spending eternity in the pit of fire called hell that you designed for Satan and his followers (Matthew 25:41).

Meeting more Spirit-filled people at my new church greatly enriched my life. A wonderful, loving, Christian couple in the area studied the Bible with me. God had clearly put them in my life for me to see how a Christian marriage looked. Teresa and Al lived in love and treated each other with respect. I also got involved with a lot more of the church activities, joining the choir and later the praise team and seeking additional opportunities for church fellowship.

I learned about tithing and grew in the understanding that everything we have belongs to God. This was a new concept for me. It challenged me to really have faith in God and not be afraid that I would not have enough money to pay my bills. That was a fear I had to overcome, by trusting God to know more than I did.

As I let go of this fear, I grasped the concept that we are just stewards in this life. As I brought all my earnings into the storehouse, my thankfulness to God for entrusting me with these worldly possessions leaped to the forefront. I wanted to show my gratitude by giving back to God my first fruits—the first ten percent of my income before paying my bills or even buying food.

As I began to really understand God's love for me, I realized that He already knows what I need. He has promised to provide all our daily needs (Matthew 6:25-34). Therefore, I should just trust Him to take care of me the way He wants to. So I decided to become obedient to the Word of God, including the area of money. I started tithing joyfully and well, it really paid off. I began doing better and better financially and could see how God was blessing me.

During this time, I avoided male relationships and appreciated my newly found independence. I quit working at the restaurant but continued selling Mary Kay products. I was my own boss rather than being controlled by bosses who did not care about my child. From 1990 to 2003 I drove free Mary Kay cars and made more money than I had ever made in my lifetime, working my way up to driving a free Pink Cadillac. I learned a lot about myself in Mary Kay; my confidence increased. I became more aware of my value, as I achieved what even my mother told me I was incapable of accomplishing. I learned to put God first, my family (Chris) second, and my career last.

Life was good, and I felt so blessed that I began telling women about Jesus when I went to do their facials and makeovers. I met more and more Christian women who believed the same as I did. Many joined Mary Kay and followed in my footsteps. I learned to face the fear and do it anyway, as Mary Kay taught us.

God had now turned this business into a ministry to women, as I had the one-on-one time to really listen to them. The feeling of being able to help other women is still one of my greatest blessings in life. I developed great friendships with these women through Mary Kay. I went on to be a very successful Pink Cadillac Senior Sales Director. It was such a great feeling of accomplishment when I proved my boss at the Italian restaurant wrong the day I parked my new pink Cadillac right next to his Porsche and quit restaurant work. Mary Kay used to say, "There are three kinds of people in this world: some that make things happen, some that watch things happen and some who say, 'What happened?' " I knew I was now a woman who made things happen. I was growing out of being a woman that wondered 'What happened?'

Recently I came across a saying that I feel describes who God has made me to be: a leader, using my God-given gifts that Mary Kay began to develop in me. "A leader is one who sees more than others see, who sees farther than others see, and who sees before others do."

It is important to know who we are in Christ, in order to be aware of what is happening around and to be able to set goals and boundaries. This helps not to be so deceived by the enemy, who prowls around looking for someone to devour. Philippians 3:14 tells us to press on toward the goal for the prize of the upward call of God in Christ Jesus. I advise the same for you as you prepare yourself as the Bride of Christ, as God was preparing me. He is still preparing me and always will until the return of Jesus, our real hero! Hebrews 12:1-3 tells us:

> *"Therefore, since we are surrounded by such a huge crowd of witnesses to the life of faith, let us strip off every weight that slows us down, especially the sin that so easily trips us up. And let us run with endurance the race God has set before us. We do this by keeping*

our eyes on Jesus, the champion who initiates and perfects our faith. Because of the joy awaiting him, he endured the cross, disregarding its shame. Now he is seated in the place of honor beside God's throne. Think of all the hostility he endured from sinful people; then you won't become weary and give up."

Today's generation of youth is looking for a hero, and Jesus is the hero they are looking for!

7

Christopher

My Son Chris

I will now go back to the birth of my son in 1983, so to dedicate this chapter on him and his 18 years living mostly with me. I had the privilege to stay home with Chris for his first two years, for which I am grateful. I loved raising him; he was so fun and learned so quickly. Like a sponge, he soaked up knowledge. He began to learn how to talk at 6-8 months old. I easily taught him to read and write before he was a year old. At 18 months of age, Chris was the smartest kid in his preschool.

Chris' education has always been a priority to me. I do believe "knowledge is power" and wanted him to have even more opportunities than I did. I wanted the very best for him and felt it was important for him to continue to learn in school while I worked, instead of wasting time in front of a TV with a babysitter. I wanted to spend more time with Chris, as I did during his first two years, but after my separation and divorce from his father, I had to work two jobs at a time in order for us to survive in NYC. The child support I got from his dad was minimal.

Chris remembers his teacher, Vicki, as being his favorite one in preschool. He was well liked by the other children and taught others to read and write some, too. He loved to read. He had quite the personality: outgoing like me, with an optimistic and joyful disposition around people. He talked to everyone; he loved people's attention. He was known as the "Little Mayor." He was such a joy and he loved to learn. All of these traits are much like my own.

Chris loved me very much and tried to please me. I loved him very much, maybe too much since up to then I never felt truly loved by anyone but him. I tried to show him that through working hard to provide for him. At times, I tried to buy material things for him as one way to show my love, although I always felt inadequate compared to his father, Anthony. He could afford to buy Chris more things since he retired at age forty-two with a side job and lived in his mother's house.

As a single mother, I was now burdened with paying full price for housing, so I had less money available for extras. As a matter of fact, his father seemed to attempt to buy Chris' love through getting him material things. Sadly, this was the only way he knew to express his love. At that time, I still struggled with whether money could buy love or not so I felt invaluable and inadequate. I know now that was the devil taunting me through this.

Because of my revelation with God when Chris was born, I believed showing my love to Chris included taking him to church with me so we could seek God's love together. I did that when I could, in Brooklyn and even later when we moved to New Jersey.

Chris had natural talent for singing and playing the piano and I was so proud of him. I have videos of him in church plays where he showed his love for Jesus through music. He had lead parts in plays, including Joseph in "Joseph and the Technicolor Dream Coat." I so enjoyed making that dream coat and all his Halloween costumes too. His music teacher at church sought him out to lead parts because he was very confident and memorized parts easily yet with such expression, much like my personality in this way.

Out of the Mouth of Babes

As he began to learn more about Jesus, he eventually began to ask me, "Mommy, why do you have to drink?" whenever I ordered an alcoholic beverage at a restaurant. I found it amazing how Chris knew right from wrong and so quickly just spoke his mind as he saw it, without rationalizing all the reasons why not to say it. He just said it like it was. I never rebuked him for it. I would just smile and say, "I'm just having one; it's no big deal." His question was a checkpoint for me that caused me to never get drunk in front of my child. Deep inside I kind of knew he was right but it tended to be a crutch for me to learn to relax in trying to keep up this stressful life I was leading.

His question also reminded me how much I hated it when my own parents drank, but I had known that if I asked them about it, I would get slapped. This just built resentment inside me. Yet as an adult, I still went out and drank, even though it caused so much havoc in my childhood. I didn't have to take my parents' orders any more but I was still acting out of rebellion. It must be the killing of brain cells, along with Satan keeping us in a place where he can manipulate us easier, by keeping our reasoning and senses dull so that we forget the lessons of our past.

If you haven't seen the movie "Letters to God" I highly recommend it. It reveals how children will turn adults around to see reality. It shows how we, as adults, allow fear to keep us from truth, especially fear of what people will say. The movie showed how a little kid gave so many people hope, when as adults we find it so easy to just give up on hope.

It also answers the most frequently asked question; if God is so good, how can He let young children and babies die? We see how God knows the bigger picture and people can only see the immediate picture in front of us so often. God's loving heart wants all to be saved and only He knew how this boy's death would bring so many salvations. In other words, many more people will be in heaven instead of hell because they came to believe in the same God this young boy did by his example. I have come to learn that "to live is Christ and to die is gain" (Philippians 1:21).

Chris' Childhood

Chris was always an A and B student, just like I was in school. He was well disciplined, respectful, loving, talented, and an eager student. Teachers remarked that he was so steady they were surprised to learn he came from a single parent home. He was always good with computers; he quickly figured out how to use technology. He never got into trouble in school, though bullies teased him for being academic and for not being "a tough guy" like they were. He never had an interest in venturing into the unknown world of testing fate, like so many boys. I was often complimented on how bright and disciplined my son was.

Chris played baseball and learned karate. Though I had him in the water from birth, he never really loved swimming. I am reminded of a precious moment when Chris and I were at a hotel for a Mary Kay function. He called out to me while we were in the pool, "Mommy, look!" The next thing I see is him swimming under the water for a few feet. Then, he popped his head up, looking straight at me and said, "Mommy, I felt the fear and did it anyway!" I had never felt so proud of him than at that moment and just so tickled inside.

Mary Kay had taught that to me and I repeated it to him periodically. There he was living it out at that moment. Over the years, he became a real city boy and tended to go along with his grandmother's and father's fear of the water. He would do things that could be done at home.

Chris loved his cats. Unfortunately, Chris lost his favorite Siamese cat on the busy road where we lived. Fortunately, he had a second cat named Bangles who our former roommate had given us. I now realize how much my son Chris' pet cats gave him that deep feeling of acceptance he so desperately needed, especially during the times when he might secretly believe it was because of him that his mom and dad were at such odds against each other. If I couldn't understand it then, how could he?

Only today, I clearly understand my deep search for Truth that always opposed his father's deep search to be right! My spirit was looking for God to control it and his father's spirit was looking to control someone. I had given his father permission to control me without even realizing it, when I had married him.

When he was 13 years old, Chris gave his beloved tiger cat, Bangles, to my Nana, his great grandmother. She had fallen in love with Bangles while taking care of him when Chris and I finally got to go to Disney on vacation together. My Mary Kay career had afforded me the $3000 for this trip by the time Chris was thirteen.

Nana asked to keep Bangles but Chris understandably did not want to give his beloved cat to anyone. However, at Nana's 90th birthday party, I sang for her the song *"Wind Beneath My Wings."* Afterward, Chris was inspired and of his own accord courageously announced, "And my birthday present for my great Nana is my cat, Bangles!" Needless to say, there was not a dry eye in the place. I was so proud of his unselfishness to do such a noble thing. Nana had Bangles with her for almost ten years. He died just months before she went on to be with our Lord.

Chris had a heart of gold. He was an extremely compassionate and kind child and we were very close. We used to sing a song together *"That's What Friends Are For"* by Dionne Warwick, Elton John, Gladys Knight, and Stevie Wonder. Even though I am his mother and disciplined him as necessary, I have always offered him my friendship so he would feel free to talk with me about anything. Since I had trouble trusting my own parents with my deepest thoughts, I wanted to do what I felt I needed from them for Chris.

Chris was around 11 years old when I found an affordable apartment on the second floor of a two family home. This was after Silvia and her husband helped us. The apartment was right down the street from the house that I had lost in bankruptcy in River Edge, New Jersey. The landlords on the first floor treated Chris, his two cats, and me very well. We lived there for quite a few years, eventually adding another member to our household, a little Pomeranian named Harley.

Chris was around 15 when we got Harley. I believe God sent that happy little dog for me to love just as Chris began to separate himself from me, when he became more concerned about what his friends thought of him than his mother.

When we moved to this apartment, he was so happy that he was no longer bullied and was able to continue his prior friendships there. He was quite successful academically. It was a blessing to move back to River Edge and for Chris to be back with his intellectual friends, as far as I could understand then.

Chris and Jesus Christ

Chris verbally gave his heart to the Lord as his Savior when he was 13 years old after admitting he believed in Jesus. He was sitting on the couch with me in our living room in New Jersey, in that second floor apartment. At that time, I had more understanding of the issue of eternal life and felt led by the Holy Spirit to help my son to also know that Jesus is the only way to Heaven so he would not fear death. Interestingly, that's the same age I accepted Christ as my Savior, as you may recall, though didn't understand His Lordship and Chris didn't either.

I believe we all truly desire to know where we will go and what will happen to us after we die at one point or another. I love my son so much; I am much more concerned with where he will spend eternity than if he temporarily gets angry with me in this life in talking about God. Spending eternity burning in hell will be far more painful than temporary anger over a misunderstanding. With all my heart, I desire for Chris to have eternal life and be in Heaven with me. I pray for God to lead him back to the truth and His Lordship so he will have peace with God, as I have found.

Because Chris tells me today that he doesn't believe like he did then, I believe he has just gone astray for a time, just as I did. He needs to make Jesus the Lord of his life and still doesn't realize that. It is possible that Chris accepted Christ as a young teen just to please me, and that it was not real to him. However, it is also possible it was real and today he struggles because of past pains that Satan has held over him. It is possible that he consciously or unconsciously blames God for pain instead of blaming Satan who deserves the blame. Only Jesus has the power to heal our deep pains but we must be willing to submit them to Him in order to be healed and delivered from the bondage deep rooted pain puts us in. That is not something that anyone can force upon another but each of us must come to that realization ourselves as the Spirit draws us. The unconditional love of Jesus is a free choice that each of us has the option to make when we truly realize we are at the end of ourselves and don't have the answers.

I believe that just as the Bible teaches us to come to Him as little children, he was sincere then but has strayed away. It is very possible that in his need to be accepted, people's opinions and the public school system, which gave him good grades, confused him about God. I later read in his schoolbooks, before throwing them out, the lies that God doesn't exist. I know it is Satan who influenced people to re-write our American history books, for my schoolbooks didn't say that.

As a matter of fact they have been re-written to indoctrinate a few generations now that God is a fairy tale made up by Christians and man got to earth through the big-bang theory or evolution. Both of these theories have been disproved yet taught as truth. Projecting

129

lies onto the young and innocent is the way Satan works to destroy generations. All these men who re-wrote them will be held accountable to God for leading children astray.[1]

As adults, Satan so often leads us astray through brokenness and by various means, all to prevent more pain. Yet, we are missing the real truth and bigger picture that there is a much greater pain than the bumps and bruises of this life. The consequences we face on earth and Hell's eternal pain of fire and torment are far greater. Those who choose Christ can consider the troubles of this time to be nothing compared to the glory that shall be in Heaven, as God promises us.

It is important to make this eternity decision for oneself for the right reasons, and then make Him Lord in growing and maturing with greater understanding of the Bible until the Day of the Lord. Being a follower of Christ is a daily journey of relying upon the reading, meditating, and application of the Word of God to our lives. This helps us to grow more like Christ, our Lord and Savior.

We are a new creation in Christ Jesus. The old has passed away and the new has come, for Jesus makes all things new. This is a transformation of our lives that we cannot do for ourselves. So often we think we can change ourselves but I found that is impossible. Jesus can change us from the inside out.

We need to renew our old ways by receiving the new truths that are all in the Word of God, the Bible. I'm afraid that I did not do well at reading, studying and applying the Bible to my life with Chris at home at that time. Going to church and praying before meals was all we did. I also still struggled with the generational sin of anger since I didn't give all my life over to God then for healing. It has been a slow growing process for me in not understanding the full Lordship of Christ over my own life until recent years.

Chris has not yet experienced abundant life in Christ or the great spiritual treasures in the Bible, or does he enjoy fellowship or serving with a church. I take full responsibility for not modeling "living for Jesus" as he was growing up. I pray it doesn't take him as long

---

[1] David Barton has some of our nations' original educational materials in his library for proof. Visit www.Wallbuilders.com.

as it did me to understand how precious and wonderful it is to give your all to Jesus Christ, by making Him Lord of your life. I am praying and trust my Lord that he will come back to his Savior and make him Lord in time.

Chris and Puberty

Chris was very close to me until about age 14, when he began rejecting my kissing him in front of his school friends or dropping him off at school. The kids teased him about riding in a pink (Mary Kay) car and called him "pinkie." So, while he was trying to look cool to his friends, my heart was breaking in feeling the separation.

I know he blamed me for the kids teasing him because of my driving pink cars. I witnessed some boys calling him "pinkie" at Dunkin' Donuts one day, as soon as we walked in the restaurant. Chris quickly ran back out to the car crying. We all know that everyone wants to fit in with the crowd in order to feel significant.

I can understand that, since I did the same by stealing a bracelet, just to fit in, when my girlfriend and I were thirteen. Out of my learning the hard way, I had hoped that I could teach Chris to not base his worth on what other people think of him. I gave him ammunition to use, suggesting that he asks those boys "What color is the car your mom drives for free?" But he refused to use it by angrily reacting with "Mom, they won't get that!"

I have since learned that our deep need to be significant actually comes from God. He has designed us in His image to be truly significant. He has put in each of us gifts that He desires for us to use for His glory, in His divine plan for our time on the earth. I see my son's gifts and they are many but he just won't believe me when I tell him. He devalues himself and I know where that comes from but it is not the truth.

Unfortunately, as he grew older, I began to see how much Chris' attitude toward me was becoming a carbon copy of his father's attitude toward me. Insecurity is a deep root that leads to bad attitudes and anger. Boys tend to emulate their own fathers. What I've now learned is that according to the Bible, this is the reason God has called fathers to be the spiritual leaders in their families, so their children will follow a spiritual example that's like Christ. I pray that God will show him these things someday, so we can have a healthy relationship

131

again. Only then, he will understand that I always desire the very best for him.

If Chris would truly turn to God and give his whole life to Him, he would then be free to have a healthy relationship with me, with my husband Steven, and ultimately with his true love one day. God knows there is a wonderful lady specifically designed for him. Please pray for him! I pray for this daily. I wish I had known this when Chris was going through his childhood and teenage years. Life would have been better for both of us.

Chris' attitude changed toward me in the way he talked to me and treated me. Like many adolescents tend to do with their parents, he acted as if I knew nothing and he knew it all. I remember feeling that way with my parents also, so I guess it somehow all does come back to us. My son's communication with me at this stage amounted to just a few statements: "Ugh" and "I don't know."

One day we had an argument and all of a sudden, he hit me. By this time in my life's lessons, I had learned that boundaries are crucial. A child is not in control but the parent is, as long as they are still in the house together. His father had verbally and physically abused me by hitting and pushing me in his anger, so I knew I had to nip this behavior in the bud right then and there, or it would be a springboard for further abuse. The Bible says there is a curse that can affect many generations (Jeremiah 31:29-30). In my studies of Scripture and generational sins, I have learned that the curses of the father come down upon their children. When one accepts Jesus as their Savior, they can be delivered from those curses. Jesus is the only one who can break those chains.

I demanded he go pack his bags and move out—go to his father's house to live. I would not take that treatment by a son of mine. By the end of the day, Chris eventually begged me not to carry out my demand. He wanted to stay with me. I was glad, since I wanted him to stay as well but he must promise he would never hit me again. He promised.

Chris didn't really have much interest in girls throughout school. His father once discussed this with me over the phone. In Anthony's eyes, this was a problem. He thought that by the age of 13, if Chris had no interest in girls, that something must be wrong with him—he might be gay. His father justified this fear by alluding to the fact that his cousin was gay. I suggested that just because he, Anthony, chased girls at a young age, it did not mean all boys must; not all boys are like him or his cousin. Some realize the importance of pursuing an education before pursuing girls.

By the age of 17, Chris began talking with a girl online. Much to my surprise, he told me he was going to get on a bus and go to Pennsylvania to see her. My understanding of the Internet and computers was limited, since I didn't even realize this was possible to do online. Chris had helped me run my Mary Kay business with the software program the company provided since he was 14. I obviously had no idea where having a computer in his room might lead.

At a NCCA Christian counseling conference, we were taught by one of the counseling experts how important it is for parents to monitor our children and their computer usage. However, I was unaware of that at the time. I am now being reminded that it was at age 17 when I hid from my parents my newfound relationship with my first boyfriend, as you may recall from the beginning of my story. Interestingly, my son is following in my footsteps in this. At least he had the respect to tell me about it so it seems I had some success in getting him to talk to me as a friend.

I finally told Chris I would drive him to this girl's house to meet her. I kept my eye on them the whole time, while trying to get to know her mother. At one point, while at lunch together, I found out from the girl that she hated her dad because of his alcoholism. Her parents were divorced and not on good terms, much like Chris's dad and I. Now I understand how this relationship online between them began—through the common bond of having divorced parents. Again, misery loves company. People naturally look for a common connection to enhance their companionship or to support their sorrows.

What I've learned in counseling is that we attract the opposite gender based on our emotional state at the time. However, a healthy relationship can continue to grow past this stage regardless of the pain we must face to overcome it. An unhealthy relationship that stays stuck at this emotional level without God's perfect standard to measure truth will never mature into a healthy relationship. It will eventually self-destruct. It takes God's standard to correctly measure truth so to learn how to grow past this emotional level, by choosing truth over emotions. I have experienced this in both ways and counseled enough women to know it is true.

Without my knowledge, Chris and this girl conveniently planned out attending the same college. When I realized it at orientation, I asked the head of the school to ensure that they not reside in the same dorm because of the temptation that might lure Chris to jeopardize his purity. Because my purity had been lost, out of love for Chris, I desired to help protect his purity in order to protect his heart. I had already experienced many broken hearts to prove it would be destructive to him and I certainly do not want my son to experience that.

Being in an intimate relationship would distract him from his studies (this I learned the hard way when I was young) and would hurt him emotionally and spiritually. I found out from the school, however, that this girl's mother wrote a letter requesting that her daughter be in the same dorm as Chris in order for him to drive her around, since she had no car. The school administration honored us both by putting her in the dorm behind Chris' dorm.

Sadly, Chris, who disagreed with my warnings, suffered a broken heart after a ten-year relationship. With all my heart, just when he was a little boy and I picked him up when he fell down and comforted him, I wanted to hold him and comfort him when his heart was broken. I so desired for him to have learned from me so to prevent him that pain rather than go through it the hard way.

I desire with all my heart for Chris to learn the truth that I finally learned: that he needs to make Jesus his first love because Jesus actually knows who the love of his life is. Jesus says, "Seek ye first the kingdom of God and all these things will be added unto you." Jesus loves us so much for He created us for a love relationship with Him and He knows the desires of our hearts. He has known us since before we were conceived in our mother's womb, therefore He knows all about us and knows who our perfect mate is. He is simply waiting for us to choose Him and trust Him first so He can reveal him/her to us. Once I did that then God sent me my lifetime mate.

9/11

Like other people around the world, my son and I will never forget what happened on 9/11/2001: the Muslim jihadist attack on the Twin Towers, the Pentagon, and the tragic crash in Pennsylvania. Our whole country was affected by this devastating event. We were attacked by Muslims following Muhammad's military agenda and his goal of establishing Islam around the world, as well as killing and/or conquering the unbelievers (those who do not follow Islam).

That morning, unlike most other days, I was compelled to turn on the TV. I don't even like TV and rarely watched it. I believe it was the Holy Spirit in me that prompted me to turn it on. Much to my shock, I saw the plane crashing into the Twin Towers right there on the screen. At first I thought it was a movie. When I realized it was the news, my first thought was "Wow, what a freak accident!"

As I watched it being repeated as a rerun, the next thing I realized was this plane hit in a different place than the first. "Oh my goodness, this is an attack! Oh God, help us! What is happening?" my heart cried out.

Immediately I ran upstairs and pounded on my son's bedroom door to wake him up. It was about 9:15 am and he was sleeping in because this was the month before he was due to go to college. He woke up and asked, "What? What's the matter?"

I yelled, "Chris, get up! I think we are being attacked!" He jumped out of bed to turn on his own TV before racing downstairs to see the news. The next thing I know, he is yelling while pacing the floor, "I am going to war! I am going to get these guys! I am going to war!"

Chris was very addicted to the "good guy, bad guy" video games; maybe that was what was driving his anger. Instantly I recalled that my cousin had gotten drafted into the army to go to Vietnam. He had no choice at the tender age of 18. I wondered, "Will they draft my son?" I started praying to God, "Oh God! Please don't take my only son, Lord. Please!" Chris was just about to turn 18.

Wow, it just now hit me! What about God Himself who gave us His only Son? I can't even imagine how God must have felt to sacrifice Jesus, His only Son. He did so for the sake of all of us, so we are able to simply choose to believe and receive salvation. While we were

135

yet sinners, Jesus paid the cost we all deserved to pay for our sins. God knew it was the only way because none of us are perfect, no not one of us. Only Jesus in his death could pay the price and overcome death through His victorious resurrection.

In my own heart, I know that Christopher is only alive on the earth today because of Jesus Christ, who influenced me to save him from abortion before his birth. When the choice of "life and death" was put before me, I chose life for Chris (Deuteronomy 30:19). And yet as he walks around on this earth today, while not choosing God's ways, his soul is empty and actually dead. It has a God sized hole in it until he freely chooses life by choosing Jesus who is our eternal life, God's love and our salvation. Without salvation, our souls are dead. Because Christ is alive, through believing in Him our soul becomes alive!

"He who has the Son has the life; he who does not have the Son of God does not have the life." (I John 5:12) In God's divine unconditional love, every person has a free choice to choose spiritual life or death. God desires for each one of us to choose life, but because He is a gentleman, He will not force it upon us. He has His arms open, waiting for us to run into Daddy's arms. Jesus tells us in John 8:12: "I am the light of the world. Whoever walks with me will not walk in darkness." Death is the darkness. The light overcomes darkness but darkness can never overcome the light.

After a while, Chris changed his mind about going to war and decided he was going to attend college as planned. I thanked God for His Grace once again for Chris' change of heart, as well as for a draft not being issued. Today, I wonder what would have happened if he had gone? Then that girlfriend he went to college with wouldn't have broken his heart. Would that had been better for him?

Adversity builds character and wouldn't that be better? I still wonder if our relationship would be better today if he did go to war and saw death in its face and came home safely, but grateful for life. Then he might have a greater appreciation for life, for my choice to choose life for him and the life of Christ that God provided for each of us to choose life. In 2011, when I had to share my own testimony of 9/11/01, I asked Chris why he changed his mind about going to war. He said, "Because they had not clearly defined the enemy." He decided it would be useless to go. America's leaders have publically deceived us all to believe we, a Christian-founded nation, are not in war with Islam. The lie that President Bush publically told America, that Islam is a peaceful religion, which had been hijacked by a few radicals, seemed to convince people to go back to normal in life.

Sadly, it all has gotten worse with the Obama administration. Based on my training in Islam, I conclude Obama is a Muslim. He is clearly not a Christian for he does not produce the spiritual fruit to prove it. He sympathizes with Islam in more ways than I can explain here and has ruined our nation's superpower standing among nations.

Because Satan is in war with God and can't touch Him, he can only go after God's people and Godly nations. America was established on Judeo-Christian principles to promote life through Jesus, confirmed in the US Constitution. Middle Eastern nations were established by the sword through this ideology called Islam (a governmental system ruling people through *Shari'ah* [law] disguised as a religion). Jesus said, 'Those who live by the sword will die by the sword."

Satan represents death. Islam promotes death. The great Deceiver has so cleverly mislead over 1.6 billion Muslims worldwide to believe his lie of Islam. So many Muslims do not know the true Islam which we see today as ISIS and are blindly following this works oriented religion in bondage to the law of *Shari'ah*.

Today, on the contrary, I know that the enemy is clearly defined, as I have studied the ideology of Islam. We as a nation given by God are in war with Islam, the ideology. It is the clear teachings of Islam that encourage young men and women to kill non-Muslims and be killed to find paradise. These deceived people called Muslims are actually choosing death when they choose to follow Islam. In Deuteronomy 30:19, God's desire is that we choose life.

Islam's ideology is the spirit of death. Satan leads people with the spirit of death in opposition to Jesus who leads people with the spirit of life. This includes suicide bombers martyring themselves for Allah (their god) in order to obtain their closest assurance of earning Paradise. If I were Satan I would lead people to kill and be killed so to take more with me to hell, out of pure hate for God, Creator of all. Wouldn't it be just like Satan to call this ideology of death a "religion" to get people to believe it is good? If I were Satan, knowing my destiny is hell, I would do whatever it takes to lead people to hell with me, wouldn't you? Satan is the father of lies and deception. We have a free choice to believe truth. Christ' resurrection power that overcame death gave us that choice.

Paradise is what Muslims believe to be equivalent to our Christian Heaven, where we will go after death. How sad that for Muslims this assurance is not even 100% guaranteed, but rather depends on whether Allah, in his aloofness, will give them grace and mercy.

I praise God that I have 100% assurance of eternity with God in accepting Jesus Christ as my Lord and Savior. God's grace and mercy has already been granted to me. All I have to do is choose it. I have received and will receive God's gift of eternal life in Heaven with God. I thank Him that I do not have to earn this eternity but that it is God's free gift. I know I am certainly not good enough to earn it. I praise God that He is truly a God of grace and mercy. That is why He offers us this unconditional love that we all are free to choose, no matter what we have done in the past. We can come to Him just the way we are.

Chris and College

I dropped Chris off at college in Pennsylvania in October 2001, about one month after 9/11. We stopped on the way at Hershey Park, where we enjoyed a nice day together on rides and eating chocolate. After getting him settled in his dorm room, he looked at me before I left and said "Mom, what are you going to do without me?"

"I don't know," I cried. He knew the significance when I tried to lighten the mood by saying, "I may be calling you to walk me through computer issues on the phone." I cried for at least an hour on my trip home alone, already experiencing the separation anxiety.

This was a very difficult time for me. I would be experiencing emptiness syndrome with no one to go home to. I realized that he was grown up now and would be learning to live on his own just as I did at 18. Now, I would need to find a new purpose in life. Of course, I could have asked him the same question: "What will *you* do without *me*?" since he had refused to let me teach him to cook when he was growing up. So, rather than eating a healthy diet in college, like the one I had provided him, he began eating Ramen noodles, canned food, and junk food.

Before going to college, he had not been sick in eight years. He was completely healthy when he had his medical exam before school. It did not surprise me however when he came down with mono and strep throat in college. I prayed that he would learn a lesson by it and eat healthy, as well as take care of himself in all ways as a responsible adult.

God loves Chris and wants the best for him even more than I can comprehend (Ephesians 3:17-20). God knew Chris before he was born, even before he was conceived in my womb (Psalm 139:13-18). I pray that he will learn to be thankful for the blessings he really does have and turn around and walk into the arms of his most loving Heavenly Father, God, just as I did when I came to the end of my ideas and myself. In that defining moment I was able to turn my life around for the better. Somehow I knew that in God's perfect time, I would be blessed with a new purpose in life and Chris would be ok.

My Son and his Dad

After Chris graduated from college in 2003, he chose to move home with his father in getting word of the death of his grandmother, Anthony's mom. Chris was extremely close to her since she played the role of mother in his dad's household. Within a couple of months, while still mourning the death of his grandmother, Chris got the news that his father had cancer. Anthony had only a year to live. So, at the tender age of 20, Chris was expected by his father to be his caregiver.

Anthony demanded this of our son for two reasons. First, he wanted to be home and not in a hospital; he did not like strangers coming to his house to care for him. Secondly, he expected that if Chris really loved him, as a son should, he would become selfless and take care of his father's every need. Anthony's idea of love ("If … then …") was conditional love.

Even though Chris had just finished college, doing a super job with a degree in multi-media, his father demanded that he forgo his career opportunities as a result and find whatever job he could locally, even if it was not in his field of interest. Anthony was not thinking of what was best for Chris, but rather his own selfish desire: for Chris to take care of him. When I think about it all, I think of how Chris is a son

139

Anthony had not wanted at birth, yet then expected to be his caregiver through to his death. Just like me, Chris was distracted from pursuing his college career by the demands or request of another person and persuaded to do so.

When Chris had gone to college, Anthony had absolutely refused to pay a dime for our son's education. I found that peculiar, since when we were married, he not only made us skim on all luxuries, but also took away my car to cut bills in order to save for college for this child from the time of his birth. By insisting that Chris become his caregiver and sacrifice his career, he was indirectly aiming to make Chris' college degree worthless. In addition, part of his vendetta stemmed from his anger at me for bringing Chris to meet the Pennsylvania girlfriend, which he was also against. I believe he feared that he would end up dying alone. The prospect of Chris going away to college and/or moving to Pennsylvania for a girl made that fear a reality.

When Anthony held a grudge against someone, as I watched him do to the two couples that came to our wedding, and to me, he held that grudge for a lifetime. He never even considered forgiveness. As a result of losing these last two male friends and me, his final wife, he feared being alone in the end of his life. He was extremely pessimistic about the number of his days because his father died young. He had deep hurts and insecurities that only an unconditional loving God, our perfect Heavenly Father, could heal, yet he rejected God!

Chris did give up his dreams in order to take care of his dad. Sadly, his dad would use this to test Chris. For example, while he was caring for his needs, his father decided to put a piece of paper on the floor, just to see how long it took him to pick it up. Chris, obviously not recognizing this as a "test", took three days to pick that silly paper up off the floor. Because he "failed" this crazy test, Anthony didn't speak to him, except to give him orders, for three whole weeks! I only know about this because Chris called me to tell me about this problem with his father. He was devastated by it.

All I could do at that point was to cry with him. Déjà vue hit me like a brick, as I remembered Anthony doing these same kinds of things to me. I knew Chris was telling me the truth. I could feel his pain, but I could not help him. Anthony was not willing to change and unconditionally love people when I was married to him, nor after I escaped his cruelty. When I got off the phone, I began gulping down sobs, crying over what my son was experiencing, similar to the hell I went through at the hands of his dad.

Later I talked to Anthony on the phone and all he could do was bash his son, telling me how selfish he was and threatening to take away his inheritance. Indirectly, I connected those dots to see that his father knew that Chris would be the only one to inherit all he had. He seemed to expect him to perform like a circus dog for it. I could not reason with him as usual. Sadly, the anger inside of him was now lashing out upon his son without any concern of how Chris was feeling about losing him to cancer.

I Do Not Regret Having Chris

If only I had not begged God for that man to marry me. If only I had run to God instead of uniting myself to this mean man who was now hurting my son. As I cried over my painful past with Anthony, I realized I never ever regretted having my son, Chris.

If I wished Anthony away, then Chris would not be alive. As I write about this right now, tears come to my eyes. I feel pain for another reason, because my son, who was once a loving, joyful, and carefree child, has become more and more like his dad in his attitude and outlook on life and toward me. At this time, Chris closed communication with me for a year, just because I said "God" is his answer to difficult times. Please pray with me against this generational sin of anger and rebelliousness against God and that the truth will set Chris free.

Chris has always been very gifted. I can see today how he has lost his belief in his own giftedness. My heart grieves that Chris, following his father's footsteps, has so far chosen to blame God for the death of his grandmother and father. When we don't understand something, just as when we don't know God, it is so easy to just blame God.

God gave us life by creating us. God is love and loved us enough to redeem us from death by sending His sinless and only Son. He emptied Himself of His divinity and came to earth to be born of a woman, only to die again by age 33. But Jesus rose victoriously and overcame death; He holds the keys to death and Hades where He will send Satan and his followers for eternity.

Satan is the author of death. Satan tempted Adam and Eve in the garden with the lie, causing them to disobey God and listen to him. That caused them to be separated from God – to lose the perfection of the garden and their daily walk and talk with God. They chose to allow Satan to convince them to turn their backs on God. They believed him instead, the author of death and lies. That was the fall from the perfect loving relationship with God. God restored us by sending Jesus, our perfect sinless sacrifice. He gives us life when we look upon Him and believe in Him.

However, I do not lose hope for my son. I can't blame Chris for the way his father was. As long as he is still breathing, my son has the choice every day to get to know God, His great love, and acceptance. My prayer every day is that someday my son, named after Christ, will run into God's open arms toward him and experience God as his perfect Heavenly Father, as my husband and I both have. I pray Chris would know personally, as I do, the great joy that fills His children's hearts, the peace that passes human understanding, and the amazing love and grace that gives us abundant life in Him.

Before 2nd Husband Died

In Anthony's last days of living, I tried to show him that I truly cared about him and his eternal destiny. Since he had hung up on me when I tried talking to him by phone, I sent him cards with the message of truth about God's great love for him. I hoped that he would take the opportunity to choose his eternal destiny privately.

Like everyone else, Anthony was free to choose to repent of his sins and turn to God. He could make it right with those he held unforgiveness toward and ask God for forgiveness. Then he could choose to believe he is forgiven through the sacrificial blood of Jesus. So, before departing the earth, he would know for sure that believing in what Jesus did is the way to God. However, Chris later told me that his dad just tore up the cards and threw them away.

God does not force Himself upon any of us. He gives us the free choice to choose Him first, so that we can feel His unconditional love. It is so simple to be with God eternally after we depart this earth, just by making a simple choice. It is like when someone gives you a gift—it is up to you to choose to take it or reject it.

Even though Anthony and I never made it as a couple, that didn't mean I wished the worst upon him. I certainly did not want him to go to an eternal pit of fire: hell. Based on what Chris told me, it was apparent that Anthony was not choosing God but only God knows for sure. Yet I cared, enough to risk his rejection again. After all, he is my son's father.

I thought I would try one more way to show him God's love: by cooking for him. So I went there with fresh food to make him a home cooked meal. Chris was home and told me he didn't think it would work, but I wanted to try anyway. I knew he might reject me, but what if there was a slight chance that he might accept me making a meal for him? God's love made it worth the risk.

As soon as I got inside the door and into the dining room—I didn't even make it to the kitchen—Anthony cursed me out of the house with rage and anger. Chris insisted I leave. I could see in his eyes how fearful Chris was of his rage. So, not wanting Chris to suffer further, I put the food on the dining room table and left.

God had sent me there just as He had asked me to send those cards to show Anthony the love of Jesus. I obeyed my Heavenly Father. The Bible says that they hated Jesus so they will hate us, too. I know that is one reason why Anthony insulted and cursed at me. Jesus said that people would insult us (Matthew 5:11).

Like God said to do, I forgave Anthony many years earlier for the pain he caused me and told him I was sorry for hurting him. My willingness to go there showed my forgiveness. However, using his free choice, he chose not to forgive me. His unforgiving heart saddens me not because it hurts me; it doesn't. Rather, I am sad because it just hurt him to not forgive and I know un-forgiveness destroys us from the inside out. Eventually, I learned more in Scripture that applies to forgiveness. In Matthew 6:15, it says that if we do not forgive others, then our Heavenly Father will not forgive us. I believe Chris' father died of unforgiveness, a choice of his very own. There are always consequences to our sin.

Our loving God, who loves unconditionally, does not force anyone to believe in Him or love Him. In Deuteronomy 30:19, it says that God has put before us life and death, blessings and curses. He desires that we choose life and blessings. However, His unconditional

143

love will never force us to choose His ways. Though God created us in His own image, every human being is born as a sinner since the fall of Adam and Eve in the Garden of Eden.

Romans 3:23 states, *"For all have sinned and fallen short of the glory of God."* Because of this, we must choose to change our sinful, wicked, and unloving ways by repenting of the past. We need to turn around to walk in the opposite direction of our past sinful ways to find peace—to walk in God's ways. God is love.

The Pharisees were always so concerned with keeping a check on people to ensure that they kept the law. Anthony was a man who acted like the Pharisees, with absolutely no grace for others. So many people are in bondage to the lies they have been raised with and the lies from those people that attract them. They need to look to the loving Creator God to help them overcome and be freed from this bondage so to develop healthy relationships. Jesus said *"If I be lifted up I will draw all men to myself."* (John 12:32)

When people, out of pride, close their minds to listening to reason instead of drawing close to God, most of them just blame God without understanding His love for them. I found that pride, though it makes a person appear so all knowing, actually comes from great insecurity. The burden of the law is too heavy for all people as we try to become perfect. Moses writes that the law's way of making a person right with God requires the keeping of all of its commands, not just one or a few of them.

Sadly, Muslims are also trying to keep the law to be holy but God knows the intent of every heart. Both He and they know they cannot. The Word says we are condemned already so that means we feel guilty. It makes people mad when they fall short of perfection. We are all imperfect and cannot fulfill perfection and therefore can never be enough. I see that anger in Muslims who believe Islam with all of their heart, soul and mind, how they lash out at Christianity with such rage! They just want to be right rather than peacefully and respectfully listening to the truth, and allowing their mind and heart to reason together. The problem is they have no peace at all while proclaiming Islam is a peaceful religion.

I sat through a five and a half hours discussion between my current husband, Steven and a Muslim proclaiming how peaceful he was to my sweet Jewish Christian friend. My friend had made lunch that day to host this discussion. This peaceful Muslim was so respectful and kind in his initial demeanor, though he was disrespectfully late. Once the conversation began between him and my husband, a former Muslim now Christian, it was very clear how offended he was by Steven. His respect went right out the window within a half hour.

My husband remained calm the entire time while this Muslim just got angrier and angrier. I had to interject in the first hour to ask the Muslim to please consider the 30 more years Steven had over him as well as his study of Islam from his childhood. I knew Islam taught respect for elders. Could he please show some respect in the manner he was speaking? As I reflected upon it later, it reminded me of arguments I had experienced with Chris's dad about God and truth, except when Anthony would have no answer he would shut me out.

This Muslim would just change the subject of argument to attack from another angle. He was relentless all the way to the front door as we tried to leave. After 5 hours, we still had to drive 3 hours home. This Muslim continued his arguments in email form. He got so nasty and verbally abusive. Steven simply forwarded it to my friend who finally realized he wasn't peaceful at all and she asked him to stop communication with her and Steven. He did.

God knew that man could not fulfill the whole law and that is why He sent Jesus as a perfect man so he would do it perfectly for us. All we need to do is except and believe in our heart that God raised Him from the dead, and you will be saved and made right with God. It is the blood Jesus shed for us that would cover us in the eyes of God, our Father, our Creator so to restore our intimate relationship back to Him that Adam and Eve lost in the garden. Then God would see us as perfect because of the blood of Jesus that paid the price we could not pay. Jesus overcame sin and death and is alive eternally. He is our righteousness so no one can boast of his or her works. His grace for us is enough and He is offering it as a free gift for us to freely choose.

You see, Anthony expected me to fold his underwear perfectly in military style and be who he wanted me to be according to his ways. He expected me to cook only what he liked, put every DVD back in alphabetical order, and never leave my clothes on the floor before leaving a room, just like my father expected the dinner to be at the table by 5:30 PM sharp every night he returned home from work. In the same way, Anthony expected Chris to pick up that piece of paper as soon as he dropped it on the floor. All these men expected perfection from those around them in order to please their flesh but even if we did those things perfectly, they would have looked for something else that did not please them about us. The truth is, I could never be enough for any man, just as Chris could never be enough of a caregiver for his father.

Without realizing it, all men are looking for perfection in others so to prove their love for each other because we are all created in God's image and God is perfect. That God sized hole in each of us will never be perfected until it is filled with God's unconditional love given through Jesus. We must receive and believe in Jesus in order to feel truly loved. Then we must be transformed by the renewing of our minds through studying the Word.

Jesus is the Word and Jesus makes all things new! The old is passed away and we are made into the new creation, becoming more like Jesus day by day. Sadly, even many people who call themselves Christians are not renewing their minds in the Word. They are tripped up by the same bondage of Satan, by not seeking God in prayer for help from the Holy Spirit to lead us into all truth by the Word. I know. I was one of them for a long time and still struggle at times.

Jesus came to set the captives free from the law and bondage. Acts 15:10 says, "*Now therefore, why do you test God by putting a yoke on the neck of the disciples which neither our fathers nor we were able to bear?*" The Jews themselves were not able to justify themselves before God by the law, so they shouldn't put that heavy, burdensome yoke on the Gentiles either.

Without accountability to another Christian who is more mature, the devil will lure us away by deceptively putting us under his bondage. We will not be free to grow and get prepared as the Bride for our Bridegroom. That is what Satan wants. Jesus said, "*Come to me all those who are heavy laden and I will give you rest*." Only Jesus could fulfill the law perfectly as the only sinless man. He did it for us, knowing we couldn't.

When his father passed, Chris inherited half of that house from his father. Later his aunt, who owned the other half, wanted him to clean it out and sell it. Chris sold it and moved elsewhere. What saddens my heart most about Anthony is that he wasted his life by being miserable. He then died from it. All I can do is pray to God that He will somehow, whatever way He has to, turn my son's life around so that he won't follow in his dad's footsteps.

God is so good and I trust Him. If God forced us to love Him, instead of giving us free choice, we would rebel and try to run from God just as a two year old does when he has a temper tantrum in order to get his own way. Anthony's resentment of my forcing him into having a child and marrying me became the same resentment he had for my leaving him.

Demands can never be satisfied, even with new demands, for the soul is never satisfied without Christ. God designed us all that way. Anthony's resentment manifested itself in the way he spoke about me to our son throughout his growing up years, and the way he spoke to me. He did vindictive things and cursed me even to the day he took his last breath.

Cancer destroyed Anthony's body. I believe his cancer was fed in part by resentment. Resentment, if not resolved by first admitting it and changing by asking forgiveness and forgiving all who are involved, has been medically proven[2] to manifest in our bodies as illness. I have seen this happen numerous times to people I have counseled, as well as to people I know outside of counseling.

The resentment and anger a person holds onto does absolutely no good. It boomerangs and kills the embittered person, physically as well as emotionally. God gives us all only good things and is always with us but a love relationship must be two ways to be true love. God is waiting for us to love Him and delights in the thought of it. He is waiting patiently for us. Love commanded is no love at all but torment for both involved.

God turns everything around for His glory eventually, for those who love Him (Romans 8:28). The inheritance that Anthony left Chris ultimately paid off the balance of Chris's college loan. God al-

---

[2] Medical   Report   from   http://www.mentalhealth.org.uk/help-information/mental-health-a-z/A/anger/

ways makes things right because He is in control, even though it may look like, for a time, the devil is winning with the evil he encourages people to do.

Satan tempts us with lies we choose to believe. We either choose his ways or God's righteous way through faith in Jesus. Satan even convinces people that they are not choosing between God's or Satan's ways but have a third choice which is "my way." God says that if we are not with Him we are against Him; therefore our own way is Satan's way.

Father Figures

The saddest part of this situation is that after puberty, Chris began emulating his father more and more. He didn't realize the destructive path his father was travelling. Many boys desire to emulate the father figure in their lives, whether that role model is doing well or poorly, whether the man is a great father figure, or a bad example. My prayer is that Chris will someday stop blaming God for his grief like his dad did, and realize that God loves him so much and is actually the source of his help. It is the devil (who does exist) that wants all people to die miserable and join him in hell, not our loving God who created us for a loving relationship with Him.

As God promises to be our provider, He has now provided Chris with a good and loving male role model in my husband Steven, if only Chris would choose to accept him. I am not saying Steven is a replacement for his father. No one can replace his dad, but I do believe that the two of them could become friends and have a healthy relationship built on love and respect. However, just like God's love, Steven has no desire to force a relationship—true love is not manipulative. Like God's love, this is unconditional love that allows free choice, as opposed to conditional love, which demands that a person "earn" it. Every time Chris calls, I encourage him to talk with Steven, who always ends the conversation by inviting him to come anytime he wants to visit. Steven looks forward to that time.

As a mom, I am so sorry for all the grief that Chris endured because of my years of looking for love in all the wrong places, as well as all the errors I made as a mother. While I am grateful that God has blessed me with a wonderful husband in Steven Masood, I also hope to someday have a wonderful relationship with my son, whom I love very much. I continue to pray for him daily, that God brings into his life a wonderful lady who loves God first and foremost so with her he can enjoy a long and happy life full of God's great blessings, just as I am finally enjoying today!

Praise God for a recent improvement in communication when Chris moved out of Brooklyn into his own house in Pennsylvania. God has answered my deepest prayers and cries to Him. Now, as I see Chris using his creative abilities in designing costumes that duplicate video game warriors, I see he is becoming a Warrior for God. He has already created his full armor of God but I think he is just missing his shield of FAITH. Lord, help him in his unbelief so that his shield of faith will become the most powerful in his armor, so he can fight for YOU!

8

Third Marriage

Is Merely Being "Christian" the Answer to Finding Your True Love?

Now going back in time to August 1997, in sharing with you my life, I decided to take a vacation to see my family in Maine. My son was with his father in Brooklyn for that month. My schedule was pretty much my own, so I had chosen to take this time off work. Being my own boss as a Mary Kay Pink Cadillac Sr. Sales Director definitely had its benefits, which also earned some sort of respect from my mother.

As for my love life, I had gotten lost in 2 husbands and several live-ins, as well as other male relationships. I was hoping to learn the "secret" of true love through reading the book, *Finding the Love of your Life* by Neil Clark Warren. My pastor had given me this book to read. The author founded eHarmony, the website that was originally a Christian website for singles. It saddens me to see where it is today, as I would not recommend it to Christians at all.

Even in my financial contentment, I had been feeling a bit lonely for someone to love and for someone to love me. I speculated about my financial ease. I could buy anything I wanted, as my tastes and wants were really not too extravagant. $75,000 a year was more than I had ever made before, and that didn't include the Cadillac I was driving for free.

I had already taken Chris to Disney at age 13. As he grew, he became more of a homebody. He was naturally interested in doing things other than hanging out with his mother. I thought about the fact that soon he would be off to college and I would be left alone. So here I was, able to do more in life than ever, yet with no partner. I had accomplished as much or more than any family member had, and even more than they expected of me. So, I pondered, "What is it all for, if I have no one to share it with, no partner, no love life?"

Looking back, I wish I could tell myself, "Stop right there, Karen! Why don't you give yourself a break? Why don't you just be alone for a while and seek God?" I obviously hadn't learned my own temperament's weaknesses yet and how important it is to cling tightly to Jesus first.

I sadly fell for the devil's trick again, since I was not wholeheartedly seeking God and still was not content in my singleness. Even this book I was reading, written by a Christian and recommended by my pastor, never mentioned the importance of seeking God and being completely content as a single, recklessly abandoned over Jesus and his love, before a man.

Here I was minding my own business, just trying to get insight into what this writer had to say about relationships and along comes… you guessed it . . . another guy—Marcus. I have to say I related the timing of reading the book with meeting this new guy as "being from God." So much for seeking God in prayer for His answers! That seemed to go out the window. The Bible says to seek God for wisdom in all we do.

Marcus had a boat and my parents had a boat. Their recreational boating included drinking together. My mother liked him and either thought we should meet or was talked into arranging a meeting by him. Marcus later told me that my mother had told him of her concerns for me as a single again. They mulled over the fact that I was still alone and why and what kind of guy I needed. God only knows what she told him.

Marcus was also divorced. He had three kids whom he believed he couldn't visit, even though he financially supported them. He feared his ex-wife's threats and he wasn't allowed to see them. I learned he was non-confrontational.

Marcus knew about my work with Mary Kay. While taking me on a romantic moonlight boat cruise on his boat, he used lines like, "Look at the Mary Kay clouds in the sky!" due to the lovely shade of pink from the sunset painting the clouds. In our conversation, I learned he had a farmhouse there in Maine and was taking care of his mother because his dad had died. She was alone and in her 80's.

While discussing my beliefs, Marcus told me he was a Christian too. He believed in respecting a lady and in refraining from sex until marriage . . . I sure *thought* I heard that. He said he had no problem going to church and that he goes to his mom's church.

About five months later I was visiting him and he kissed me for the first time. Well, you know how that story goes. We seemed so attracted to each other that I thought at last I had it right this time, since he was a Christian. At least, he said he was a Christian.

After getting engaged, I felt pushed over the edge to be intimate before marriage. He rationalized and convinced me that since we were engaged, it would be ok. Remember, the "Christian" counselor down the street had told me this very thing from where I lived in New Jersey. To this point, I had not understood the distinct line. The wedding plans convinced me it was fine. Just a little truth sprinkled with more lies can easily lead us astray. When a woman wants marriage more than Jesus, the devil tempts her as he poses as the "angel of light."

My Third Wedding

We were married within about 9 months of our first meeting, in Maine at Marcus's mother's little church. The counseling session with his pastor amounted to this:

"Well, Marcus, I know you've been married and have learned it isn't as easy as it seems, right?"

"Yes sir!" answered Marcus.

"So Karen, I understand you've been married before as well. Can I assume you learned the same?"

"Yes," I replied.

"Okay then, you two are consenting adults, so let's get on with it." The full counseling session was basically along those lines. We were out of the place in minutes.

We held the reception in Marcus' family barn, with both of our families. Some of my Mary Kay friends from New Jersey came, along with all his boating friends. I made the cake and bought the dress and a hat at a bridal store. My son stood up with me and gave me away.

My dad danced with me that day and cried. It seemed so authentic, like this was it for a lifetime.

Marcus was willing to move to New Jersey and find a job there. My apartment seemed too small for the three of us, along with my dog, so a friend helped us find a house to buy together. We moved out of the 2nd floor apartment to a house near the railroad track on the cheaper side of town. It was within walking distance to Chris's high school. Life seemed good and on the right track. It seemed like my dream came true.

Difficulties with Marcus

As time went on, Marcus and Chris never seemed to find a common bond. Marcus was a country boy and Chris a city boy. Unlike Chris, Marcus was not computer literate or well read. He liked New England sports teams and Chris liked the New York teams. Although Marcus was personable, I am sure that Chris was by this point tired of getting used to another guy out of the many I had dated. Can you blame him?

After some time together in the first year, I realized Marcus was a poor money manager. He used credit loosely and generously in order to look "good" to others, but he had difficulty paying it off. When he was in trouble, I bailed him out with my earnings a couple of times. He rarely paid for the mortgage or our household expenses while he continued to pay for his house in Maine. His reason for not selling that house was because his mother still lived there. He understandably didn't want her to have to move. However, little did I realize, in his mind, it was "his way out" if necessary. He had one foot in the door and one outside the door: a recipe for trouble ahead or even disaster.

Marcus was charming with everyone and loved to drink socially. He soon hooked up with the alcoholic neighbors who loved sports like he did. His laid back personality just adored sitting around watching sports and drinking beer. When he was home, he never took the initiative to fix anything or keep the house maintained. While I did appreciate that he was not a controlling person, I had no idea before marrying him that he was out of control in so many areas of his life.

As for church, he didn't mind going to a traditional church, but forget the Spirit-filled church. He was certainly not going to pray out loud, nor tithe, nor spend too much time in church. We did not see eye to eye on spiritual matters. Our goals in life were not the same. Our commitment level was not the same, nor headed that way.

Because the Bible teaches that God hates divorce and I was now serious about obeying God, I decided that divorcing was not going to be an option for me. So I committed myself to sticking out this marriage, even though I realized I had made yet another mistake. Hopefully, somehow it would work out.

However, our lifestyles were very different. We began to argue about spending time on spiritual things, as opposed to drinking and having a "good time." We argued about his needing to make a concerted effort to fix something in the house, but he just never found that motivation. His heart longed more and more for his life in Maine and less and less for his life in New Jersey with Chris and me.

We argued about his trying harder to get along with Chris. He told me that my son was a brat and needed to be disciplined. Even though I knew Chris's attitude was not great, because he emulated his dad more, I also knew that it was up to Marcus as the adult to push through and try to get along with him. I felt like I had two children now instead of one, yet I had hoped I had found a better role model for Chris. I supposed there was something more to the reason Marcus never saw his own kids, besides fear of his ex, which may have contributed to not getting along with Chris. It could have conjured up his true feelings about his own loss of his relationship with his children. I instinctively knew that man needed to see his kids.

One day, despite his fears, I took him to see his children, which he protested at the time. Just two years later, he would tell me, "I want to thank you for opening the door for me to have a relationship with my children."

Abandoned: the Third Divorce

One night when I came home from a Mary Kay appointment, Chris looked at me and said, "Mom, he's gone."

I asked, "Where did he go?"

My son informed me, "He's gone with his truck and all his things. He said he is going for good. He is not coming back." This was in the year 2000.

Marcus abandoned our marriage about two years into it. That was the longest I had ever been with any one guy other than Chris' dad. I never saw him again. I filed the divorce as Pro Se at his request and with his consent.

I couldn't believe it. I had failed at love again. This was my third divorce. I was devastated emotionally! Three strikes and you're out is what they say. I felt like a complete failure. I actually talked to my mother at that time. She did insinuate I must have done something to cause it. She then recommended I get some drugs to calm me down. I had never taken drugs since my experimentation with cocaine after college. I refused to have anything to do with drugs, especially seeing her life and how prescription drugs controlled her moods and caused her constant problems, side effects and dependency.

A girlfriend from Maryland recommended a natural relaxant from the health food store. I took one and went off to choir. I passed out on the stage while singing, on that one natural pill. So, you can see how sensitive I am to any drug. Sedating my pain was not going to be my answer.

After a couple of days of my son consoling me and trying to convince me how wrong Marcus was for me anyway, I began to feel better. Chris was making a lot of sense. I greatly appreciated his caring for me. I was able to find comfort in the prospect of spending more time with Chris, as well as burying myself in my Mary Kay business. However, I knew deep inside I needed to change something.

Back to the Drawing Board for Real Help

Everything I had ever tried in relationships failed. I was now ready to listen intently to God. I was broken. I had been humbled and knew change was what I needed: to repent—turn around and begin walking in the opposite direction in the area of my love life. Now I really knew that I needed to go back to the drawing board. I really needed God to be my concrete foundation. I had come to the end of myself and it cost me yet another broken heart. I needed to seek truth wherever that would take me.

All my ideas that ultimately came from Satan gave me a broken heart; they came to the dead end of emptiness and of my facing God alone for judgment. I faced the reality that pain always came when I chose to follow my own way. Somehow, I had been convinced that my way was a third choice over God's way or Satan's way.

It was finally sinking in that my ways were Satan's way, because it was not God who desired pain or evil for me. Satan was the one who tempted me and desired evil for me. I had been lured over and over again, yet somehow I still just believed I was a good person. So many ask why bad things happen to good people. I was now seeing more clearly that it just might be our own choices: rejecting God's wisdom in His Word and choosing the bad for ourselves.

I did not have the answers. I knew that if I didn't sincerely start seeking God for answers, I would only self-destruct. I'd fall into the abyss of depression, self-pity, and resentment. I could clearly see what resentment had done to Chris's father and even my mother, who just continued medicating herself to mask the problems she faced. Both went into a downward spiral, exactly where Satan wants us all. This is a victim mentality of our own choosing. I sure didn't want that kind of life.

The way I saw it was: I had failed at my own route so I had no place else to look but up to God and seek His route. I was now ready to commit whole-heartedly to God's way, wherever that would take me—even if it were not popular with my family, friends, and acquaintances. I freely decided to choose to commit to God's way.

The first thing I did was to go back to the wonderful Spirit-filled nondenominational church 45 minutes away. Every time I was in church there, I would just break down, crying profusely during almost every message. I felt each message was speaking to me. As healing came over me, I eventually got back to singing on the praise team. There was always a joy and peace that I felt when I sang.

A woman at my church was just beginning to lead a class on *Boundaries* by Townsend and Cloud. She realized that my situation showed I needed to learn better boundaries, so she invited me to join her class. I did and was shocked at what I learned. This class, along with the book, really helped me to learn how to say "no" and mean it, as well as how to be much more discretionary with "yes," especially when it concerned men.

Looking back, I believe that understanding and implementing healthy boundaries can really help a lot of people. Sadly, many people grow up in dysfunctional homes and their parents have great difficulty with establishing boundaries in their own lives. My parents demonstrated that for their children. Therefore, we generationally inherited bad boundaries. God, however, created us to have healthy boundaries.

Through studying this Biblically based book on boundaries, I realized that I never really understood where I ended and another person began. I did not know what boundaries I needed to put up so I could recognize the difference between what is right and what is wrong in God's eyes. I did not understand the natural consequences I would suffer when crossing certain boundaries that God never intended for me to cross.

For instance, if I had been taught early on that sex should never be approached outside of marriage, I might have understood that any enticement by a man in that area clearly meant that man was not the one God had for me. Satan cleverly uses men to lead women away from the perfect plan God has for us, just as I had experienced.

Throughout my life, I felt that in the eyes of my parents and family I had no value unless I was married or with a man. Parents with bad boundaries usually produce children with bad boundaries. Unless the church body intervenes and teaches good boundaries, how can children know? Clear Bible teaching is vital. This is a crucial part of discipleship, as the Bible teaches us to "go and make disciples." It is vital to learn about God-given boundaries through the body of Christ and studying God's Word.

Divorce Care

God directed me to *Divorce Care* at another nondenominational church near my home. On my first night there, I became rebellious against God. When I saw that the leaders of the group were a happily married older Christian couple that had known each other since age 14, I argued with God, "What do these people know about divorce? They have been married all their lives." I thought they could never understand the pain I felt and the betrayal I had been through.

That week however, God rebuked me and clearly directed me to go back, as all other roads were a dead end. He was not going to allow me to rationalize my way out of this one. I felt guilt and realized how the opportunity came to me just as I had asked. So, I went back and it became very clear that God was putting this happy Christian couple in front of me as another precious example of the kind of marriage God exhorted, so that I could see what a healthy marriage from God looked like.

This thought came to me as I felt the warmth of their love. They had such a heart for divorcees - hence so much love for us. They invited us to their home for several socials. We all sang and ate and praised the Lord together, just like a big family. There was so much peace and love there that none of us wanted to leave! We would keep them up late talking with us. About twelve of us gathered and shared our life stories. It was obvious they were passionate in their calling from God to do this.

An unsettling situation occurred at one such gathering. A fierce man, one of the participants in our group, started ranting and raving about how his separation was justified. He wanted his wife to submit to his authority and move to Florida, because that is where he wanted to pursue his work. He felt that she was obligated, as his wife, to do what he demanded no matter what.

Before meeting the couple leading *Divorce Care*, I really believed it was normal for men to be dominating and controlling over women, even though I didn't like it. But finally, when this man was ranting and raving about his wife, I now understand he was wrong. In my past, something inside of me seemed to switch on when I had "enough" and I would run. I would have flashbacks of my father abusing my mother. When I was a child, although I never jumped in front of my mother to protect her from my father's abuse, I sure cried out to God for His help. I was always too scared to do anything else. Today, I have learned healthy boundaries and realized God answered my cries with the freedom I live in Christ.

I recently read *The Imam's Daughter*, by Hannah Shah, which I highly recommend, especially for those who want to learn more about the oppression of women in Islam.[1] In this book, the three-year-old daughter jumped in front of her mother to protect her from her fa-

---

[1] http://hannahshah.com/who-is-hannah-shah/

ther's abuse. She then became the victim instead, only worse than her mother experienced by far! You must read it to see how far this male-dominating abuse goes in Islam. What shocks me most is how Satan uses such extreme abuse. Man has the audacity to call it religion.

I know there are many women out there who believe the lie that abuse by their husband or boyfriend is normal, especially after generations have just kept quiet about it here in America to present a "good face" to the public. This is actually hypocrisy and God frowns upon it. Our covenant with God and in marriage calls for complete transparency.

Abuse is a huge issue that is hurting the church in America. It is so sad that even people leading the church often don't have access to adequate counseling to address abuse, because of their reputation in the church. I am saddened by the number of Christian women who contact me these days that marry Muslims after being abused by their Christian husbands. Unfortunately, they go from the frying pan to the fire because now they will face worse abuse in their marriage to the Muslim. Remember I mentioned that over five hundred thousand American women have married Muslim men and it is mostly Christians that are in the statistic.

This man at Divorce Care reminded me of the dysfunctional men with whom I had been involved; he made me very uneasy. The male leader was aware and asked him to stay afterwards for a talk. This seemed to calm him down, as he was quieter after that until he eventually left the group. This reassured me that the authoritative controlling type of attitude for a husband is wrong. The relationship of the couple leading the divorce care group gave me a clearer picture of a healthy and peaceful Christian marriage, and gave us all hope. The *Divorce Care* curriculum made a huge impact on me in learning how to forgive.

I now had a broken and willing spirit, and was determined to learn why I had gotten myself in and out of three marriages and divorces and so many other relationships over the past 25 years. In my brokenness, I finally completely surrendered my entire life, including my love life, to God. By recommitting my life and trusting Jesus as my Lord and Savior, I have received the power of the Holy Spirit living in me to give me spiritual discernment and a clearer understanding of Scripture.

As a growing Christian, I have realized the importance of accountability and discipleship. I realized I couldn't walk this Christian life by myself. Much to my surprise, there is clear Scripture that teaches God's children to not forsake the fellowship with other believers (Hebrews 10:25). That's so Satan can't isolate us to deceive us.

God's Word is so powerful; like a two-edged sword, rightfully dividing the Truth, exposing the lies of this world. It promises to never return void. Now, through studying the Word and applying it to my life, I was beginning to learn about the Lordship of Jesus Christ over my whole life. I understood exactly what I was saved from. My overwhelming gratitude to Jesus drove me to want to please God with my life. I didn't allow the devil to convince me of excuses not to go to the meetings. Rather, I made attending them a priority. After going through *Divorce Care* twice, I began teaching it to women at my church. I could see how God used me in the lives of several of these women. Seeing the positive change in their lives felt so wonderful. Serving God has immense value. God was using me to "set the captives free" as I began to teach others what I had learned. God was beginning to turn what Satan meant for evil around to be used for His glory in the lives of other women, through the word of my own testimony. (Romans 8:28)

My life began to feel more joyous and my Mary Kay business also began to feel more like a ministry as I shared Christ with those I met who were struggling in different areas of life, especially with relationships. When you learn something, it is best to immediately teach someone else the same thing. This is a great way to know if you have really learned it and to make sure it becomes part of your heart beliefs, not just head knowledge.

At this point, I really felt that this was the calling God had placed on my heart for using my broken past: to help other women. They opened up to me, recognizing that I had been where they were, so I truly knew what they felt. Through the words of my testimony, I shared how God remedied the problems I also had faced.

Forgiveness and Other Important Lessons Learned

The biggest lesson I learned in *Divorce Care* was that if I don't forgive others, my Heavenly Father would not forgive me (Matthew 6:14-15). This will hinder my prayers to God. This was a very serious issue for me, since I prayed constantly. I knew I needed Him to listen and answer me. So, I learned to forgive. I realized that what God means by forgiveness differs vastly from our own inclinations. Jesus told us how many times to forgive in Matthew 18:21-22 …seven times seventy….

How the world sees forgiveness (just say you're sorry and then avoid the person so you don't have to deal with them or your deep feelings) is completely different from how God sees forgiveness. The world thinks that if we pretend to forgive, the whole situation will just go away. I guarantee you, it won't. It will come back to bite you over and over, until you truly repent by turning around and going in the opposite direction, doing things God's way.

I was finally truly learning to trust and obey God. Understanding His great love motivated me. My biggest sins that kept me from His blessings were my own disbelief and my fears. Satan was using them to keep me in bondage so I could not truly be free. Satan was using the same temptation he used with Eve in the garden: the lie that I knew more than God and could find my own spouse, my own true love. That is a lie from the pit of hell.

Satan is still up to the same old tricks. There is truly nothing new under the sun, as the Word says (Ecclesiastes 1:9). I still see all these same traits in my Mom today, so I can see how this has been a generational curse. I needed to stop it with me. I could only do this through Jesus Christ.

I feel it is important for everyone in this world to understand that we all have only two choices. Daily and minute-by-minute, we can choose God's ways or Satan's ways. There is no third way to choose, like we might believe. Our own way is selfish and selfishness comes from Satan. If we believe our own way is good and therefore must come from God, then we will find this good way in the Bible, since all good and perfect things come from God. The Bible shows us God's way.

I realized God had given me grace. He had forgiven me for much more than I deserved. Concerning divorce, His Word states that when a non-believer departs, to let him go (I Corinthians 7:15). So I did. My third husband walked away, so I forgave him and let him go.

Why did my marriages fail, including this third marriage? I believe they failed because they looked too much like the world. Deep inside I was searching for truth and the man I was with was not. I saw this scenario played out in a movie called *God's Not Dead* by the professor's girlfriend. I saw myself in her role.

I was seeking the right path in life to discover truth wherever that might lead. As the professor in the movie made a mockery of his "Christian" girlfriend in front of others for her beliefs, I always felt that same kind of condemnation by male relationships also. 2 Corinthians 6:14 says to not be unequally yoked. Our loving God wants to protect our hearts from being broken by the ungodly. This was one of the many great lessons taught in that movie.

Time and again, I had disobeyed God and given in to premarital sex, even in engagement before marriage. God cannot bless disobedience because He is just and loving. His rules are for our protection and wellbeing. The Bible says do not defile the marriage bed (Hebrews 13:4). I had freely chosen to give in to Satan's taunting rather than pray and listen to the Holy Spirit's voice leading me to all truth. I gave in to my feelings to want to be loved rather than seek out truth in God's Word that would teach me Jesus needed to be my first love.

Satan uses our fleshly desires to overpower our spiritual souls that know right from wrong. Our carnal wants are the tools Satan uses to tempt us. He wants to keep us separated from God, our Creator and our perfect loving Father. Satan deceives us with many lies, including the following:

- "If it feels good, do it."
- "We are engaged, so sex is fine."
- "What is the big deal in getting involved sexually?"
- "As long as you're happy, it's all fine."

Our minds create all sorts of justifications and excuses to keep us from reading God's truth in the Bible and obediently applying it to our daily lives. The Bible is our standard of right and wrong, truth and lies that God has given us so that we know how to live.

The Bible is clear about sexual immorality being any sex outside of marriage. In Ephesians 5:3 it says, *"But among you there must not be even a hint of sexual immorality, or of any kind of impurity, or of greed, because these are improper for God's holy people."*

When I called myself a "Christian" yet became intimate sexually before getting married, I was committing sin against God. I was making a mockery out of Christianity, since others saw me as an example of Christianity by the use of my words to describe myself. Jesus said to his disciples that whoever wants to be my follower must turn from selfish ways, denying their selves, and take up their cross and follow Him. (Matthew 16:24; Luke 9:23)

I was "causing my brother to stumble" by leading others into an ungodly way of life and claiming it to be Christian. The Bible warns us of these things. Sexual temptation is very strong, but God gives us warnings to avoid taking that route. Song of Solomon tells women three times, "Do not awaken love" before its time (Song of Solomon 2:7; 3:5; 8:4). This thrice repeated warning is very important to heed. In addition, God's word teaches us:

"Flee from sexual immorality. All other sins a person commits are outside the body, but whoever sins sexually, sins against their own body. Do you not know that your bodies are temples of the Holy Spirit, who is in you, whom you have received from God? You are not your own; you were bought at a price. Therefore honor God with your bodies." (I Corinthians 6:18-20)

I also carried around a lot of fear, unbelief, and anger while I was claiming to be a Christian yet living in disobedience to God's Word. I know that I might have acted righteous in some ways, because of the head knowledge I had gained about being a Christian and about the Bible, but I don't believe that people could always see "Jesus in me." I was not humble.

The humble/meek will inherit the earth (Psalm 37:11), not the proud. Jesus confirms that the humble will inherit the earth, recounted in Matthew 5:5. Pride does come before the fall, as Proverbs 16:18 says. It does not attract anyone and never looks like love, nor feels like love.

I believe that, just possibly, if Jesus were to have returned during the almost 30 years I wandered in the wilderness, messing up my life, my son's life and affecting others' lives wrongly, I may not have made it into Heaven at all. Or, I would have just "squeaked by" with a lot of "*esplainin'* to do, Lucy."

I would have been in big trouble from the just side of God, with plenty of reason to feel guilt and shame. Some may think that I would be innocent of not knowing the Word because I didn't read or study it. But consider what Jesus says:

> "*If you try to hang on to your life, you will lose it. But if you give up your life for my sake, you will save it. And what do you benefit if you gain the whole world but lose your own soul? Is anything worth more than your soul?*" (Matthew 16:25-26 NLT)

I know for a fact that nothing is worth losing my soul to hell for eternity. I am assured today that my soul will go to eternity with God, my Creator. How about you? God has given the Bible to us so that we can know the answers that will bless us. We don't have to like God's answers, just like we never had to like Brussels sprouts or spinach as children. A loving parent loves their children enough to feed them healthy food to help them grow, even though junk food often tastes better and is more appealing. If you, as a parent, love your child enough to feed them healthy food even if that is not what your child wants, how much more will your loving God who created you want what is best for you, because that is His character.

Satan is crafty and deceitful; he has made sin pleasurable, fun, and addictive in order to feed the lusts of our flesh. Just as candy tastes good and Brussels sprouts don't, what feels good oftentimes is truly bad for our wellbeing. That is why sex outside of marriage, getting revenge, stealing what one wants, and getting addicted to drugs and alcohol can give a temporary "feel good high" while they poison our body and souls. However, sex within God's plan, letting God be the avenger, and obeying God's commands are blessings that bring nourishment to our souls instead of damaging them.

God's promises are true. It is our free choice to obey His Word. His unconditional love leads us to the one true love that He especially designed for us here on earth. It is our unbelief, our fears, and our disobedience that gets in our way. I know this because I have again and again experienced the consequences of my own selfish choices. Though we are free in Christ, we should never use that freedom to indulge in fleshly desires. In Galatians 5:13 it says, "*For you, brethren, have been called to liberty; only do not use liberty as an opportunity for the flesh, but through love serve one another."*

For the doubters, Satan does truly exist. He wants the worst for you because that is his character. He cannot hurt God, but he can hurt the creation that God made and loves. Satan is a liar, a deceiver, and a manipulator. He surely isn't going to be up front and tell you the truth about himself. Satan prowls around looking to destroy every person and every relationship.

In America today I see clearly Satan's attack on the family, the body of Christ, and Christians' personal relationship with God more than ever. He is on his way to hell and he wants you to go there with him. He knows his time is short. Lies come from Satan only. The Truth comes from God only. The Truth will set you free from the lies of the Devil. Satan wants bad things for us; God wants not just good but the best for us.

We all have the freedom to choose to do what Satan wants us to do or what God wants us to do. We will all one day be accountable for our choices in life to our Righteous and Holy Father, our Creator God. It is appointed once for man to die, and afterwards comes the judgment (Hebrews 9:27).

Before we die or the world ends, we have the opportunity to learn from our life choices. We have the free will not to continue to make the same mistakes, but to make better choices and grow in living for God. Or, we can choose to become bitter and blame God and/or everyone else for our circumstances. We can always find friends who will join us there. All that will do, however, is eat us up inside, causing us to die in our sins, and those friends will go to hell with us. Remember, His way is the best because He loves us so much and desires to reward us with Heaven.

Today, I am truly grateful that God gave me grace in allowing Marcus to walk away from our marriage. It was a clear turning point in my life to seek complete truth, not just partial truth. It did strengthen my character and led me to persevere closer to my Father God. It taught me that God was looking out for my best interest, although I could not see it at the time of the break up. I praise God, that He used it to teach Marcus the importance of his relationship with his children also. I praise God that He taught me that just because someone calls himself or herself a Christian doesn't mean they are, any more than a man in a garage makes him a car. We must see their fruit. What fruit is their life producing for God's glory? Is the way they live making a difference in other people's lives?

Abba Father does know best and continues to prepare me, His daughter, for her Bridegroom. He was strengthening me so I could help other women to recognize the truth from the lies, to recognize the difference between what Satan sends to tempt and get us off track and what God sends us to bless us and make us stronger for His glory.

God taught me to stay with my covenant commitments under God and wait upon Him alone. God orchestrated this break up and showed me His grace in His Word. I Corinthians 7:15 says, "*But if the unbeliever departs, let him depart; a brother or a sister is not under bondage in such cases. But God has called us to peace.*" I learned so much from this one incident, which God clearly turned around to be used for His glory, as you will soon see (Romans 8:28).

Everyone's lessons will vary slightly since God created us all uniquely different. But all these trials were part of God's preparation to purify my life for my soon coming Bridegroom, Jesus, as well as for God's choice for my earthly husband so to glorify Him.

Prayer for God's Way

If you would like to choose God's way now, I will lead you in a prayer below. First please consider the following thoughts:

- If you do not know for sure that you are walking with God, but you want to believe the truth and pray to the one true God, then join me and pray.

- If you are tired of the brokenness (in other words, "sick and tired of being sick and tired") and truly want to find God's peace, pray this prayer with me now.

- If you sincerely want to be guaranteed in the here and now that you will for sure go to be with God in Paradise (Heaven) when you depart this earth, then pray this prayer.

- If you want to know your wonderful Heavenly Father and walk with Him every day, talk with Him about everything, and clearly see Him working in your life, then pray this prayer.

- If you thought Christianity was only a religion and not a personal one-on-one relationship with the living God who created you and the entire universe, yet now you want to truly experience Him and have an amazing relationship with your most awesome Heavenly Father, then pray this prayer:

Dear Heavenly Father – the one TRUE God,

I am broken and lost. I have been selfish and have followed my own ways in life. I confess that I am a sinner. I am tired of all the ways of the world. They have never satisfied the depths of my soul. My soul is parched, dried up, and desperately needs its thirst to be quenched by Your living water! Please fill me with your HOLY SPIRIT that Jesus promises.

I repent of all my own ways. I want to live YOUR WAY now, oh God! I want all You have for me, for I know that what You want for me is the very best for me. Just like the struggle of the butterfly to break through its cocoon to freedom in order to be the beautiful butterfly YOU intended and created it to be, I know I will have struggles in becoming all that You want me to be. However, I am WILLING to do whatever it takes for I KNOW with all my heart, soul, and mind that You keep Your promises, as our Covenant God!

You have promised in Your Word that You are with me and will never forsake me. I know Your Word says that with Christ, all things are possible! I surrender completely to You, Oh God, as a "living sacrifice" to You. Thank You for sending Your only Son, Jesus, as the pure sacrifice to pay the price for all my sins. I am so sorry for (insert your sin confessions). My sin is all my rebellion against You and Your ways. Please forgive me!

Please free me from all of Satan's bondages upon my life so that I can be free indeed, as Your Word promises when I turn everything over to You! Please heal me Lord from my fleshly addictions that are unrighteous in Your eyes. Thank You in advance for Your healing, Your forgiveness, Your protection from the evil one and from all generational sins. Thank You that the Truth sets me free to be all You have created me to be!

I look forward to communicating with You daily and learning who You are and who I am as Your child. Help me study the Bible, Your unchanging Word: the Truth. Help me learn what my gifts are that You have given me. Help me to use them only to glorify You and not myself. Help me to be selfless and not selfish! For it's all about You, Lord! Help me to help others by sharing the Truth in Love also.

Third Marriage

I gratefully receive Your forgiveness and the free gift of eternal life with You now and forever! Thank You God for loving me so much that You sacrificed Your only begotten Son for me. Thank You that You see me as Your precious child, Oh Father God, because of Jesus' blood that covers my sins. With Your help, I will never take it for granted but rather will cherish You. I pray in the Precious name of Jesus Christ, my Savior! Amen.

[Author unknown]

9

Healing

Empty Nester

After dropping my son off at college, one month after 9/11 in 2001, I spent about five months, including Thanksgiving and Christmas, with some dear friends from church, Terry and Al, learning the value of a healthy, loving marriage by watching them. It really gave me a sense of security, love and Christian family life like I had never personally experienced in my own family. We had a lot of deep conversations about life and problems without arguing or yelling. I never felt devalued or dismissed or cast out in their home. I always felt heard. Castles of space were available in their hearts for me. Healing flowed over me like a warm shower of water. I never felt so loved. So many of you out there need to be heard and valued for who God made you. Only God's love can bring that love to you.

Alcohol was never involved. I began to learn more about dealing with conflict when two people disagree without losing the relationship. Conflict resolution, a crucial part of love and peace, can actually strengthen a relationship when done God's way. I believe it's crucial for the body of Christ to be taught peaceful conflict resolution while maintaining a loving relationship between brothers and sisters in Christ. This is what God means by loving our neighbors as our self and laying our lives down for one another, just as Terry and Al did for me. Being a peacemaker (Matthew 5:9), not a peacekeeper, would be the result as Jesus demonstrated for us. In other words, we seek to understand each other so that all feel valued and respected but never compromise the truth and learn how to still love those who disagree with us.

Terry had compassion for me, a single parent again, due to my recent divorce. She had spent enough time with Marcus to know what I went through and how he tried to pull me away from God rather than closer to Him. I felt God's Spirit leading me to put my house up for sale in order to lighten my responsibilities and she supported me in that. It sold the first week, without a realtor, to a Christian couple who moved in by Christmas.

Terry graciously offered for me to move in with them for a while, to seek God's direction in my life. They had a big 10-15 room Victorian house. So often I regretted the fact that I was not born during the Victorian Era. Living in it was like living out a dream I had of being a southern belle like I saw in the movie *Gone with the Wind*.

I began spending almost all of my time with Terry and Al as part of their family: in church, studying the Word, and listening to Christian radio and TV. My Christian life grew by leaps and bounds. Terry and I became even closer friends. My other friends would come over and Terry would engage them. Many of my friends became her friends, too, and they began learning about Christ. Terry and Al understood and accepted me. They welcomed me into their family, inviting me to spend family gatherings and holidays with them.

I loved helping Terry cook for and host family and church gatherings. I learned more about eating healthy as she had learned in the healing of her cancer. Terry and I were nuts for dressing in Victorian hats and dresses and going to Cape May, enjoying antique shopping together. Like I had felt the mercy and shelter of a bosom friend, Susan Johnson, in high school, I experienced this same mercy and shelter of a bosom friend in Terry as a Christian.

In addition to studying Scripture together and listening to radio teachers and Evangelists, we also went to Bible Study Fellowship-International (BSF). This is a nondenominational organization that studies Scripture verse by verse.

As I grew in Christ, I repented of my sin of premarital sex at the altar of the church we attended. I really felt total conviction that this was where I had been disobedient to God and certainly experienced the consequences for it. This is why my love life was still not honoring God, so I needed to learn that lesson. I realized from assessing my life that if I did not begin to be obedient to God's Word,[1] than I would continue to fall flat on my face again and again in my love life.

My deep need for love needed to be submitted to God, in order to learn to love Him first. God's love through Jesus is the only perfect, safe love. His unconditional love nurtures our souls. He has commands for our good, not our harm. The Lord says, "If you love me, keep my commandments" (John 14:15).

I realized that my flesh was weak, so I put up boundaries based on God's commands for purity. I decided to no longer watch secular love stories, which always made me yearn for lustful romance. I gave up listening to secular music, especially love songs, so not to trigger past memories. I didn't allow myself to be alone with a guy, so my weak flesh could not tempt me.

By spending time with these loving friends, my new family in Christ, I received the attention and love I needed and others could not so easily exploit me. This loving, Christian family was essential for me to begin to trust the love of God's people. Agape love among Christians is one of the greatest needs of the church today: the only way many people are able to grow and trust God and His people again.

I grew in living the love of Jesus. It was much later that I learned about my particular temperament that God created for His purpose, which had a stronger need for affection than most people can give.

eHarmony

In about January of 2002, I heard an advertisement on Christian radio for eHarmony, an online site originally designed to help Christian singles meet. The founder convinced me he had a heart to help Christian singles find the love of their lives. At this time I didn't realize the founder had also written that book I had read before meeting Marcus. I heard that the site would allow singles to choose whether to put their picture up for public viewing or not.

---

[1] http://www.openbible.info/topics/obedience_to_god lists several verses that apply to obedience

The screening process, before a potential couple could even talk to each other, included a lot of questions. These questions could be asked in the first stages online—with no phone numbers or even personal information to be shared—until you got past that stage of the decision process.

The idea seemed brilliant to me, especially since I had finally learned the hard lesson that I needed to put up boundaries. I thought these questions would also help me scrutinize better before jumping headlong into a new relationship. It sounded pretty safe. After all, this was supposed to be a Christian website, advertised on Christian radio.

My greatest boundary, I found, was not even to put my picture on the site. I deliberately did this so that men could get to know my heart and what I believed in first. Maybe someone would actually like me for who I am on the inside and what I believe before seeing my outward appearance. This would help me to know who was really from God.

Years of bad experiences convinced me that my God-given beauty was a curse in regard to getting to know men. They seemed drawn to me because of my looks. As I learned later, God made men "visual" and women "emotional." This is why God's perfect design is for all men to be focused on loving God through Jesus first. Then, with the Holy Spirit directing him, he would know who his wife is. God doesn't lie, tempt, or lure anyone.

On the site, I decided to simply ask this question of every suitor: "Do you believe in premarital sex?" If they said anything else but a clear "No" I would just delete them. So, that question was very important for me to determine which men were not looking for a Godly relationship. They had little faith in trusting God and were not truly interested in following Biblical principles for meeting one's mate.

The deleting option enabled me to select only the men who were compatible with my ideals. I deleted the majority of those who matched my profile, including many just because they were annoyed that they did not get to see my picture. Some suitors would answer my primary question with a "No" but then further into the dialogue questions their beliefs were revealed by perverted language. I ended up talking to only a few men out of the hundreds that were matched with my profile. At this stage of my growth in Christ, "deleting" felt like power.

I believe God's Spirit was leading me. His drawing me unto Himself through revelation after revelation, as I was going through my sanctification process, was what repelled undesirable men from me and me from them. Out of the mouth, the heart speaks. Just like a former smoker or drinker would be the most critical of people who smoke or drink, so I was now. Formerly being immoral in my relationships with men, I was hard on everyone who still believed in premarital sex.

The book written by eHarmony's founder, *How To Find the Love of Your Life*, was not a successful tool for me. Eventually, eHarmony began advertising on public TV for all people. I believe this Christian got "money hungry." Non-Christians increased his business; this compelled him to expand into non-Christian arenas to promote it. Sadly, most of these people were actually exploiting innocent Christians by lying.

I experienced this myself and eventually discontinued this matchmaking service. What concerns me is how non-Christian men use the site. A friend's son bragged to me once about finding Christian women on this site. His theory, he explained to me, was that they were more honest. He didn't feel he would have to be concerned about his being taken advantage of, but would have more control himself. At least, a Christian woman believed in submitting to her husband. He was not a Christian. In other words, he was actually just looking for a woman he could control - exactly what I escaped from. This is a man led by Satan to lure Christian women away from God's perfect plan for them.

As for me, I only talked with four men from eHarmony on the phone. Out of these four, I met three in public. Out of these three, I liked two. Out of these two, only one, Ross, showed interest in me also. He was respectable, very kind, humble, and never even tried to kiss me. We became Christian friends online and on the phone.

Eventually, for my birthday, Ross invited me to Florida, where he lived. He offered to pay for it all, including two separate rooms at a hotel. I felt he had proven himself to be honest so far, so I went. We had a blast at Sea World, like two kids! Since he did not pursue me physically, I appreciated that and just learned how to be friends with him.

Later, I decided to go on vacation and use my timeshare to spend a week alone in Florida on the beach, to seek God's direction. I loved the sun and the beach. If I could get to know Ross better while I was there, that would be fine, but I didn't want that to be my priority. I did enjoy the time hanging out, walking, singing Christian songs while he played the guitar, and going out to dinner. While I was there, we visited Calvary Chapel in Ft. Lauderdale. He knew about it because they had a late service when he wanted to sleep in and miss his own church.

Growing at Calvary Chapel in Fort Lauderdale, Florida

At Calvary Chapel Pastor Bob was straightforward with his messages while he wrapped truth in humor. He taught verse by verse from the Bible. At that service, I just felt like I was home. I never wanted to leave there! I had never before experienced a huge church—about 17,000 people at that time. I decided to stay for another week and went to that church a few more times, even midweek. I just couldn't get enough.

I felt the Lord was drawing me there. I never had so much fun listening to the Word of God. Pastor Bob kept me laughing at myself and scrutinizing myself for any sin in my life. I felt God was speaking to me through him. I found I was so thirsty, I became like a sponge. My hunger and thirst for righteousness was ravenous. I really felt that God was drawing me to Florida and to this church in order for me to grow.

I called my son and asked him how he felt about my moving to Florida. He said it didn't really matter to him. I decided to put out a fleece (Judges 6:36-40) to the Lord, in order to make sure it was not my flesh talking and that I was not thinking of moving to Florida just because of Ross or because I loved the beach.

I put out this fleece: I prayed to the Lord saying, "God, if this is my flesh and not You, please make it clear to me and close the door. If it is You, let me go into a real estate office and find an apartment on the beach that will take me and my dog and that will not cost me any more than the monthly mortgage I was paying in New Jersey."

Sure enough, the second place I saw was perfect and I had complete peace about it. It was furnished and completely fit the criteria and cost even less. I was thrilled! Ever since I started seeking God's direction and listening to His voice, He directed my path. He moved me to Florida and I was finally going to realize my life-long dream of living on the beach and more than I ever could have imagined. I signed a year contract to rent the place and see what God had in store for me.

I went back home to New Jersey and told my friends I would be moving. They thought I was crazy! Terry said I needed to just rest for a while longer and stay there in New Jersey with them so they could nurture me a while longer. While I really appreciated her kind offer, I knew God had called me to move to Florida. I had perfect peace about it and smiled as I said, "Thank you for your kindness, but I feel God drawing me there." I really appreciated her sweet friendship and all she and Al had done for me, but I felt God's Holy Spirit leading me. After all, I knew we would always be friends, with or without distance between us, and we still are.

I moved on July 1, 2002 to South Florida. God had given me perfect peace in that church He led me to in order to continue my journey with Him. Now I needed to follow through and attend this church regularly to see what God was up to in my life. Once I started doing this, I found I was hungry for more of the Word and never seemed to get enough. I was learning the Word like never before. I bought the CD recordings of the sermons so I could listen again and again. The huge numbers of people attending did not intimidate me, because I thrive on interacting with people. At least now, I could find lots of Christian girlfriends to hang out with!

I did go to hang out with Ross once in a while, but I could see he was starting to get more distant now that I had moved there. One day at lunch, I simply asked him what he thought about our friendship and did he think it might grow into a potential marriage relationship. He frankly said that it was just a friendship; he didn't see it going any further than that. I was so thankful that I had never crossed my boundary of morality with him. It was so much less painful than any other breakup. Thank You God for Your wisdom.

Ross had introduced me to Sarah, a Mary Kay Rep, and we had become friends. Interestingly, she mentioned that he seemed to hang out with girls but had never made any commitments as long as she had known him. One lesson I had already learned in New Jersey: friends of the opposite sex were dangerous because someone could get hurt and that just might be me, so I decided not to hang out with him any longer. I can't say I didn't feel a sort of rejection, because I did, but my daily growth in my relationship with Jesus soon freed me from that.

Being Discipled and Mentored at Calvary

I began meeting a lot of women friends in the different Bible studies I attended in order to receive more discipleship. Groups of ladies took the time to discuss what we were learning. I went to small groups at people's homes. Eventually, I even got involved in a home group of women who studied the Word through Kay Arthur's *Precepts* class.

My life was totally consumed with study after study. I found I had less and less interest in finding new customers and recruits in Mary Kay. Mostly, I just serviced my existing customers. My focus was now on learning more about our loving God with whom I was so intrigued.

Jesus became my passionate love, and I began to seek after Him every morning in my walks, watching the sun come up. Jesus became my husband. I sang to Him and talked to Him and read my Bible there on the beach where I lived. I never felt closer to God. I just wanted to please Him with my whole life. I was hearing the still small voice of my Lord more and more regularly.

Of course, this became a conflict, not only with my unsaved family, but also with my son. Sadly, I could see his college experience tugged him away from what he had believed as a child. My parents called me a "brainwashed Jesus freak" and began persecuting me, especially in their drunken state when I would visit them. They even got their friends, mostly Roman Catholic, in their retirement park to join in with them against my beliefs and me. Jesus tells us that a prophet is not accepted in one's own land (Luke 4:24) and that they hated him so they will hate us (John 15:18). Yes, I said Roman Catholic Church friends helped my parents persecute me. Our beliefs are distinctly different. Being born again, mine are based on learning the Bible and theirs on traditions and confessions to a Priest rather than God.

At Calvary Chapel God directed me to speak to one woman, Sharon O, in a church class to ask her if she knew how I could get discipled through the Bible. I wanted to understand more of how to handle life God's way. It was obviously God who was directing this, as she was delighted to do it with me. She began walking me through a discipleship program that the church offered, keeping me accountable to her on a weekly basis. She listened intently to me and even shared her own feelings that we had in common. Sharon was married, very personable, and talkative like me. I felt so comfortable asking her questions.

Discipleship is also called mentoring. The program at this church uses a blue book called *One on One Discipleship* that guides you through a thorough understanding of the Bible, who God is, and who you are in Christ. Since it is a one-on-one program, it can be very personal.

The mentor can clearly get to know you and how you think. She can help you distinguish between a Biblical worldview and a secular worldview, and direct you to what the Bible gives us for answers. Being discipled and memorizing Scripture to help me through difficult times greatly aided me in understanding God and myself better. Today, I do this mentoring with other women and highly recommend it as a start for discipling new Christ followers.

Anne Shirley

My friend Tammy introduced me to *Anne of Green Gables*. I found a friend in Anne Shirley, the star, and her melodramatic speeches, such as "I am well in body although considerably rumpled up in spirit, thank you ma'am." She gave voice to my pain. I so wished I had known her in my younger days.

Anne's deep sensitivity to rejection and insults reflected my own. She truly inspired my soul. I would think that since her character was so popular to others, so I myself could also be accepted. She gave me hope that my own deepest feelings expressed outwardly in expressive fire could also be an inspiration to others. Maybe I too could prevail one day.

I also found comfort in getting to know Anne Shirley through this movie series. I feel as if she is a kindred spirit with her dramatic speeches, flowery imagination, and heart noticeably worn on her sleeve. She seethed like an ocean with waves of joy and pain.

God eventually brought me two dear close kindred spirits in South Florida. One was Tracy and another was Kim. I could share my heart and deep thoughts without condemnation. I could express myself with all my fervor and flowery expression and be completely understood. What a precious gift is such a friend!

Avoiding Temptation

In New Jersey, before moving to Florida, I had gone dancing with a few girlfriends for the exercise and because I always loved dancing. We wanted to learn ballroom dancing, so we went to a place where we dance with professional dancers. We just tipped them at the end of the night. We liked it there because there was no commitment to any one guy. Now in Florida, before meeting the two kindred spirits I mentioned, I learned about a local dancing class being offered for Christians. I found the advertisement in a Christian newspaper I had picked up at church. I probably got too excited and really didn't take the time to ask God in prayer about it. The thought of dancing again and getting exercise, this time with Christians, compelled me to go.

"What harm could it do?" I thought. The teacher claimed to attend Calvary. As I began going, I found it to be great fun and exercise. I greatly enjoyed dancing with other Christians who also loved to dance. This teacher also offered private lessons. It wasn't long before I realized he was after more than my lesson money; he was after me, too.

I began sharing my concerns about his behavior with my accountability partner, Sharon. She was able to help me discern a bit of this guy's motives. Thank God, I was now comfortable opening up to her. I also decided to seek a Christian counselor, advertised in that same newspaper, to see what she had to say about my getting "sucked into" this situation.

Note to my beloved reader: I hope you are learning from my experience. Our battle is not with flesh and blood, but with principalities in the Heavenlies, a battle between Satan and God (Ephesians 6:12) for our eternal souls. Satan was using my flesh in my isolation and the idea of having fun dancing and getting some exercise to lure me into sexual temptation. The naïve question "What harm could it do?" and fleshly desires are Satan's deadly weapons that can cause a Christian to fall.

While I yearned for true love in my heart, as I was created to do, my fleshly addiction to sexual immorality had kept me in bondage for so long, like a drug. I rationalized my way into anything that attracted my flesh—it was the same old familiar generational curse. Remember that if you try to save your life, you will lose it, but if you lose your life for Christ's sake, you will save it (Luke 17:33).

The Christian counselor used Scripture and prayer in our sessions, and made it clear that this man's use of his dance classes was to attract women. He was a man with a serious problem, so I needed to flee temptation. Although he didn't give up easily and still looked for me at church, I found it easy to avoid him in such a big crowd.

God convicted me that I needed a stricter boundary, to not even touch a man in dance, for this may be causing a brother to stumble. I tried to convince God I could handle it, so I just avoided that guy at the dance studio. Then other guys would approach me and try to get closer to me. After two or three other attempts to avoid them, I realized it wasn't working. So I quit going to the dance place, as I felt God directing me. Being in the Word so much and having this accountability really helped me to not even get upset about the issue.

My first love, Jesus, consumed me. We can do all things through Christ who strengthens us! (Philippians 4:13) I was now truly denying my flesh. God lead me to this new friend, Tracy, at church about this time. She and I loved to play tennis and ride our bikes to the beach together! God also sent Kim to me and she would pray with me a lot. Both girlfriends were dear to me and helped me stay on track.

I had been reading the necessary books and taking the required classes that would equip me to serve in the church. At a certain level, I qualified to volunteer in the bookstore. This I enjoyed very much, since I loved meeting all the people. While volunteering also at the bookstore, I got close to one of the managers, Claudia. She had met her husband at church and I admired her relationship with him. We had such fun when stocking the shelves, talking about all the miracles God was doing in and around our lives.

Because I had served in New Jersey as a leader of *Divorce Care*, I felt that was really where God wanted me. So I continued to do the studies necessary to serve in *Divorce Care* at Calvary. Interestingly, when I got to that level and began serving, the devil was still trying to tempt me. I met a guy at a singles retreat who happened to be a leader in *Divorce Care*. He actually headed off some annoying phone calls from the "dancer" who was still pursuing me relentlessly. As I began innocent conversation about *Divorce Care*, it turned out that he pretty much pursued me during the entire retreat and even convinced me to ride home with him.

I figured, as a leader, he certainly would know better than to try anything. This is where I learned how strict my boundaries had to be, for he was very persuasive. He took me to his home, not mine, and got a little too close for my comfort. Although I did convince him to take me home, he continued his pursuit through emails and the phone to the point of my having to report him to a church pastor. This was when I learned to never be alone with a guy, even for a ride from a church event.

I was directed to serve in the women's ministry instead of anything co-ed. Pastor Bernard King showed me in Titus 2 where it talks about older women speaking into the lives of younger women. I got involved in women's Bible studies as a table leader.

When I think about the battles raging around women today, I know firsthand that nothing is new under the sun, as Satan is still up to the same old tricks to deceive women in their area of weakness—their emotions. "Band of Survivors" by Twila Paris, is an impressive song that addresses the spiritual battle and how we can survive it: through Jesus Christ.

Biblical Counseling Classes and Session

I believe God used these situations with men to lead me to a class called "Biblical Counseling." My lifetime struggles of trying to hold a healthy relationship together, combined with all the counseling I had been through over the years after my breakups, compelled me to serve God by serving other women in this ministry. I wondered what the

Bible had to say about counseling issues and how to help others through Biblical counseling.

Pastor John Chinelly was the teacher. He was a gentleman in his late 50s who had been a real estate agent. He humbly admitted his past alcohol addiction that had in part influenced him to commit adultery in his marriage. Yet, his wife was still with him; their love for each other had grown in spite of his failings. His past also included all kinds of troubles in handling life's responsibilities.

I could envision Pastor John as being a once arrogant alcoholic with controlling rage of his poor wife, much how I saw my father control my mother. Thank God, he admitted he was wrong in the way he treated his wife and how he handled family responsibilities. He transparently shared with the class how he first admitted he had committed these sins and then asked forgiveness from God, his wife, and his family. He turned himself around to walk in the opposite direction. God healed him and blessed his life abundantly for it.

The fact that a man like him was so humble and made himself so vulnerable by sharing his feelings with a whole room full of people absolutely flabbergasted me. I had heard women being this vulnerable before, but never a man. I really admire Pastor John, and I also greatly respect him for sharing his testimony so openly. I was hungry to learn everything I could from him so I could understand how to change my life that dramatically. I wanted to understand more about how God transformed an arrogant alcoholic man into a humble healed man.

It turns out, as God would have it, that Pastor John and his wife, Connie, are close personal friends of Sharon O, my mentor and her husband. God would bring both couples into the path of my future husband and me.

As I began to intensely study what the Bible taught about counseling, with all the Scripture to back it, I realized that there was a worldview that taught people to pay for "professional help" to get their life "fixed" after losing a relationship. They call these paid professionals: psychologists, psychoanalysts, therapists, psychotherapists, and even some Christian counselors. I had been to them all with very little true help.

Worldly professional doctors charge lots of money. Unfortunately, their testimony holds up in our courts as "professional opinions" and a growing ungodly court system respects their opinions over Christian teachings. People's very lives are at stake, based on them. I learned that if they aren't using the Bible as their standard, they couldn't bring healing to anyone, including themselves.

I had paid high prices for professional help, and even the Christian counselor I had, I did not pray or give Biblical direction. That counselor even told me that premarital sex was fine within the context of engagement. I don't know what Bible he was reading, but I've learned since that just because someone says he/she is a Christian does not mean that person truly follows Jesus Christ and all His ways.

In total opposition to that, this Biblical counseling course was teaching me that God's complete counsel is in the Word of God. The answer for every one of life's dilemmas can be found in the Bible. Pastor John pointed out that counseling is a ministry that every church should offer to its people free of charge, because of the need and because of the spiritual gifts God gives His children to help each other.

Looking back at all the professional help I paid for to try to "fix" me, I could see more and more how people had manipulated me and used me to earn money off my problems, and not just mine but the problems of millions of people in desperate need of help and healing. Worse yet, none of it would or could heal anyone. It hit me like a big newsflash, or better yet like a light bulb just turned on. I then realized that I had never been truly healed from any of my broken past.

Especially since I almost got suckered into temptation by that dance instructor, as well as the *Divorce Care* leader, I saw how I seriously needed Biblical counseling. I finished the entire Biblical Counseling course. I learned more than I could have ever imagined about how much God loves us and cares so deeply about us that He has given us the answers to life in His Word. The Word of God is actually our healing balm!

The next day, after my light bulb moment, I decided to go to a Biblical counselor. In the counselor's presence that day, God was very present. I poured out as much of my whole dramatic story as I could fit into an hour and answered a few of her questions for clarification. For the most part, I talked and she listened. She referred me to several scriptures in the Bible that she felt God was giving her for me. She encouraged me with the truth that God, my Perfect Heavenly Father, loves me more than anyone could ever love me. She reassured me of how special I am to God just as I am, the way He made me. She reassured me that God wants to use me for His glory. I truly felt I had value in God's eyes and He had a great plan for me.

The final and most important thing she did was to lead me in prayer. She asked God to direct her in what she needed to share with me, so to help me heal and experience the freedom in Christ that He promised me. I don't remember all the specifics of the prayer.

When we opened our eyes, she did not know why, but she felt God was telling her to give me a leaflet. As she pulled it out of her drawer and handed it to me, I looked at it. The title was "Walk for Life." It read something like: "Help save a baby with your donations to help prevent (some phenomenal number of) abortions."

Not Just One Abortion

The "Walk for Life" leaflet totally baffled and stunned me. I asked her, "God told you to give this to me?"

She said, "Yes."

A tear or two or three began to roll down my cheeks. "But I never told you anything about my abortions. How could you know?"

"God told me," she said. "God knows."

As Psalm 139: 7-8 comes to me now; where can I go from your Spirit Oh Lord? Where can I go from your presence? If I go up to the heavens you are there. If I make my bed in the depths you are there. Yes, I realized God must have known all about them, but no other person knew except the fathers of those babies, men whom I've never seen again in my life, as well as Chris' dad.

God sees and knows everything. He uses others to reveal the truth to us if we seek His help. There are no secrets with God. Jesus says, *"Seek and you will find, knock and the door will be opened to you"* (Matthew 7:7). This woman, my Biblical counselor, had only known me for one hour, yet God revealed to her the sins of my past since 1979. That is 23 years' worth of history. I knew without a doubt God was speaking through this woman, just as the woman at the well could hear God's voice to her through Jesus. She testified, *"I can see that you are a prophet"* when He revealed her entire history of five husbands to her (John 4:18-19), as well as the man with whom she currently had.

I said to myself that day in the counselor's office, "She must be a prophet. I hear God speaking loud and clear." My awe or fear of God kicked in and I said to her, "I will call there tomorrow. I know this is God speaking directly to me, and I know I can help any girl who thinks she needs to have an abortion understand that it is a lie from the devil. Every woman needs to know the truth about it."

A woman may think a baby will ruin her life, but the truth is that aborting that tiny little life will destroy the mother's life, too! That is two lives ruined, not just the one. It eventually haunts the men also but it takes a lot longer. It could take up to twenty years for them. I lived through this experience personally far too long. Abortion caused me so much anger toward men and the world around me that I couldn't keep any relationship together. I had also lost my relationship with God because of my sin and was controlled by Satan's deceptive games. I couldn't recognize the good from evil.

You see, while I told you about the first abortion earlier, I didn't tell you along the way who else, of those men I mentioned to you, forced me into aborting for the following reasons:

- "It's fairly early in the pregnancy, I know people who have just taken this morning after pill and it just flushes out in the toilet. Then 'poof!' It's fixed!"
- Another said, "I can't possibly allow my prestigious position to be jeopardized! This is just not in the cards for me. Here is the money. I don't want it to affect my own children's lives. Go get rid of it." When I said "No. I'm just going to have it, without your consent," I was tormented and then pushed abruptly to terminate the pregnancy early. The excuse was to do it while it was just "tissue" and didn't develop too much.
- Another excuse came hand in hand with "support": "I'll come with you and pay for it, but I just can't afford another child."
- Anthony, Chris's dad, said he could not afford another child because he said we couldn't even afford the one we had. He pushed it further, saying, "No way, I'm too old!"

The second baby with Chris' father was conceived very soon after Chris was born. The doctor said that is a time when one is the most fertile. Chris could have had a little brother or sister, but his father pushed me to abort again. This time I gave in to his pressure. I cried out to God for help but didn't wait for His answer. Human rationalization won over my weak love for God, and for this child forming in my womb.

Anthony had already lied so much to me. Knowing by this point that he was 15 years older than me, he smoked and drank, as well as argued all the time with me and tried to control me by intimidation, I realized I made a big mistake in marrying him. Because of his threats, I just couldn't even imagine how I was going to get out of this situation alive with one child. What would I do with two?

When I was married to Anthony, I never even had the guts to talk to my pastor's wife about this. I just felt so trapped and intimidated by him. Praise God, I have learned so much since then and know God loves and cares for all these children who were conceived in my body. I, their mother, never allowed them to grow, because of their fathers' pressure, except for Chris, the one for whom I took a firm stand to save and nurture. So you see, there was a much bigger secret sin I was harboring that affected my life in more ways than I could even understand at this time but God would soon reveal it to me. This secret sin was the thorn in my flesh that caused my life to be a living hell just as Satan planned. I will share more later about the literal thorn in my flesh God allowed to teach me a lesson.

Forgiven of All My Sins

As I write this, it is the first time I have thoroughly remembered all these terrible malicious memories again since my healing. I am doing so for your sake, to help my beloved readers. It is certainly not to gain any self-pity or to draw any attention to myself. This book is not about me but a testimony of my life to help you understand God and your own life so that you might choose rightly and be set free from the lies of Satan you have believed and feel God's incredible unconditional love for you. If you have had abortions, please know there is forgiveness and healing in Jesus Christ! Don't waste another day without it! There is hope!

If you have not had abortions, please do not do what I have done. I am so ashamed and embarrassed to even admit all this to you right now but I share it so to save some souls. My prayer, is that my public confession will help someone learn from my mistakes and understand clearly how the enemy, Satan, works to destroy and devour our lives. The Word also teaches us that others are saved by the blood of the Lamb and the word of our testimony.

It is so important to point out how merciful and full of grace God is. He forgave me, a person full of sin, who disobeyed His laws, many times including the Ten Commandments (paraphrased):

- Thou shalt have no other gods before me.
- Thou shalt not make for yourself an idol…
- Thou shalt not use the Lord's name in vain.
- Remember the Sabbath and keep it holy.
- Thou shall honor your parents.
- Thou shalt not murder.
- Thou shalt not commit adultery.
- Thou shalt not steal.
- Thou shalt not bear false witness.
- Thou shalt not covet your neighbors' spouse or anything.

I broke all Ten Commandments, yet God has redeemed me through the precious blood Jesus Christ shed once for all, and blesses me over and above my own human understanding. My past, as you can see, is quite messed up, yet God has thrown all my sins as far as the east is from the west and remembers them no more (Psalm 103:12). It is only man who wants to pick them back up to compare them with other people's sins.

We need to come just as we are to Him with our secret sins and let Him heal us. We can then be free to help others and to really love others just the way they are. Some of the feelings we harbor over abortion and other sins are grief, denial, anger, guilt, regret, feeling unworthy to be loved, and the desire to keep running from God. Some people believe God wants to spoil our fun. No! God wants to protect us from destruction.

We either stay so busy that we have no time to think about our issues and sins, or we go into deep depression and turn to drugs, alcohol, and/or suicide, making things so much worse. Christians need to humble themselves and seek God's face, pray, and repent so He can heal our hearts. It takes one healed soul at a time coming to His throne to eventually, together, become the united body of Christ Jesus prayed for. (John 17:23)

God loves us so much that He gave us in advance, years ago, His Word in human form, Jesus, and in literary form, the Bible, for us to read and heed. He also gave us His Spirit to be in us. The key is we must choose to read the Bible and abide by it in obedience. Jesus tells us, *"I am the vine and you are the branches, abide in Me and I will abide in you"* (John 15:5). Obedience proves we love Him. If we abide, the fruit in our lives will show it.

God gave His Word to us so we could get His whole counsel to apply to our lives here on this earth. I learned that because of God's love for us, He wants the very best for us. He has given to us all the answers to life so we can be led by Him, while He keeps us safe and heals us. He has called us to help others as we have been helped. His Golden Rule is to do unto others as you would have others do unto you (Luke 6:31). Jesus commands us to love each other (John 15:12) as He loves us. Our own healing and the Holy Spirit help us do that.

When two people love each other unconditionally, they communicate and listen to one another. Our interaction with God, our Creator, is relationship, not religion. The Bible and the Holy Spirit teaching us is God communicating with us. Prayer and living for Him according to the Word is our communication to Him.

The Pregnancy Center
I followed through with my word to help girls thinking about abortion and called the Hope Pregnancy Center the next day. Sharon S, the director, spoke with me. This is not the same Sharon who mentored me at Calvary. We became instant friends. She is still my dear, dear friend to this day.

Sharon S is a very good listener, which I really needed. I felt her compassion immediately. I told her that I want to help pregnant women make a better decision about carrying and having their babies, rather than aborting them. She believed I would be a great blessing. We talked for quite a while and she told me that I first had to attend the one-week training class before I would be able to counsel anyone. It just happened that this was Thursday; the classes started on Monday. God's timing was perfect.

I showed up on Monday. The classes were from 9 am to 4 pm for one week. By the time Wednesday came, a lady named Maria shared her own testimony about her abortion, right before lunchtime. She described the place where she was at the time of the tragedy: in the Florida Keys, where I had lived with my first husband.

She recounted the details of what her boyfriend had told her and how he had pressured her into having an abortion. When she described what the doctor had told her, especially about this just being a "quick procedure" and they would just be "removing tissue," I could feel myself getting choked up with painful tears.

She described her fears and the thoughts she had then, including so many other details that brought back my memories. It was as if she were describing my own experience and procedure. All of a sudden, I just began to break down crying right there in my chair where I sat in the front of the room. I couldn't stop crying through the rest of her whole story. When she finished, I just lost it completely. She immediately came to me and comforted me as the others went to lunch. She took me to a private room in the back and asked me to share with her my feelings.

She listened and then discussed with me how I was going to have to go to another class after this week, if I chose to finish this week out. It is called PACE (Post-Abortive Counseling Education). I would have to begin the healing process specific for women after abortion before I could ever counsel anyone. She explained how it is important for me to not lose it in the counseling room with others. I sure wanted to get that healing. She assured me of the benefits of going to this PACE class.

The healing process is always necessary after abortion, no matter how long or short of a time it has been. This process relieves her of anger, bitterness, unforgiveness and so many deep-rooted pains, including grieving over the loss of a child. Most women have no idea the long-term effects all this pain has on their character and their lives.

Again God's timing was right on the mark, because the class was beginning in a couple of weeks at my church. It would be behind closed doors. No one there would know who was in the class. Since I didn't know too many people, it was fine with me. I looked forward to being healed so I could truly be freed from this past bondage.

Abortion, Lust, and Love

I recently saw a new documentary put out called "Blood Money." It shows pure evidence of exactly how and why abortion began in this country. In the early 1900's, a woman by the name of Margaret Singer had ideas much like Hitler. She wanted to "purify" the human race and allow only the "elite" to live.

Margaret Singer focused on killing off the babies in the wombs of African-American women through the Planned Parenthood organization she started. Eyewitnesses testify on this film how the name of the organization was strategically given, so as to make people think that she had a "good" purpose: to help people to plan their families. It reminds me of the Scripture that says that Satan sometimes comes as an Angel of light to deceive people. Really, she wanted to greatly diminish the offspring of people she did not esteem.

Abortion is not about love and caring for family, but rather about control and selfishness, destroying the family. Abortion comes straight from Satan, as it is the spirit of death that he represents. God said, *"Be fruitful and multiply."* (Genesis 1:28) Satan in defiance and rebellion to that has given people the rationalization in their minds of why it's ok to kill that one like he is whispering "God didn't say that" just like he did to Eve in the garden.

The battlefield is in your minds with those thoughts you think. Reading and receiving truth in the Word helps us to overcome those lies because the Word of God is a two edged sword that rightfully divides truth from the lie and never comes back void as God reminds you of that truth over and over until you get it.

Through my healing I learned why I could not, from my very first marriage onward, stay in a relationship with a man for more than a year or two. Deep-rooted anger against men and other people had clung to me since my first abortion. Desperation for love from a man, plus this anger, led me into confusion and more failed relationships. If I had had a strong love for my Heavenly Father, I could have been sustained without any other love.

Believing that sex was actually "love" only superficially fed the lust of my flesh. I always realized after I succumbed to the temptation that I ended up unfulfilled and very empty, rejected again and left with an even greater need to be loved. I often felt used and guilt and shame but didn't understand why. Lust of the flesh always wants more; it is never enough to fill our emptiness for love. But I kept going back and committing the same sin, over and over somehow still believing this was love. This is known as "habitual sin" in the Bible.

I was not abiding with God, nor proving my love for God, while disobeying His commandments. Therefore, God was not abiding with me, for I had chosen Satan's way, not God's. That lust of the flesh separated me from God to go my own way, so He allowed me to suffer the consequences in order to teach me. We, like sheep, have gone astray and gone our own way (Isaiah 53:6).

Paul pleads with us in Romans 12:1-2 to give our bodies to God. Let them be a living sacrifice — the kind God will accept. When you think of what He has done for you, is this too much to ask?

"Love the Lord your God with all your heart, soul, and mind" and *"Love your neighbor as yourself"* are the first two commandments that Jesus said are the most important (Matthew 22:37-39). The second commandment requires you to love yourself. If we do not love ourselves enough to get healed so that we can love others as ourselves, we can never fulfill this second commandment, or the first.

God loves us first and knows us before we are even born. "He Knows my Name" by Tommy Walker is a lovely song that comes to my mind as I meditate on God's love for us. Tommy beautifully describes how much God loves us and knows everything about us. Check out this precious song.

God knew us before we were formed in our mother's womb: as a person, not tissue. Through meditating on Psalm 139:13-16, you will understand how much God loves you and knows you more than you know yourself. He wants you to come to Him for your healing, so you can truly be free indeed.

PACE: Post-Abortion Counseling and Education

I went through all the classes and found out I still had a lot more forgiving to do. I really had to face the whole trauma all over again in order to do the work to forgive and heal. This included the painful process of writing letters to my unborn children who I now knew are with God. That was the hardest part, to really look at each one as a human being, my children, whom I will see again when I get to Heaven. What would I want to say to them if they were alive here today? Could I even face them? It was the most painful thing I had ever done for my emotional state, but I had to do the work for the ultimate goal of healing for myself—so I could love myself, as well as others.

It was so important that I not abandon the ship, because that is exactly what Satan would have wanted me to do. I saw others drop out in anger, in denial, and with human rationalizations that were ridiculous when compared to a lifetime of healing and freedom from Satan's bondage. Satan didn't want me or anyone else there healed. He wants everyone to be defeated, as he is.

Satan even used my Mary Kay National Sales Director to call me and demean me for leaving behind my goal of becoming "National Sales Director." I left in order to pursue healing, but she called me foolish, and the idea ridiculous. She said, "Suck it up! Get over it and move on!" Even though she hurt my heart with her words that day and made me question myself, and then cry about losing all I had built up, including the car, I wanted to be healed even more. So I continued. I just avoided her and the others beckoning me away from my pursuit of God's healing. I was determined to be completely healed and set free from all the pain, un-forgiveness and bondage these sins had kept me in, blinding me to what God's plan was for my life.

God clearly told me at that time that He wanted me to step down from Mary Kay. My identity had become tied to my position instead of to Him. The natural progression for quitting was that I lost my income, as well as my free and lovely pink transportation. In 2003 I bought my first car since getting free ones from 1990. I felt the immediate emotional pain and I counted the cost, but I kept my eyes on the goal that lay ahead and persevered in the race to receive the prize (Philippians 3:13-14). Being completely healed and set free from my past would be the prize that became my priority. All other things perish.

Friends, it is so important for you to understand that Satan wants you in bondage and defeated. He wants you to give up on anything that is good for you. Satan is a liar, a deceiver, and is looking to destroy as many people as possible before Jesus returns for us, or before we die. Satan is the author of every bad and evil thing in this world. Jesus wants to set us free!

God Wants the Best for Us!

God is the Author and Giver of every good and perfect thing (James 1:17). He wants the very best for you and desires you to be victorious over evil. Although God can use even evil for His glory, we must fight the devil by allowing God to speak to us through the Holy Spirit who lives in us as Christians. He leads us to all truth and nurtures us to maturity so to grow more like Christ daily. Without Christ and the Holy Spirit leading us to all truth, we can do nothing.

We must stand firm, dressed in our full armor of God, against the fiery darts of the enemy (Ephesians 6:10-20). We need to put the armor on every morning before getting out of bed. God is our refuge, our fortress, and our strong tower (Psalm 61). He will protect us from our enemy, but we must seek Him first.

We must trust Him to do what His Word promises He will do. We must study and thoroughly know the Word in order to take strength from His promises. He has given us His Word so that we may know Him personally. The Word says in Matthew 6:33: "But seek ye first the kingdom of God, and his righteousness; and all these things shall be added unto you."

We should receive His grace with gratitude, and we should repent of our unbelief and our fears. Perfect love casts out all fear. (1 John 4:18) We must have a willing spirit (Psalm 51) for God to guide us. God is a perfect gentleman. He will not force His love upon us. Yes, He knows what we need but He wants us to ask Him for it. We cannot do any "works" to gain His favor. A study of Romans and Galatians makes that clear. Rather, we must simply receive His gift of eternal life and know that His grace is sufficient.

In His foreknowledge, He knew we would sin and would not be able to keep the law. However, He loves us so much that He sent His only Son to die in our place, to take the punishment for our sins. God sent Jesus to fulfill the law perfectly, knowing no man could. We need to simply choose to believe in Jesus and His ways for our lives.

If we love our sin too much and choose to live in our sin instead of receiving Him as our Savior, we shall not be in Heaven with Him. We must choose. The choice is yours to choose freely. If we feed our flesh, we can't get enough. You will always be left "empty" inside.

The emptiness you feel is the God shaped vacuum that can only be satisfied with God's perfect love.

God created us with the built-in desire for what only He can fulfill. He is our Heavenly Father, our Abba, which means "Daddy" (Matthew 6:32-33). He longs to hear you call out to Him. He has His arms stretched out, waiting for you to come running to Him for all your answers in life. He wants to give you the answers; they are found in Jesus Christ, the Word.

Volunteering and God's Provision

When I received God's healing, I was truly free indeed. I had no guilt or shame, for I had confessed my sins, repented, received God's forgiveness, and turned around to sin no more. Proverbs 28:13 says, "*He who conceals his transgressions will not prosper, but he who confesses and forsakes them will find compassion.*"

Healed by God's grace, I felt as if a house fell off my back! The chains were gone and my eyes were opened to the uniqueness God had designed me for, His divine plan for my life. I was blind but now I could see. I was lost but now I was found. The pain caused by my deep rooted sin was healed by Jesus, my Jehovah Rapha, my healer. In Exodus 15:22-26 Moses had led the Israelites from the Red Sea and they came upon bitter waters. The bitter waters were made sweet through the piece of wood symbolizing the tree Jesus hung on for you and me to heal us. Jesus made a decree with His people as He did with me that day. He said "If you listen carefully to the voice of the LORD your God and do what is right in His eyes, if you pay attention to his commands and keep all his decrees, I will not bring on you any of the diseases I brought on the Egyptians, for I am the LORD, who heals you" My joy came back to me and I remembered who I am: God's child. I was free to love and help others experience the same freedom God had given me. I felt like a little child, full of joy and peace, without a care in the world and forgiven. The world around me seemed brighter and the joy of the Lord became my strength as God gave me new mercies every morning.

After my healing, I sought God for what was next in my life. I began to volunteer two days a week at the pregnancy center, beginning my Crisis Pregnancy Counseling by being mentored by Sharon S. I watched while she counseled women until we both felt I could do it on my own. While Sharon listened in on my counseling, I was incredibly amazed how all these women I did not know at first, so easily opened up to me with their feelings and confessions. This gave me the ability to speak honestly to them, and I begin educating them on abortion while they waited for the results of their free pregnancy tests.

Once we saw the positive results, we could then discuss the options. Most all of the women changed their minds about aborting, and decided to keep the baby once they realized that this was a real baby, not just tissue. I shared with them the center's desire to help them with supplies and support in raising their babies.

I know that if someone had talked to me like this when I was in my own crisis pregnancy, I would have had more confidence to raise a child on my own without any help from the father so I sure had a deep desire to help others to have that kind of help. Praise God, many of them decided to follow Jesus. This gave them more confidence in God being with them, to help them in motherhood as well in life.

Day after day I left the pregnancy center crying with joy to the Lord, praising Him for how He was using me to help change lives so miraculously. I could see God's real purpose for my life here on earth. I felt such an honor to have this privilege, that God trusted me with the souls of these precious women and their children.

Since God had not given me the motivation to start building my Mary Kay business in Florida, I just serviced my existing customers, but that income was not enough. God, knowing all my needs, gave me a great job at an architectural firm, through a Christian friend at church. I thank God for all His provision.

Somewhere around this time, as my apartment lease was going to expire, I began to search for a small house close to church and the beach. I preferred to own rather than rent. The perfect ad popped out at me in the local paper. When I saw it, I fell in love with the house and signed a contract to purchase it on the first of May 2003, even though my lease was not up until July.

The owners moved out and let me have my furniture delivered from New Jersey early so I could stop my monthly payment for the storage. My job at the architect firm started at the beginning of that same year. The house was even closer for commuting to work.

The job was a perfect fit for me at that time, since I was allowed to continue my Biblical studies in my spare time at work. Wearing my Mary Kay business suits, I answered phones and greeted visitors, working 35 hours a week. I was also able to continue my volunteer counseling after work.

God provided this security for a season and I felt blessed by the way they treated me. It was wonderful to work with Christians and, in the slow times, share the blessings of God! "I Am Not Afraid Anymore" is a song by Twila Paris that reflects my state of mind set free from the bondage to sin.

This time of healing was the most significant step of my journey that had to happen for me to not only be ready to meet my true love but also was a part of my wedding preparation for eternity with my soon coming Bridegroom, Jesus. Now I had complete transparency and freedom in my walk with Him. My Bridegroom is coming for a spotless Bride full of purity, holiness and righteousness, aligned with New Covenant truth.

Now my secret sin of murder through abortion has been confessed and repented of. God has turned it around to be used for His glory to help others. Praise His holy name full of righteousness and truth! He was preparing me for something greater than I could ever dream or imagine. God is good and merciful for those of us who listen to His still small voice and obey Him. That voice comes from the Holy Spirit within true believers. He promises to lead us to all truth. We are responsible to listen to Him.

My Bridegroom is faithful and true and His promises are everlasting. My heart skips a beat in just thinking of the marriage supper of the Lamb (Revelation 19:9), the lamb who takes away the sins of the world (John 1:29). His unconditional love and grace-filled arms are opened wide, waiting for you and me to choose to love Him, by obeying His New Covenant that He has written upon each of our hearts when we are in Christ. He must continually cleanse us from all unrighteousness in order to prepare us for our Bridegroom, Jesus.

My body yearns for Him and my soul thirsts for Him like a deer pants for water (Psalm 42:1). My thoughts are consumed with my royal wedding with the King of kings and the Lord of lords. All that matters now in life on earth is my heart's desire to please Him in all my ways. What a glorious and delightful dance with my Savior! Come with me, my dear sister, and join in the dance, for eternity.

10

My True Love Story

How Did I Meet Steven, My True Love?

Here it is . . . finally the answer to the big question I am often asked: "How did you and Steven meet?" I must first point out that I had learned to be a very content single woman, blessed by many Christian friends and blessed through ministering to others. I loved my life of counseling women at my church and at the local pro-life pregnancy center. I was using my spiritual gifts given to me by God for the good of others and it was so fulfilling. I was about the Father's business.

I enjoyed playing tennis weekly, riding my bike along the beach with friends, and spending my spare time on the beach alone with God. Through so many sunrises I admired God and sought His wisdom and heard His voice. I sang to Him and He danced over me. These activities, along with my job, church, group Bible studies, and personal time with God, which included reading the Word daily and spending time in prayer, kept me busy and satisfied.

I could see that ministering to women's pain and broken hearts was my real God-given purpose in life. Out of my own pain and broken hearts, God was using "the blood of the Lamb" (Revelation 12:11) and the word of my testimony to speak into these women's souls for the sake of the gospel. God has designed every one of us with a God-given purpose. (I Peter 4:10, Romans 12:4-8) When we are living that purpose, there is joy and a sense of contentment like nothing else can give.

Now, you will see how God used something else that the devil meant for evil (the 9/11 attack) and turned it around for His glory in my life. This truth is shown in Romans 8:28, which is not only my life's verse, but is also one of Steven's life verses. The verse says *"And we know that God causes everything to work together for the good of those who love God and are called according to his purpose for them."*

Let me take you back to that infamous day, the day everyone in America who is over twenty should remember. 9/11 is the event that drew me into studying Islam and eventually to Steven. My compelling question was: How could any human being kill in the name of their god in such a way? When I heard that the men who attacked the United States that day did so because they believed that their god, Allah, was directing them to do it to "judge" America for their sins against god, and Islam so they themselves would end up in Paradise, I just couldn't believe it! I passionately wanted to find out more about Islam and the Muslims who follow this belief. I was seeking out the truth no matter where it would lead me. God heard my prayer and would answer it His way, far beyond my human understanding.

On 9/11/01, God awakened me to who He, the true God, is. He confirmed to me that day that He is not only the loving God, full of grace and mercy, who I had begun to know, but He is also just. I believe the hand of God's protection over our nation had been lifted that day and that His allowing the United States of America to be attacked was the natural consequence of our disobedience. I understood at this time that I needed to listen intently to the Holy Spirit in me so He could direct my path and change me from the inside. I had to do this by submitting all of my life to God, not just the parts I wanted to give Him.

I needed to become a living sacrifice for Him. I was shaken that day to the core. I feared Almighty God and His mighty power like never before. I just knew in my spirit that the Holy Spirit, who promises to lead us into all truth, was speaking loud and clear. God was in control and He had allowed this attack on our nation that day, and He now had my attention. Did He get your attention too?

I learned more about God, our Heavenly Father, who chastens those whom He loves, as I studied in Proverbs 3:11-12, in Hebrews 12:5-6, and again in Revelation 3:19. I realized there were great consequences for my own sins and I had better straighten my path. It comforted me to know Abba Father loved me so much that He wanted me to choose His best for my life for He saw me as His own daughter.

After the attack, in February 2002, for ten weeks our church invited a speaker to come after our Sunday service to share information about Islam in order to help us understand it more. The classes were very informative, but the concepts were certainly foreign to anything I had been taught in America. However the perpetrators had killed themselves in it, so it was up to our government and military to punish those behind the plot whatever it took. It seemed war was inevitable.

These teachings opened my eyes to why Muslims committed this crime on 9/11, but the most impressive thing I still remember about a particular Sunday teaching was the demeanor of two former Muslims who shared their testimonies. I went up to talk to them afterward just because I was so amazed at how humble these two men were, and I was amazed at the love I saw in their eyes for Christ and others.

What a contrast to how destructive those terrorists were on 9/11. I could see what a difference Jesus makes. This observation caused me to be very curious about Islam. At that time, I never dreamed I was being prepared to work for the Lord in a ministry reaching Muslims with the truth of the Gospel and equipping other Christians for the same.

Even though I had now learned about jihad, the sixth pillar of Islam, I still did not understand how any human being could actually believe it is right to kill in the name of their god. What kind of god was this? These two questions lingered in my heart from then until God would answer it in 2005.

In 2011, I was led to some very important messages about 9/11 which confirmed what God had told me that day. Four days after the attack, God gave Pastor David Wilkerson of the Times Square Church in NYC a message he called "The Towers Have Fallen" about this attack being allowed by Him as punishment for disobedience as a God-given Christian nation. At the same time, God gave to Rabbi Jonathan Cahn, a Messianic Jewish believer in NJ, a similar message and the two men discussed it with each other.

Interestingly, both these men lived and preached in the same areas I frequented with my friends Terry and Al. We went to NYC to Times Square Church at times for a powerful message from Pastor

David, and other times I went with them to their new church, Calvary Temple, across the street from Rabbi Jonathan's synagogue. I was not led to Pastor David's message until 2011, or Rabbi Jonathan's until 2012 when he began to speak of the Harbingers. I do find it fascinating how God spoke to me that day of 9/11/01 just as He also spoke to these two men the same message "God had allowed this 911 attack to chasten His children in this God-given nation." I wonder how many other people heard the same message.

It sounds to me like the Holy Spirit outpouring bringing a message from God to His children. It sure seems like God is up to something and must know a bigger plan than I do. Do you think the Creator of the universe just might have higher thoughts and bigger plans than we do? Whether you know Him some, a lot or not at all, I dare you to ponder: "How big is your God or how big could He be to know so much more than all of us?"

God Opens the Door
In October 2004, in Florida, one of the Christian women I worked with at the architectural firm suggested I check out a website that included a chat line for Christians discussing both political issues and God. It was there that a discussion concerning Islam intrigued me because my son, Chris, had completed college and moved back to the New York city area to be with his father, so I was still concerned about further attacks there. I had already learned about the jihad of Islam, so I began chatting with the people on the site.

From my previous teachings I surmised that one of these people, Steven Masood, seemed to be more knowledgeable about Islam than the others. I looked up his site and discovered that he was born in Pakistan. Formerly a Muslim, he became a Christian at the age of 23. His Ph.D. is in Comparative Religion with an emphasis on Christian/Islamic relations. As I observed his manner of chatting with people, I noticed how polite and humble he was, as well as the high level of respect he displayed to everyone. This stood out to me and made me feel very secure in asking him questions. He was always courteous and gentlemanly in his answers.

After a while, he seemed to get tired of answering my many questions. He suggested that he send me his books *Into the Light,* his testimony, and the follow up, *More Than Conquerors*. He added, "If you still have questions after reading these, I will answer them then."

I gave Steven my address and email in order to continue to communicate privately and to follow up on his books. I decided to get off the chat line due to unsolicited marriage proposals from several Muslim foreigners, probably to obtain an American passport and try to marry beautiful women, as Islam teaches. I did notify Steven I was leaving the site and would be eagerly awaiting the books arrivals.

In December, I went back to Maine for Christmas, spending this special day and my week off with my beloved Nana. As I had been walking much closer with the Lord, my Nana and I had gotten closer and closer as well. From Florida, I had spoken with her almost every Sunday on the phone. I have fond memories of spending Christmas with her that year, just like I did in my childhood, only this time it was at her assisted living home. It was a sweet, sweet time for both of us, as we bonded again, surrounded and housebound by mounds of snow. We talked about the Lord now, instead of my latest turmoil. My Nana celebrated her 97th birthday that year.

When I got back from Maine in January, I realized I still hadn't received those books Steven promised me, so I emailed him again and asked him about it. He was puzzled, as he verified my address and confirmed that he sent them, so we couldn't understand what had happened. Today, I know it was the enemy who diverted those books, but he didn't get away with it the second time, since they had been covered in prayer. They reached me in January. I am grateful to God that Steven kept his word, no matter the extra cost for him. Steven showed by example his obedience to Jesus' teaching of letting your yes be yes and your no be no (Matthew 5:37).

Reading Steven's autobiography, *Into the Light,* consumed me. I had a hard time putting the book down. The Holy Spirit moved in my soul upon the completion of both books. When reading *Into the Light*, I was so anxious to find out what happened I found myself taking it in the car with me to finish it at the stop lights, which typically were at least 2-3 minutes long in South Florida.

I read his follow up book, *More Than Conquerors* lying on my couch while sick from work. That was certainly no coincidence based on what the Lord did to arouse my emotions and lead me by His Spirit at the end of this book. With God there are no coincidences but divine appointments. It is up to us to embrace them no matter how beyond our human understanding, while lining up with the Word of course.

For several reasons I felt great compassion for this man I was reading about that day. I could clearly see he was undeservingly treated unjustly by Muslims including his own family. I cried profusely at the end of *More Than Conquerors*, which drove me to my knees in prayer. In doing so, I first felt compelled to reassure him that the Holy Spirit had confirmed to me the eternal destiny of his best friend, before his death. In addition, I was amazed that as I read in the last pages of the book, just as God had reassured him through Romans 8:28, He had also used that verse to reassure me after my troubles. Finally, I felt I needed to let him know that it was perfectly fine with God, as I had also discovered, that we had every right to ask "why" of our earthly authorities so to understand, regardless of what people tell us.

I found myself having flashbacks of my own childhood experiences when I would ask "why" when my parents would demand that I not do the very things I saw them doing in the home. I was literally told, "Because I said so!" This is clearly hypocrisy. Steven's dad actually sought to kill him for questioning their religion by asking "why" and for discovering the flaws in his parents' way of life. Although my situation was most definitely not that bad, I also recognized and questioned the flaws in my parents' way of living and felt condemned for doing so. The closest I got to being physically hurt by my mother was when she emptied an entire drawer of kitchen gadgets, large spoons, spatulas, et cetera, by throwing them at me. I was about 12 years old. I don't remember why she was mad at me that time. She came after me and threw me across the room. I landed against a sharp metal drawer handle, with my ear split open. Blood oozed out all over the kitchen floor. Suddenly, she came out of her "demonic state" of outrage and embraced me saying, "I'm sorry! Are you ok?" Only then could I really see her fear of seriously hurting me and feel her regret. Most of the time I never really saw any remorse for all the times she or my father lost their tempers and took it out on us kids.

I remember thinking, "How *could* I be okay?" Yet I just whimpered, "Yes." It very negatively impacted my relationship with my mom. At the time, I couldn't have imagined any worse situation. This haunting experience came back to me as I was reading Steven's book. However Steven's relationship with his dad was threatened by death.

Looking back, we are so grateful to have gained new spiritual parents and families. They say they get to love us because we lost our parents and family who were supposed to love us. Losing our original family is felt deep in our bones.

I was now crying out to God for an opportunity to talk to Steven so I could share these things with him. My heart cried out for him with compassion. What kind of father would plot the death of his own son, who just wanted to understand "why"? God spoke to me through His Holy Spirit communicating with my spirit. He simply led me to check Steven's last email to me. Sure enough, I found he had sent a general email to all of his ministry supporters, including me, announcing that he had just moved to Florida! His address and phone number was typed directly under his name!

Questions flew from my mind to my Heavenly Father: "Lord, when did You move him to Florida? How is that possible? He lived in England when he sent these books." I was so excited that he now lived so much closer. I simply heard, "Call him," so I did, just as the Holy Spirit directed me to do. Steven answered the phone. When I said "Hello" and introduced myself, he went silent. After a pause, he said "Karen? Em ... Karen from the chat line and emails that I sent my books twice to?"

I said, "Yes," and then proceeded to ask him my questions and share what was on my heart. I don't remember much from that conversation, except that I was relieved to express my inspirations and I felt heard, very honored and respected by him. He didn't say anything suggestive or invite me on a date. For the first time, I felt completely "safe" talking to a man, this man, and free to be myself. This is how God's peace feels.

God Works in Mysterious Ways! [1]

Only a week or two later I got another general email from Steven's ministry, this time announcing that he would be teaching at a seminar

---

[1] It is a paraphrase of a 19th century hymn by the English poet William Cowper. "God moves in a mysterious way, His wonders to perform."

at a church in central Florida with a couple of other scholars. The topic was "Understanding Islam." I was so amazed at what God was up to, moving him to the state in which I lived! Would I really have an opportunity to meet the man whose testimony I just finished reading?

Only now, as I look back can I see the plan God had for me in using His orchestration of every detail to write His own "love story" of how God's love unites the East to the West given to Christ followers by God. It actually just came to me after our church pastor, Pastor David, preached on the book of Hosea. He spoke of how God called a godly prophet of God to marry a promiscuous woman (adulteress). He pointed out how God was teaching Israel of His undying love for them to forgive and embrace them, even though they had committed adultery on their husband, God. Watch and see in my love story ahead if you might agree; there are similarities.

As a "Seer" of God, I believe God sent America a "Warner" and "Equipper" to prepare them for the influx of Muslims into this nation in 2005. That Warner and Equipper is Steven Masood, a former Muslim and a scholar in Islam. Though He might have sent others also who could help equip us, I knew of only a couple others by 2005. God orchestrated Steven's marriage to me so to use *Jesus to Muslims* for this purpose. Steven extensively studies both the Bible and the Qur'an.

Because of God's love for Muslims, His other sheep that He must bring into the sheep pen (John 10:16), He has brought them to the freedom in America to seek after their Savior without major persecution. Although people may disagree with me, I feel the Holy Spirit has given me this WORD from the LORD, our GOD to His nation, America, and His children.

Let those with ears to hear and those with eyes to see receive God's Word. What matters to God is the salvation of souls and that is the "calling" He has put on us. That is our daily burden: the salvation of souls, including Muslims, and the discipleship of Christ followers so they will be ready to share their faith with the lost, especially Muslims.

When I checked my calendar, I discovered I was already scheduled to be at my parent's retirement home in Zephyrhills, Florida the same weekend as the seminar, the weekend after Easter. They still believed in drinking their way through holidays, so I tried not to be around them when they were drunk, in order to avoid being persecuted for my faith. I had learned to set boundaries with my parents by now, so I had decided to drive the five hours to see them the weekend after Easter, when they would less likely be drinking with their friends. After checking *MapQuest*, I was amazed to find that the church in New Port Richey, where Steven would teach at a seminar, was only one hour from their house.

I decided this was too perfect an opportunity not to go! I was excited about learning more about Islam. I was also excited for the God-given opportunity to meet this amazing man whose autobiography I had just read. The Lord gave me complete peace about it. I emailed Steven after the deadline and asked him if there were still seats available at the seminar. He emailed back and said he would personally reserve a seat for me. He told me he looked forward to meeting me.

The evening before Easter, someone robbed my house while I was sleeping. Harley, my Pomeranian dog, was extremely protective of me and was a very good barker, but he didn't bark at all. The robber must have known the dog or known he was there and probably came prepared with a dog treat. The robber emptied my stolen purse on my side lawn, taking only the $15 I had in it, as well as my brand new bike from the lanai where he climbed in.

In the morning, I asked my neighbor, Danielle, if her boyfriend could possibly have been the thief. She and I went bike riding together almost daily and her boyfriend didn't approve of her new friendship with me. I know it was really Jesus in me that intimidated him, since that threatened his drug and alcohol addictions. She said it sure didn't seem like something he would do, but we could have the police check him out. The police said the footprints didn't appear to be made from the shoes they found on him. After the police came, we still had time to go Calvary Chapel Ft. Lauderdale's Easter service as we had planned.

Danielle accepted Christ as her Savior that day! It turned out to be a mightily blessed day for me, just knowing that she now had eternal life and that I could help her grow. It was so exciting! I had taken her to see "The Passion of the Christ" the week before and I knew she was incredibly moved by it from her silence. As I look back on it today, I see that Satan did all he could to prevent her salvation, but he lost that battle. Since then, I have lost contact with Danielle. When I think of her, I pray for her and for her growth in her faith walk. I look forward to seeing her one day in God's presence.

Returning home, I was still concerned about the robbery. There was an eerie atmosphere in my apartment, and I felt violated. However, I remembered I had felt a certain security when talking with Steven, so I called him. He prayed with me for protection, which freed me from the worry. Steven even offered to pay to replace my bike with some money he had just received, that he said God must have intended for me. He asked me if I was alright. Steven was so sincere, kind, and truly concerned for me; he emulated Jesus. I felt safe with him and I trusted him that day. I was absolutely certain he knew the same God I did.

During the week before the seminar, I decided to email him and attach one of the pictures a friend had taken of me on Easter Sunday at church. In a lovely Victorian dress, with a Victorian hat in my hand, I had posed in front of a colorful flowerbed in front of the Calvary Chapel church office. I thought that sending the picture would help him recognize me at the seminar.

Due to my feeling of security from our phone conversation, I also felt compelled to send Steven a picture of my son in his graduation cap and gown with his friends, my dog, and my favorite picture of my Nana, because these were the most important people in my life. I remember a passing thought, "If he has any fleshly lustful thoughts about my outer beauty, all my Nana's wrinkles that I would probably inherit should destroy them all!" Although I really had no clue whether this connection would ever go anywhere and had not thought about it in that way.

Meeting My True Love in God's Divine Providence

When I finally got to the seminar, I was late. MapQuest and I just didn't understand each other. I even parked on the wrong side of this big church and ended up having to walk the long way around to find the room where the seminar was already in progress. When I entered the room through the back door, I planned to just sneak in and sit in the back. After I opened the door, Steven stood up and looked at me. I felt like he acted as if the Queen of England had just walked into the

206

room and he was the only one who understood it was proper to rise in her presence. I was so embarrassed!

In seconds, a woman came to me and asked, "Are you Karen Johnson?" I confirmed her suspicion. Lo and behold, she escorted me to the front row seat, right in front of the current speaker. So much for being discrete! Steven was sitting at a table to my left, facing perpendicular to the front. When I turned slightly to my left, I could see him out of the corner of my eye. Every time the speaker would talk about something I had either read in Steven's book or discussed with him in conversation before this, I would turn and smile at him as if in agreement. My hair, cut in a bob, would swish back and forth with each turn of my head, as he described it.

Little did I know that Steven was fighting with God and telling Him, "Lord, this woman is a distraction to me! What will I do about it when I have to speak?" Later he told me that God said to him at this time "You call my creation a distraction?"

In a later phone conversation, Steven told me that God had given him a dream three years earlier, while in England, in which he was walking on the beach with a woman in a Victorian dress and hat that covered most of her face, with a cross gracing her neck. That day he received it, he felt strongly that the picture of me that I sent him fit that dream, though he didn't mention it on this day. Can you see God's plan, His love story, begin to unfold here?

Steven was scheduled to speak last, but at lunchtime I was aching to ask him a question and went to the book table. The question I asked was, "Please Steven, could you just show me where it says in the Qur'an that if I, an infidel, as Muslims call me, don't bow down to Allah, I can be killed?" Steven showed me several verses.[2] As I read it for myself, my heart dropped to my feet. I could not believe my eyes! It really says that. How can anyone follow a god that teaches them to kill other people who may not choose to be Muslims? What kind of god is this? For a few years ahead through studying Islam deeper, these were still my lingering and nagging questions in my heart.

---

[2] For example, Sura 8:12, 8:39; 9:5, 9:14, 9:29, 9:123; 33:60-61; 47:7.

The lunch break was over. It was Steven's turn to speak. The other speakers' teachings had intrigued me, but I was completely enthralled with the gift this man had to teach with such compassion, love, dedication and humbleness. He has such a gift for explaining details and intertwining his own personal experiences into the subject.

When Steven taught *"The Role of Women in Islam"* and talked about the lack of freedoms of Muslim women, I began to get more and more angry at what I was learning concerning the lies of Muslim men who force innocent women into bondage to them as part of their religion. I was now realizing that this was a male dominated ideology that subjugated women. I could only imagine how many women must be innocently deceived into believing these lies. I never learned about this part of Islam back in New Jersey in 2002. Only God would know the perfect timing of this teaching for me would be now.

In the seventh century, satanic spirits had influenced Muhammad. These generational curses and lies have been carried on to this day. Muslims are brought up with these lies from the time they are born and deceptively believe they are serving the real god in following the ways of Islam.

As I am writing this today, my heart cries out to my Abba Father, to help me to help them and that He would bring other Christ following women to join me in my passion to set these captives free. After all, the truth is Jesus came to set the captives free. The Spirit of the LORD came upon Isaiah (61:1) because the LORD anointed him to proclaim freedom for the captives. This prophecy was fulfilled in the favorable day of the LORD, when Jesus read it in the scroll and proclaimed it fulfilled during His ministry on earth (Luke 4:16-21).

I know that there is nothing impossible in Jesus' name. I trust Him to use you and me today to continue to carry out that prophecy by using us to set these Muslim women free. They are clearly captives! When I watched a film called *The Stoning of Soraya M* again recently, the Holy Spirit showed me something profound about the innocence of this Islamic woman in the film, in a comparison to the innocence of Christ dying on the cross.

I believe God is leading me to lead a specific group of Christ following women in a mission today to set these captive Islamic women free. I ask you to pray with me about His will in it all and whether you are one of those women He is calling to join me in this mission. In obedience to God Almighty, His Father, Jesus laid his life down freely. He remained silent to the untrue accusations against Him.

When you watch this film, you will see how Soraya silently allowed herself to be led to the slaughter, completely innocent of the crime for which she was accused: adultery against her husband. How cruel it was to watch her own husband stand by and even take part in stoning her, knowing she was innocent.

Her husband accused her of adultery because he wanted to marry a young girl and his wife did not agree with his desire. It just breaks my heart to see this man manipulate and influence his sons to cast stones at their own mother. I would so much rather be judged by God than man, for man's heart is deceitfully wicked. This is such a demonic ideology, where Satan leads man with the spirit of death.

Yet Jesus came to give life and life abundantly! If only these Muslim people could learn about the real Jesus, the only man to ever fulfill the law perfectly because God knew none of us could keep the law perfectly. Jesus came to set the captives of this satanic ideology free!

The Holy Spirit: "This is Your Husband"

At the book table again, after Steven's teaching, I asked him a whole lot more questions, mostly about the way Muslims treat women. I exclaimed how wrong that was and that this is America! They cannot treat women like that here, can they? "It's all against the law of this country!" I proclaimed, probably prideful.

His comments were that they are treating women that way everywhere, even in communities within the United States where Muslims flock, including Dearborn, Michigan and many other places, just as in foreign countries. I just couldn't believe that our "Christian Nation" would allow such an atrocity here! Then I went on to explain that I had experienced much abuse from men in America, even some men who called themselves Christian, who were abusive in their treatment of me and many other women I knew.

As I got worked up, Steven calmed my spirit when he changed the course of the conversation by eloquently stating: "However, what I believe is as the Bible states, a Christian man should be willing to lay his life down for a woman, as Christ laid His life down for the church!"

Wow! He was quoting from Ephesians 5:25, with personal conviction like I had never heard before from a man. I was instantly calmed and felt the fresh fragrance of peace come over me. I was mesmerized inside, knowing I had waited a lifetime to hear those powerful love-in-action words. They so directly contradicted my previous experiences, as well as the bitter ranting and raving of the fierce, angry man that day at Divorce Care in New Jersey, who was demanding his "right" of dominance over his wife, while still calling himself a Christian.

God had used the Divorce Care leader's peaceful spirit to clearly explain about submission and a healthy marriage based on love, as Christ loves the Church and gave Himself up for her. Now I was hearing those very words, right here out of this Godly man's mouth. The Biblical truth coming alive here is; the Word from my mouth will never return void. Right then, I heard the voice of the Holy Spirit tell me loud and clear: "This is your husband." I heard it three times.

Suddenly, I felt weak in my knees and leaned on the table. Just then, Steven had to leave. Quickly he gave me, in my left hand, his other two books and a padded envelope under them (which I later discovered). I walked him and the couple who brought him out to the front of the church and stood there, still awe struck by the words of the Holy Spirit. Steven said goodbye in his polite, kind way and then he picked up my right hand and kissed the back of it! They all whisked themselves off into the car and left.

As I stood there in a daze, I didn't quite know what had just happened to me. I got this incredible fluttering feeling inside my heart. Today, I see it as God's Cinderella story in my life. As I sort of came to, I looked around to find my car so I could sit down before falling down in weakness. I spotted it all by itself in the far left field of my view. I slowly walked over to it, thinking over all that had just happened, including what Steven had said to me, that I clearly recognized as Scripture (Ephesians 5:25-32). He had said it as if it were second nature to him.

I opened the car door and got in, relieved to finally sit down. A prayer poured from my soul, "Lord, he actually kissed my hand! What is this feeling I feel inside? I have never felt like this in my entire life! What is this all about?" I began to cry out to God by asking, "How can You tell me this is my husband? I hardly know him! What is happening here? Why am I feeling like this, Lord?"

Tears came to my eyes and I began to cry. A waterfall of tears fell on my new books. I looked down to wipe them off and noticed the padded manila envelope under the books. I didn't have a clue as to what could be inside this envelope. Curiously, I opened it. As I looked in, I saw the most beautiful zirconium cross necklace ever! The cross was about two inches long on a silver chain. It was just gorgeous, sparkling in the sunlight through the car window. Wow! A bookmark appeared next. It said: Love inspired and proclaimed I Corinthians 13:13: "There are three things that endure—faith, hope and love—and the greatest of these is love."

When I saw this cross and read that verse, I realized that God was doing something in the heart of this man, and I had been rather oblivious to it. I did not come to that seminar that day to seek out a husband, but rather to learn more about Islam from a kind, respectful Christian man who had been a Muslim and who had suffered horrible trials and persecution for the sake of Christ. I had come to get answers to the plaguing questions in the depth of my soul. How could anyone kill in the name of their god? What kind of god is this?

Godly Advice

At that moment, while still sitting in the parking lot, I became so overwhelmed with all of these feelings, thoughts and emotions that I began crying uncontrollably. I didn't even know what to do next. After calming down a bit, I thought, "Who can I call? This just doesn't even seem real! I need accountability. I may be going crazy and need an anchor to pull me down from all this."

I thought of my new pregnancy center director, Reatha, who had mentored me through a Biblical study called "Sexual Healing." Sharon had moved away. Like Sharon, she knew me very well. I called her and she answered right away. I began to tell her what had happened, detail by amazing detail. She listened intently. When I finished telling her about what I held in my hand, she said "Don't you see,

Karen? This is the Lord! The Lord has divinely orchestrated this whole thing!"

"How do you know?" I asked.

She replied, "Do you remember the day that you completed the final assignment I gave you in the Sexual Healing Bible study, to write a list of all the qualities you felt a man should have if God were to send you a husband?"

"Yes," I said "I gave you that list and then I laughed like Sarah when God told her she would have a child at 95 years old! I said that there was no such man like this that existed on this earth!" She then reminded me, "Then what did I say?"

I was convicted and repeated her exact words: "How big is your God, Karen?"

"That's right!" she said, "So this is it! God has sent you the one!"

I told her that I realized that I did not believe that God was big enough to give me my heart's desire, as the Word says He can. I then realized that I was really limiting God by even saying that and still grappled with my worthiness of anything this holy, this good for a wretch like me. This is where I struggled with my promiscuous past haunting me, as Satan would have it, and why God would want such a godly man to marry me. Today, I recall how God told Hosea to marry Gomez being a similar scenario although she was still committing sins in her marriage to him.

Suddenly, I became overwhelmed again and began to cry. She asked me "What are you crying for now?" I cried and blurted out, "I don't know what to do with it now."

Reatha calmed me, "How about if you start out by just calling him and thanking him for the cross? Do you think you can do that?"

Gazing at the beautiful cross again, I replied. "Yes, of course I can do that. Of course, I want to do that."

"So what are you doing on the phone with me? Call him and thank him, and let the Holy Spirit do the rest!"

"Thank you Reatha!" After she said, "You're welcome," I hung up.

I said a prayer to my precious Father in Heaven, asking Him for the words to say. Then, I dialed Steven's number. He picked up and when he heard my voice say, "Hi. It's Karen." I could hear the smile on his face.

He told me, "Let me say goodbye to my friends. I'll be right back!" I could hear him speaking in the background saying, "Thank you very much for giving me a lift; that was so kind of you. I have to take this call."

He came back to me and we had a very sweet conversation, as I thanked him for the beautiful gifts. From that day on, we have had constant communication! This was only the beginning of the beautiful transparency between us.

This was God's love story to create something beautiful out of ashes here in the West to paint a picture. This is God's picture of His divine love for a nation of people in the West who have committed adultery against Him, like Gomer did (Hosea 1:2), and to prepare them by teaching them His eastern moral and Biblical ways through another nation of people.

God created a love story picture like Hosea & Gomer by bringing this Christ follower, who is moral and gifted, a teacher from the East, to his formally immoral, now redeemed, bride. God would show His love using this man to wash her in the Word (Ephesians 5:25-32), adorning her with forgiveness and an abundant life of everlasting love in preparation for her ultimate Bridegroom, Jesus Christ. This marriage unites two people groups, East to the West, in the unity of one faith, one Lord, one Spirit, one baptism (Ephesians 4:4-6) to the one way to eternity through Jesus Christ our LORD and Savior (John 14:6).

This is the wedding preparation for eternity in a restored perfect love relationship with God our Father through the one door of Jesus Christ, the sacrificial Lamb of God, who took away our sins and washed us white as snow, pure and holy and set apart for the marriage supper of the Lamb. Jesus prayed for this perfect unity of those who believed then and who would believe today to be united as one with the Father as He, Jesus, is one with the Father (John 17:20-23).

Courtship and our Second Meeting

From that moment on, I felt complete peace, security and a "like spirit and mind" as Steven and I talked for hours over the phone about the Lord. We began a long distance relationship by phone. We even did my weekly Kay Arthur Bible study together that way, which was on the book of Romans. On one of our phone conversations, Steven shared with me how my picture that I had sent him reminded him of a dream God had given him about three years earlier where he was walking on a beach with a woman in a Victorian dress praying together.

I knew I had heard the Holy Spirit speak to me on the day we met at the seminar, but kept it to myself. He explained that while in the dream he had not seen her face, that when I sent the picture of myself to him, he was moved that the woman in the dream just might have been me. I felt we had a confirmation of spirit but still felt hesitation of speaking out about what I had heard that day. Because of what I had learned about fasting, I fasted and prayed about this relationship. God's complete peace filled my soul.

Steven and I talked at lunchtime almost every day, as well as in the evenings. He wrote me poems and sent them in emails and in text messages. He was so romantic that way and has always conducted himself as a gentleman: respectful and God honoring. Only God would know that one of my love languages is "words of affirmation" – just as had been confirmed to me in Mary Kay.

Here is a poem he wrote to me ten days after we met. It is titled: *A dream that has become a reality*. The standard of English and composition of words may be ignored.

> I dreamt a dream like the day light
> The sun was shining down so bright
> You were in rays of His splendor light
> The wind blew softly upon your face
> And when I looked at you my dear
> I was showered with grace to bear
>
> The boat floated gently down the river
> I desired to stay in the moment forever
> Then the sun soon started to set in
> I asked Him to grant us His day
> Please declare Lord that we may
> Be forever together in His bay
>
> Soon the sun was fully gone

But the boat still floated on
The only light that could be seen
I was indeed amazed to see
It came from the candles held
By the angels on the edge of the sea

Holding your hand that you raise
In prayer towards the Heavenly
I raised it with mine towards the sky
Thanking Him I pushed back your hair
And in your eyes indeed I saw it all
A sea of love, His love with no despair

O, I see it all, certainly He dwells in you
Karen, after Jesus, indeed I feel
That there is none for me better than you
And indeed without a doubt I admit
There is nothing precious than you
I know now the promised beauty is you

My heart skipped a beat after reading his words. I was being romanced like a girl desires in her dreams. It was so sweet and I cherished the moments. Well, it wasn't long before my Bible study leader began to notice that I was floating on air and more joyful. She knew something was different with me, so she asked me to stay after class that night and told me to fess up. I told her all about Steven, sharing with her what the Holy Spirit had told me about him being my husband.

She insisted that it was close to impossible for someone to meet in such a short time and jump into marriage so soon without any consideration of what the Holy Spirit had confirmed to Steven or me. She was about to move back to her home state of Michigan, to be near her grandchildren, and insisted that I take her free voucher for a four-night stay at a hotel. She wanted to get Steven down to the Ft. Lauderdale area in order to meet him and make sure he was "the real deal." I was grateful for the kind offer and called Steven the next day to invite him. It is actually touching to my heart that she cared so much.

On April 28, 2005, I picked Steven up at the airport. I decided to wear that same Victorian dress and hat that I wore in the picture I had sent him, so he could easily find me. I knew I would get strange looks at the airport, but the most important look to me was the one I got when Steven met me at the airport that day. It was the second time I had seen him in person in my whole life.

We were both full of joy and thanksgiving to the Lord. We left there and drove straight to the beach in Ft. Lauderdale. It was of course my favorite place to be. It was no coincidence that in his dream, he saw me in this outfit on the beach. We had a beautiful time together, talking about everything, never at a loss for words.

We both love to talk, especially about the Lord, and it was a perfect sunny day with a huge breeze to soften the heat of the sun. After a while, as it was still morning, we had breakfast together on a peaceful restaurant veranda overlooking the beach. I enjoyed his subtle sense of humor and loved listening to his adorable accent. He has a way of saying things that is so cute and different. There is certain innocence about him. When he smiled, he just made my heart skip a beat. I remember just how respectful and polite he was as well as humble for a man with a higher education. I felt completely safe with him.

We had a great morning at the beach and then I took him to my house to meet my Pomeranian, Harley. He cuddled right up next to Steven and as Steven petted him, he gave his approval. My dog did not normally approve of men, so to me this was a good sign. Little did I know that Steven was never too fond of dogs, because of his previous Muslim culture, but in his mind he reasoned, as they say parabolically in the east, "Well, if you love Lila, you have to love her dog."

We agreed to watch a Christian movie. I put on one of my favorites: "*Love Comes Softly.*" This movie is about a newlywed lady who moved out west in a covered wagon with her husband to claim land for a home. Upon their arrival, her husband tragically died, leaving her alone there. The next day, a caravan brought back her dead husband on a horse. One of the men with the caravan, a widower with a young daughter, felt God calling him to ask the lonely widow to join his daughter and him, by marrying him. Having no other choice, she accepted his offer, but her love sickness over her own dead husband caused her difficulty in adjusting.

Just as the Bible teaches that God leads the husband spiritually, and a woman is designed to be his helper and submit to his lead, this movie depicted it along with the bountiful blessings for all when God is the center of a home. For, as God would have it, the couple found love; peace and harmony after the formerly unhappy widow gave her life to Christ. I could see the prophetic nature of how it would be for me with Steven in the gentle, soft way he would love me, just the way I needed, as God knew.

I had felt led to watch this movie with Steven. Steven's willingness to please me by watching a "chick flick" together touched my heart. Seeing the movie again reminded me of God's plan for marriages: to bless both the man and woman and their families. To this day, when we watch a "chick flick" it always reminds me of our first big day together.

We just recently watched this movie again for the second time. The way the movie depicts love coming so softly and gently and slowly made an impact on me. This is not the typical worldview, nor what my mother taught me about love. I know that deep inside me, I was yearning for that same respect, honor, and gentleness from a man in my life. That is exactly what God gave me with Steven.

That first day, after watching the movie, we drove down to the local beachfront and sat on the sand, looking out at God's beautiful creation together. We walked to the lighthouse and back, communing with nature and talking a lot. We never seemed to run out of conversation. We then went to a local restaurant. I took him back to his hotel about 30 minutes away.

That evening, as I thought back over the day, I sought the Lord for His leading. I felt complete peace with God. That day was Thursday and Steven would leave on Monday. While my Bible study teacher insisted that I bring him down here, she ended up not being able to schedule time to see us because of her job. She never did meet Steven, although all my other friends did and they instantly loved him. We are grateful, though, for Kathy's generous gift!

Until now, I had hesitated to bring up anything about what God had told me the day I met Steven. However, as it was clear God was speaking to both of us at separate times; I told him what God had told me. We both, at that moment, felt in our own hearts that God had His hand on us. We had a confirmation of spirits.

As we parted that evening, we both realized God had divinely brought us together. He had confirmed it in speaking to both of us separately, and now as we shared with each other, we realized how God had perfectly orchestrated our union. That night, I went to our Lord in prayer, and really sought His will in it all. I felt something I had never felt before this. I just knew that I knew that this was from God. I was not in lust but felt I had found my best friend whom I just loved being with, as I was free to be myself. He loved me for who I am and my deep search for truth that led me to Christ and we both wanted to grow in a deeper relationship with Jesus.

We both agreed that we loved each other after Jesus first. I love Jesus and so does he and we were both free to speak everything and anything that comes up without restrictions. It is complete transparency and freedom to be who we are in Christ, allowing the Holy Spirit to lead us to all truth wherever He may lead us. I could see in faith the exciting adventure ahead and trusted God to lead us, without knowing where we could go, like Abraham was asked to go to a land only God knew.

The amazing thing to me was that nothing about this relationship was like anything in my past relationships: no kissing, no touching, no sex talk, and no "chemistry talk." We had pure honor, sincere respect for one another, and a mutual understanding of God first in our lives. We hadn't even held hands! He loved listening to me and I loved listening to him and we loved learning from each other.

Both of us had an earthly life goal to reach souls for Christ. My goal is reaching and counseling women through the Word and his goal is reaching Muslim men through the Word. God would later bring that together in calling us both to reach lost souls; particularly Muslims, as well as disciple Christian men and women to reach souls, especially Muslims.

Steven and I prayed together about every concern, in thankfulness for meals, our circumstances, and upon departures from each other. We discussed our faith, the Bible, and what God was teaching us day by day. Steven was willing to openly share what God had shown him: for us to have a relationship built on God's love. We prayed together about our relationship.

Unlike other men I met before and who seem to have a one-track mind that is all about sex, Steven's one-track mind was all about God. For the first time, I felt understood by my man, as the woman God made me. It was so good! This was freedom and peace like I had never experienced before with a man in particular. It was a pure miracle sent from God.

Giving Appearances over to God

Now I had to bring to the Lord all my thoughts. I opened up, telling God everything that came to my mind that night. Going over my list of qualities for a husband, I verbalized them, one at a time, to the Lord. Did I see these traits in Steven? Yes, except the one that I needed to completely surrender to the Lord was "good looks." It came to me that I did not think he was my fleshly idea of "good looking." I wondered if I could overcome this obstacle. The more I thought about it, the more it occurred to me that I actually resented all those men who only liked me because of my good looks. All my life, my "good looks" had been a curse.

Now God was asking me, "Do you think it is right to judge a man because of his looks?" I agreed with God that this was wrong. The Word says that man looks on the outside and that is the flesh and God looks on the inside and that is the spirit.

So I asked God, "If, by the time I pick him up tomorrow, You will cleanse me of this sin entirely, then I will know that he is clearly the one you have sent me for eternity. I trust You God and Your sovereign will for my life. Lead me where You want me. I completely surrender it (my flesh-my life as a living sacrifice) all to You, Oh God! My life is in Your hands. In Jesus name, Amen."

The next morning, I picked Steven up from the hotel in my car. When he got in and sat down in the passenger seat, saying "Good morning!" and smiled while looking into my eyes, all of a sudden I fell deeply "in love" with his kind gentle spirit! As I looked into his eyes, I could see his heart of love and he became the most handsome man I had ever met! My heart fluttered with excitement and joy and peace flooded my heart. Yes, God was clearly directing this ship!

"I Can See Jesus in You" is a song that Twila Paris sings. It came to my heart at this moment concerning Steven and has continued to do so throughout our relationship. One line says, "I can see His love on your face." I could see Jesus' love in Steven, and that made him irresistible!

Engaged!

Steven asked to take me to breakfast. After we ate, when we got back in my car and looked at each other, Steven asked, "Do you want to go to get a ring?" I got very excited inside and smiled, just as I am smiling right now, thinking about that moment again. I said, "Ok, I have a girlfriend around this area who has a jewelry store. She told me if I had a need, to come to her." Steven enthusiastically exclaimed, "Let's go!"

After digging out her card from my purse, I called Violetta and she gave me directions. When we arrived there and walked in, Violetta came up to me and hugged me hello. I re-introduced her to Steven. She is such a bubbly joyful Christian gal and she got so excited for us! We began looking for a ring of my taste, with baguettes and an antique look. She found me one that I liked so much, but it was more than the $400 he had in hand. I didn't want to choose a ring more expensive than what he had to spend, so I said "No that is too expensive."

Steven however told Violetta: "its fine, if she likes it."

Then she suggested we get a wedding band too, so we picked that out also and she held it for us for later. She took the engagement ring to the back in order to adjust it a bit.

When she brought it out and handed it to Steven, he got on his knee right there in the store and asked, "Will you marry me?"

I excitedly said, "Yes!" Everyone in the store clapped and cheered, then embraced and congratulated us both. It was official! We were engaged just 27 days after meeting the first time! The perfect love story from our perfect God!

I invited three couples to dinner that night: Violetta and her husband, Sarah and Roger, as well as my friend Nicole and her friend. At my house, Steven and I cooked together. Steven did the cutting and arranging of an appetizer of tomato, fresh mozzarella and basil, while I made my vegetable lasagna and garlic bread. We had a great evening together and they all just loved Steven. On Sunday, Steven and I went to church, where he met a lot of my friends, and everyone instantly loved him.

The hardest thing about the entire four days was leaving Steven at the airport on Monday. Before he left, he told me that even though we had gotten engaged, he wanted to ask my parents for my hand in marriage. He did not want to disrespect my parents. That is the Eastern way. That is the Biblical way.

Steven Asking my Parents for my Hand in Marriage

Now keep in mind, I was 47 years old! I began to warn him, "Don't forget that my parents are not Christian. Also, I must tell you I have only known them to be prejudiced in the past." I asked Steven if he was crazy, but he insisted in honoring my parents this way. I prayed for the Holy Spirit to overcome it all.

So, we went to my parents' house the day before Mother's Day. Steven thoughtfully bought a lovely bouquet of flowers for Mom. At their house, we hung out and talked that evening. That night, Steven slept on the couch while I slept in the spare room with my niece, who was also visiting. The next morning after eating breakfast, Steven got up from his chair and went around to my dad. Getting on his knees, he asked my dad for my hand in marriage!

My dad, looking down at him without understanding, sarcastically said in his quick slurred speech (because of a medical condition) and his Maine accent, "This is a free country!"

Steven asked, "Excuse me, sir?"

My mother chimed in, "Oh, just say yes!"

My father replied, "Whatever."

I felt so sorry for Steven, as I could see how nervous he was by his shakiness. My father was acting like he was laughing at this sincere respectful gentleman. I prayed for God to help him.

Steven went around to my mom and did the same thing. My mother looked down at him, enchanted. She said, "Yes, ok." The whole time, my niece, who was twenty-one at the time, stared at Steven in unbelief, with her mouth wide open. When I think about it now, it was just so precious. One year later, God blessed her with a godly man also.

After breakfast, my parents had to drive my niece to the airport. By the time they returned home, I was cutting up vegetables at the kitchen counter. Mom came right over beside me and began speaking to me quietly while Steven was in the living room reading.

My mother seemed to have changed her mind on that ride. She began trying to talk me out of this marriage, or at least out of the August 7th wedding date we had set. She objected to the place, the timing, and the marriage itself in that "he might be just trying to get American citizenship."

I refused to listen to her objections and felt upset at her lack of support. I then very firmly reminded her, "I no longer take my direction from you, Mom, but from God. God is my authority – not you – thank you. He told me that Steven is my husband. There is nothing you can say to change my mind!"

Then she went into the living room to try to talk Steven out of it. She started by opening a big can of worms, telling Steven that I was not right for him because I had been married and divorced several times and in and out of relationships. She implied that I was no good, basically trashing me.

Steven stopped her and said "Mom, I don't care about her past. All that matters is from today forward." He addressed my mom with the utmost respect and kindness.

She then approached it from another angle by saying "Karen has been hurt too many times. I don't want her to be hurt again!"

Steven reassured her that she shouldn't worry, because he was going to take care of me for the rest of my life. He said, "Don't worry, Mom. I will take good care of her. It will all be alright." He put his arm around her shoulder and walked her into the kitchen, calming her down. God has given him this gift of calming people. Steven's standing up for me made me feel so safe and loved. My father stayed out of the whole thing.

In being created in God's image, I needed His love, but I sought love in all the wrong places, as Satan led me and deceived me. Every time I chose my fleshly desire to find love in the world, in a man, I was worshiping man over God. God's desire is for everyone, including me, to seek love through Him first.

Through my seeking God's love first, He led me to His hearts' desire for me: the one man He designed to love me the way I need to be loved. God loves me for who I am, as a sinner saved by the grace of God. When I finally became a "living sacrifice," the man God sent to me said to my mother, "I don't care about her past." Steven understood and accepted me. He is keeping his promise that he would cherish me forever.

Just as God loves me for who I am, Steven loves me for who I am. He knows I am growing daily in Christ. Let us all be reminded of Jesus' words in Matthew 19:6 'what God has put together, let no man (or woman) separate'.

When it was time to go to bed that night, Steven went to the couch and began to spread out the sheets. Mom came in and offered for him to sleep in the bedroom with me. Steven looked at me in surprise with discomfort, although I wasn't surprised. I told my mom, "No. We will not sleep in the same room." She thought that was ridiculous because we are all adults here. This is the same mother, I thought, who used to fight with me when I was a teenager, demanding that boys couldn't be alone with me in their house.

Instead of pleasing God, when people give into pleasing others, they fail in comprehension of making distinction between right and wrong. I am saddened of how my mother has changed so much in going further from God's principles. I was so embarrassed by such a notion, because I had surely changed and could see God's purpose in protecting me now. My mother was simply not accepting those principles at all, which are based on God's Word. I know even today that she was trying to mock God in me. Maybe she would feel better about herself if I were the same as she. Steven and I together won out, however, and slept in separate rooms, as we did until our wedding night. Honoring God by not sleeping together was not a priority to her, but it certainly was to us.

When Steven and I left the next day, we talked about all this. As far as Steven was concerned, he took my mother's first answer: "Yes" as the answer from the Lord. He considered her second answer: "No" as the flesh fighting back against the Spirit. I am still amazed today at how the Holy Spirit can come over anyone for God's glory, even the ungodly. So we were both convinced that God had called us together in marriage and had big plans for us.

Nana and Steven

Although Steven didn't meet my Nana in person before our marriage, she talked to him on the phone. When I shared we would be married she was very happy for me and affirmed Steven on those calls. Several months later when Nana met Steven, I could tell right away that she was at peace and had an instant love for him. She now saw that God had sent the special man He had for me. Later, she never forgot, even when she was almost 100 years old, to send her love and greetings to Steven when I would call her weekly to talk to her on the phone.

Before God brought Steven and me together, my Nana once looked me straight in the eyes and asked me, "Karen, how can you be with all those men?"

I looked into her loving eyes and cried out to her from my heart. I passionately exclaimed with tears, "Nana, I just want to be loved!" Those words resonated in my spirit many times over in those years to come. I will never forget that conversation. I feel that at the time, her question really got me thinking more about the future before jumping into another relationship.

Before my Nana passed, I know she was also very concerned for Mom, as these were some of the last words she said to me about her "Karen, I am really concerned about your Mother."

I answered, "Yes, Nana, me too."

"Who does she remind you of?" Nana asked.

"Grandpa," I replied.

"Yes," she answered sadly.

My grandfather was a very bitter and depressed person most of his life. His disposition, however, never seemed to affect Nana's attitude of joy. I have now begun to cry. Tears are rolling down my cheeks as I reminisce about Nana. She was so dear to me. I miss her so. Now God brings me the thought about being with her in Heaven. Yes, she will be there, waiting to see Steven and me too! Somehow, I think she remained on earth a little longer just to see me turn my life around. I also know that if Steven weren't with me to comfort me at the time of losing her, I would not have overcome it well.

God's Purpose

We all have choices daily to allow life circumstances to grow us and make us a better or a bitter person. If we desire to become better we must seek God's help through His Word, prayer and in fellowship with godly people. When people choose to become bitter, they hold grudges by blaming others. Rather than taking responsibility to choose right they set themselves on a path of self-annihilation.

Steven and I were so blessed recently by a new movie we saw together called *The Song*. It was extremely moving. Parts of *The Song of Solomon* were narrated throughout the movie, as the lead male role experienced the consequences of his choices, both good and bad. As God directed his good choice in marrying his wife, he was so blessed in it. He was inspired in the gift God gave him to sing and made a hit love song that rocked the world.

Like Solomon in his taste of success and prosperity, as the devil would have it, the temptation came to rob him of his blessings. Everything depended upon his own choice to be tempted or not. Because I had already seen this same scenario and been tempted in my own life, I screamed at him inside, "No! It's not worth it. You already have God's blessing upon you. Don't risk it!"

The luring of the devil's taunt that I saw on the screen gave me the creeps inside. I was reminded of how I was once so susceptible to Satan's taunt. Although, the movie concluded on the man's return to his family by following godly principles, I could still feel my body trembling when departing the theater, being on the lookout for the evil one who may be prowling around, looking to destroy me, as I gripped my husband's arm tightly. Quickly, the Holy Spirit filled my soul, reminding me of how truly blessed I am in my life. I made sure I let my husband know that night and we praised God together of how blessed we both are to be walking with Christ in our calling.

God's Word in I Thessalonians 4:1-5 (NKJV) says:

"Finally then, brethren, we urge and exhort in the Lord Jesus that you should abound more and more, just as you received from us how you ought to walk and to please God; for you know what commandments we gave you through the Lord Jesus. For this is the will of God, your sanctification: that you should abstain from sexual immorality; that each of you should know how to possess his own vessel in sancti-

fication and honor, not in passion of lust, like the Gentiles who do not know God;"

Lord help us, Your children, to be holy and walk in Your will as we ought and that nothing the devil does to tempt us away from walking in sanctification with You will take us away from Your beautiful perfect blessed will. Please help us to exhort You and help our brothers and sisters to walk worthy of the calling that You have laid upon each of our lives to keep us holy and set apart as your unblemished Bride, blameless before You, in preparing us for the coming of our Bridegroom.

God's purpose for all people has always been for all of His children to spend eternity in His perfect divine presence because of His eternal perfect love for each one of us. He created people for a love relationship with Him. For Christ, our Bridegroom's love for the church, the Bride, caused Him to give Himself up for the Bride, as we read in Ephesians 5:25, to make her holy, cleansing her by the washing with water through The Word, and to present her to Himself as a radiant church, without stain, or wrinkle, or any other blemish but holy and blameless.

It is up to each of us to freely choose to trust and obey the Word, Jesus, whom God sent to restore that love so He can have relationship with us, His creation, His children made in His image. Jesus willingly laid down His life as a sacrifice for you and me. Are you willing to lay your earthly life down for Him as I did and make Him LORD? We are all guilty of sin and deserve death. Jesus is completely innocent of all sin, yet as an innocent lamb led to the slaughter, He willingly took the punishment you and I deserved to set us all free of captivity to Satan's power.

The final sacrifice has been paid so we don't need to die and go to hell. God is asking you to choose to believe, to trust in Jesus and allow Him to lead your life as He wills so that He can bless you abundantly, as He has me. He continues to do so. Won't you join me and choose today to give up your earthly life for Jesus so He can use you too?

11

Marrying My True Love!

The Lord sent you into my life,
As an angel sent from heaven above,
Easing my journey into Life,
Enveloping me with wonder of love,
Love that I had never known.

When we first held hands,
I felt a touch only you could provide.
Grown has our fellowship in Him,
And our abode in passion of His love,
Indeed only HE could provide.

I wait the day when we begin our life,
With that special first kiss on the day,
When He will bring us together,
With the intensity of our love,
And His love so incredibly clear!

Karen, when I look into your eyes,
I see a caring and unconditional love
That shines from them.
That makes me long with excitement
For our life together in Him to come.

With our first kiss on the day we wed,
Promising my unconditional love,
Cherishing each day
That the Father gives me with you,
In our little piece of heaven on earth.
I will love you always.

This is one of the many poems Steven wrote to me over our time of courtship and even after marriage. I pined over Steven during the weeks before marriage, pouring over his deep, emotional expressions of love through his poems. Every time I would receive one of these expressions of his love for me, my heart would skip a beat. This was one of the benefits of his gift of writing. God is so good and He knew oh so well the needs of my heart, so abundantly more than I could dream or imagine.

The Enemy's Attempts to destroy our Love Story

Practicing Muslims hate apostates even in the West. A few weeks after our engagement, Steven flew to England for his last speaking engagement on Islam there. Although the advertisement was sent by the organizers to churches, they did not realize that one of the church buildings was now owned by Muslims and converted into an Islamic center.

When Steven went to the venue where he was scheduled to speak, he was almost pelted by protesters with fruits and vegetables as the hall was adjacent to the fruit and vegetable market. Being quite concerned I texted him asking how he was. Steven texted back that "the fruits & vegetables they were throwing at him could have been much more wisely used to feed a lot of *starving* children!" While his humor was endearing, I urgently started praying for God to protect him, so he would not get hurt.

As it had happened in the past on several occasions, the police escorted him back to the home where he was staying. The organizers decided that the event should be cancelled. I praised God for protecting him but it is sad to see life and freedom of speech in danger. I can clearly see the writing on the wall in this that we will soon face similar problems here in the US, especially since Christians are not only being violently persecuted to death in Middle Eastern countries but Christians are now being taken to court for hate crimes and for speaking the truth in this country. Two days later he was on the plane back to the USA.

The next day while I was at work, Steven sent me a text saying that he was at the airport in Philadelphia making a connecting flight to return to Florida. About a half hour later, he sent me a text that immigration officials were taking him into a room after checking his bags. Then I didn't hear anything more. I began to pray with all my might, "Oh Lord I know he belongs to you, so I pray You will protect him from any harm. He is in Your hands now, Lord."

I was concerned, but knew I had no other choice but to trust our Father God to take care of him. When I got another text telling me he was now on the plane to Florida, I took a breath. A sigh of relief slipped from my lips and I thanked God for His protection!

In the weeks to come, the enemy tried to destroy our marriage before it even happened. One of the Bible study leaders at my church invited Steven to one of the more expensive restaurants in town. His whole intention was to sit down with Steven and bring every Scripture he could find—taken out of context—to convince Steven that he was "in sin" if he planned to marry me. This was a guy in the singles group who had actually told me that my views of purity were strong enough to "qualify" me to be a part of his exclusive home Bible study. Now, he was "stabbing me in the back" in trying to talk Steven out of marrying me.

It definitely triggered every bit of fleshly anger I had, though Steven helped calm me. Steven shared the details of the meeting with me, saying that this man did not understand the context and meaning of the Scriptures in question. However, this man never agreed and told him he would never go to our wedding. God must have dealt with him though, because much to our surprise, he did attend our wedding after all.

Then, another guy with whom Steven was staying told him that he needed to toughen up, by putting his foot down and "shaping me up" to be much more submissive. He said Steven was wrong to let me have so much *say* in the relationship. It is amazing how men who have experienced nothing but failure in their own relationships with women have so much advice to give others. Praise God for Steven's strong Scriptural background and study. None of these trials even moved him or disturbed him. Solomon writes in Song of Songs 8:7 "Many waters cannot quench love nor can the floods drown it".

The most severe way Satan tried to destroy God's love story for us was through the objections of the board members of Steven's ministry. Steven's trip to England included a sit down meeting with the board members of one of the key ministries in which he served. They told him that if he married me, they would not support him in his outreach. Their reasoning was due to their specific denominational views against divorce and remarriage. They believe that a person who has been divorced should never marry again.

The above are three examples of well-intended but misguided interpretations of Scripture by other Christians. My observation of the lives of the two men in my church revealed they had issues with male pride, exhorting themselves as being more knowledgeable of the Word than others or maybe just a bit envious. Only God knows the deep-rooted issues that plague them. I pray for them to see the light so they can be blessed as God has blessed us. Again, let us remember: what God has put together, let no man separate (Matthew 19:6).

Premarital Class and Counseling
We had already begun our premarital classes before Steven's trip to England, but Steven only missed one class. We were taking the classes in Fort Lauderdale at my church. Steven stayed on the couch of one of the single guys who co-led one of the home Bible study groups I attended. This was a true blessing for us.

Around 100 couples attended this premarital class. Different pastors and leaders taught it. The Biblical counselor head, Pastor John, put on skits, performed by various people, to address different topics. The class was divided into table groups, each led by a couple who had already had training and a solid marriage. There was discussion and prayer time after the teaching.

The leaders followed the workbook we read, asking questions for the couples in each table group to answer. Sadly, many of those couples were not living according to God's commands, which He gave to protect us. Steven and I just couldn't believe how freely some couples would talk about going away together and staying in some hotel together before marriage, without batting an eye. Thankfully, Calvary Chapel encouraged people not to live together before marriage, as well as to abstain from sexual intimacy until they were wed.

Not all people heed this Biblical advice. They are accountable to God for their choices. That's the thing about unconditional love: it always gives people free choice. It never forces itself upon anyone. God's love is unconditional and pure.

A huge part of the premarital class was using Biblical counseling and also included an accountability program with a pastor of the church. God chose Pastor Bernard King as our accountability pastor. This was no coincidence, due to the large number of pastors in this specific mega church. I greatly admire and love Pastor Bernard because his sermons are just so passionate; I always related to them. He is also the one who counseled me to serve in the women's ministry rather than a co-ed ministry two years earlier. It was just the right advice!

In our counseling accountability sessions, Pastor Bernard told us we were a rare couple, based on our belief in purity and the way we conducted ourselves prior to marriage. Steven was shocked at this statement. I, too, was disappointed, as I really thought it would be different for most Christians than in the world. Christians are to live what they believe and follow God's commandments. His commandments include purity.

Through my own experience, I knew that the world of people outside of Christianity do not live a life of purity. I explained this to Steven. When I was living in disobedience to God, my "old self" never thought there was anything wrong with premarital sex and living together. It seemed to be the way of the modern culture of America. In the Song of Songs, Solomon expresses the power and beauty of true love with the context of marriage. It also exposes the perversion of love and intimacy outside of marriage as in our culture today. Steven found himself surprised at how this ungodliness was rampant in what he thought was the only real Christian nation in the world.

Although I had lived outside of God's rules, God restored my purity as I grew in my relationship with Jesus Christ. Following God's rules that protect people from temptation, Steven and I did not even kiss. We lived separately until our wedding night. We stayed away from temptation out of love and reverence for our wonderful Creator and for each other.

As for Steven, even when he came out of Islam, he stayed separate from women. I thank God that Steven, in his surrender of his flesh to God through the power of the Holy Spirit, did not struggle with this fleshly weakness, unlike many American Christians do today. The Christians in the West used to heed the standards of males and females remaining separate unless married, which is Biblical. This is where the East has to re-teach the West. God is clearly calling His true followers in America to be set apart from our immoral culture and follow the Biblical standards. Being pure and following God's commands concerning sex causes us to shine as a "beacon of light" in the growing darkness around us. Be holy as He is holy is what the Word says.

I pray daily for the unity, as Jesus prayed for in John 17:20-23, and the purity of the body of Christ. The *bride* of Christ should be pure and holy, set apart in preparation for her *Bridegroom*, Jesus the Christ, our soon coming King. Are you living holy and set apart as a follower of Christ, as His Word teaches us in Leviticus 20:7,26, I Peter 2:9 and Romans 12:1-2 and throughout Scripture? Are you ready as His holy Bride for Christ' return? For the Word says that many will say, "But Lord, I cast out demons in your name" and He will say, "I never knew you" (Matthew 7:21-23).

The Shepherd knows His sheep. His sheep know His voice and have the Peace of our assurance in Christ. I hope you will submit and surrender all of you and your earthly life at the cross so you can take the hand of your Bridegroom on that great day. I am praying for you today.

Sinful Lifestyle Does Not Follow Christ's Example

The grim reality, according to the leaders of this premarital class, was that only about one out of every four couples in this class of a hundred couples was actually going to get married and was living right for God. From our table, only one other couple got married besides us.

How sad this is. I remember quite a few of the attendees sharing that they were there together as a couple just to see if they were right for each other, almost like an experiment. Steven and I were appalled and saddened at the lack of commitment to God's leading in these believers. Because of the worldly principles we heard coming out of their mouths, we were not surprised when we found out later that the majority of the couples in our premarital class did not get married.

For me, sharing in the class with fellow believers was very new, as was having a male relationship based on the Word of God. You see, I found that God restored "what the locusts had eaten" (Joel 2:25). I felt completely brand new! My youth had returned, and I felt like a young adult who had just met the man God had designed for me, even at 47 years old. I felt like I was in a true and healthy relationship for the first time. I was experiencing firsthand Jesus making all things new (Revelation 21:5) in my life through this marriage and this calling.

Who Jesus really is and how He makes all things new was shown in the movie *The Passion of the Christ* by Mel Gibson. Jesus tries to carry the cross through the crowded streets after being beaten almost beyond recognition. In this scene, Jesus' mother, Mary, sees Him pass by; she is absolutely devastated. Just then, Jesus falls down under the weight of the cross. As He does, her thoughts go back to a time when He was a small child. In this memory He falls down, and she runs to Him and picks Him up, holds Him, and comforts Him. As the memory ends, she is on her feet, running to Jesus as He lies beneath the cross. When she grabs hold of Him, Jesus looks at her through His blood and pain and says, "See, Mother, I make all things new."

I cried the hardest at that very moment in the movie as my own pain gripped me, remembering how I was also there to pick up my son when he was a boy. His choice as an adult to be estranged from me just broke me inside. However, I turn my attention to what the prophet Isaiah says in Isaiah 43:18-21:

> *"Do not remember the former things, nor consider the things of old. Behold, I will do a new thing, now it shall spring forth; shall you not know it? I will even make a road in the wilderness and rivers in the desert. The beast of the field will honor Me, the jackals and the ostriches, because I give waters in the wilderness and rivers in the desert, to give drink to My people, My chosen. This people I have formed for Myself; they shall declare My praise."*

What a privilege it is to be a chosen child of God! Because of this, God's Spirit moved me to care for His children, other women who also needed to be made new, by being transformed by the renewing of their minds to prove His good, acceptable, and perfect will (Romans 12:2).

When we choose to turn our lives around and become a "living sacrifice" to Him, we need to commit to following the Bible's principles for our lives, no matter what our friends or families think. I had learned the hard way that I could not trust anyone to tell me what is right or not, for Satan can use anyone to tempt me to let down my guard. I had experienced this all my life.

In order to live God's way, I had to deny friends and family and had to make the conscious decision to choose to follow the principles in God's Word, as I did before Steven and I were married when my mother tried to get Steven and me to sleep in the same room together at her house. If the intention of one's heart is to truly be obedient to God's Word alone, not to any other philosophy or person or book, God will give us all the power and strength we need to do so. His Word says He does not let us be tempted beyond what we can bear (1 Corinthians 10:13).

Wedding Preparation

During our courtship, I am so grateful God provided a place for Steven to stay so we could spend time together, going to Bible studies and out to eat at restaurants, where we began planning our wedding within that three-month time period before August 7, 2005. We also went to different stores to order the flowers and decorations for the big day.

This was going to be a low budget outdoor wedding, to be held at my friend Nicole's house. I just loved the layout of her house for a party. The outside beauty is perfect for pictures. Since we did not have the funds to pay the $500 it would cost to rent the banquet hall at my church, Nicole graciously offered us the use of her lovely house and yard for free. Steven and I greatly appreciated this thoughtful gift!

Since we were both limited in our finances, we decided to ask our guests, mostly all my friends who were becoming his friends too, to each bring a covered dish. I think they call this a "football wedding." We rented tables, outdoor fans, and a tent that we would set up to extend from the garage over the driveway to cover the guests from weather.

I asked my favorite pastor, Pastor Bernard King, to marry us and he agreed. He saw God's divine matchmaking working beyond any human understanding. While I was living in obedience to God, focusing on ministering to women by using my gifts to serve Him, God sent me my "Boaz" from afar, all the way from Pakistan in the far East to the West - first to England, then to Florida - where God brought us together.

God brought us together through equipping me in understanding Islam, a common interest and calling upon our lives. It started out as Steven's passion—to help Muslims come to assurance of salvation through Jesus Christ. Human understanding might have reasoned that I would find my "Boaz" in the mega church I attended. However, God sent him, not through a large congregation, but through us individually seeking to serve Him by reaching the lost with the gifts God gave each of us.

We need never underestimate the Power of God Almighty. Yes, God was clearly preparing us both all along for our wedding as well as for the Wedding supper of the Lamb in our eternity with our Bridegroom, Jesus.

My Wedding Day: How Did I Get Here?

Only now I am getting a flashback of where God took me from – up out of the miry pit of being a woman with many husbands and lovers like the woman at the well, or like Mary Madeline.

Mary, who out of her incredibly deep gratitude for her Redeemer's grace and mercy, was possibly sopping up off the ground the blood of the only man who could save her and restore what the locust had eaten, Jesus. The "Suffering Servant" (Jesus) had been beaten beyond recognition (Isaiah 52:14). His innocent blood was poured out for her and for me (Isaiah 53) as He was crucified. How amazing is His grace!

Is it all a dream? Here I am with the man I love, in front of our Pastor. "I promise, from this day forward, for better or for worse, in sickness and in health, till death do we part," I repeated.

I had said these words before, yet this time was different. Today, I knew that unlike before, I truly meant every word I was saying, in my heart and not just in my head. Most importantly, I knew that he meant his own promises to me and truly meant them for a lifetime. I had a joy and peace like I had never felt before. I had no doubts.

I knew that this time was forever after. Just like a dream I had as a young girl, it felt like a fairy tale came true. I truly felt like Cinderella. God had sent me my true Prince Charming in His perfect plan of our male and female union in divine Covenant. God had created our incredible relationship. But this time, my carriage wouldn't turn back into a pumpkin and I wouldn't go back to being a slave to a male master. Thank You God, thank You!

In a flash, as my thoughts went back to my previous marriages, I compared them to the here and now and the beautiful truths of this day. There was no comparison! I refused to allow myself to go there anymore, focusing my eyes and thoughts on the man in front of me, and how much I adored him and everything about him. This man, the humblest man I had ever met, loves me. His sweet nature is evident to all who meet him and is not just a performance to get me. I love him so much. Our love is more than just a feeling.

Defining love as merely a feeling is the lie the world believes. Feelings come and go, but Truth remains forever. True love never fails and is unconditional.

Love is patient, love is kind. It does not envy, it does not boast, it is not proud. It does not dishonor others, it is not self-seeking, it is not easily angered, it keeps no record of wrongs. Love does not delight in evil but rejoices with the truth. It always protects, always trusts, always hopes, always perseveres.

My favorite part is that it rejoices with truth. These truths come out of the mouth of God in His Word in I Corinthians 13:4-7. I can finally be free to speak truth with my true love without condemnation.

On our wedding day, these thoughts engulfed me with warmth: "This day is different because today is the first time we kissed each other! Tonight, the first night of our marriage, will be the first time we are intimate with each other. This day is different because we never lived together first, as I did in the majority of my past relationships."

This marriage is different than my past relationships because we pray together and have total transparency with each other. We now live together, sleep together, eat together, and work together in God's calling upon our lives. This marriage is different, because according to the world, people cannot spend this much time together without "killing each other."

Even as I write this book, over ten years after our wedding day, I am amazed at how much I am in love with this man whom God so beautifully brought into my life, without my help. Yes, Father God surely knows what is best for His dearly beloved children, of which I know I am one. It is such a beautiful truth and it is available to you too. He waits only upon you to choose to make Him LORD over all of your life so He can bless you too.

Handsome From the Inside Out

I had learned from my mother: "You can marry a rich man just as easy as a poor man." My father was handsome but poor. I learned in the American culture in which I was raised that the ideal man should be "tall, dark, and handsome" and I was always given the counsel, "You've got to have chemistry." My heart desires that all women will realize these are lies from the world to keep you in bondage.

I heard from my family and my friends all of my life the questions: "When will you marry?"

"Who will you marry?"

"Have you met anyone special yet?"

"Had any 'hot dates' lately?"

"Do you have a boyfriend yet?"

These questions made me feel as if I would never really be complete unless I was married or with someone, and that those all around me would talk if I didn't have someone special. Is it any wonder why I searched the world over for "the love of my life" yet ended up searching for love in all the wrong places?

Another reason my wedding day with Steven was different from any of my previous experiences is because Steven is so handsome on the inside. Society certainly frowns upon such a notion as to value the heart of the man more than his outward appearance. Steven does not fit the ideal American man on the outside. He is short, dark, honest, and far from financially rich, but he is incredibly *spiritually* rich. As a matter of fact, he came to America with only a suitcase and a few dollars in his pocket. He owned nothing but a laptop computer. He wasn't well established in a powerful position in America, according to the world's standards. Although he was highly educated, his only source of income was from an internet ministry and part time teaching position. As you now know, he lost even that income two and a half months after he married me, against the will of the board majority. Not one member of his side of the family or mine, including my parents or my son, came to our wedding. While that might be understandable from his side, since he was a foreigner, my parents had retired here in Florida, the state in which we married. I did not get so much as a card from my own family members.

Beautiful Wedding

The delicious food, the beautiful flower arrangements, the awesome photography, the wonderful location, and wonderful service were all free - thanks to our lovely friends. The other costs were nominal. Our wedding gifts paid for our honeymoon. This day, along with our honeymoon week, was the most exciting and happiest time of my whole life before this. It is very possible this day was an answer to the prayers of my grandmother, Nana. It was most certainly an answer to ours.

God provided everything we needed for the wedding to be the most perfect and beautiful day of my life. Steven and I had around 125 Floridian friends with us from church. Steven's spiritual parents from England came as well, and we had a wonderful time. Thank God for them and that God protected their travels, even though they almost missed their flight. They have been divinely involved in Steven's life; God used them to help rescue Steven from attempts made on his life by his enemies, who hate him for accepting Jesus as his Savior.

The color scheme for our wedding displayed God's grace: black for sin, red for the precious blood of Jesus Christ, and white for Jesus washing our sins away and making us pure in Him. All who choose Jesus as their Savior are made pure through His blood, shed once for all of us.

My friend Sarah professionally arranged all the flowers: delicate red and white roses gracing the backyard while yellow roses, both of our favorites, decorated the head table. I made the wedding cake and Sarah added real flowers to it, which gave the cake a lovely touch.

I had gotten my wedding dress at a local bridal store. A woman at a local shop made the Victorian hat to go with the dress. I wore the beautiful cross that Steven gave me, all as a visual to remind him of the dream God had given him years earlier. The guys wore formal black tuxes with white shirts and red cummerbunds. By the sweat on their brows and the looks on their faces, I could tell they were "praising me" for that brilliant idea on this Floridian hot summer day! The girls wore vibrant red dresses with red hats and just looked beautiful!

As I write this today, I am reminded of the Revelation from Jesus Christ that God gave John through the angel of what will soon come: "I saw the Holy City, the new Jerusalem, coming down out of heaven from God, prepared as a bride beautifully dressed for her husband." (Revelation 21:2) There I was standing before my husband beautifully dressed just for him. I am also reminded of the Prophet Isaiah (61:10) foretelling: "I delight greatly in the LORD; my soul rejoices in my God. For he has clothed me with garments of salvation and arrayed me in a robe of his righteousness, as a bridegroom adorns his head like a priest, and as a bride adorns herself with her jewels."

We stood adorned under a white wooden arched arbor to get married, with red and white flowers and tulle all around it. Pastor Bernard, with the bridal party standing on either side, stood under a big tree, all in the front of the house. My good friend Tracy was my maid of honor; Reatha, my accountability partner and pro-life director was my bridesmaid. Steven's best man was Bruce, his longtime friend from England; Tony, Steven's housing host, was the second fellow standing up with Steven.

We hired a DJ from our church group. My friend Eunice took the pictures, along with our friend, Bret. Our wedding albums are full of beautiful memories, perfectly taken by our dear friends for free. We are immensely grateful!

Picture of 1 Peter 3:7

Though it was extremely hot on our wedding day, there happened to be a pervasive breeze, especially near the candles we were to light with our butane lighter. As I tried to light my candle, I didn't seem to have the strength to get the lighter working. Steven would help me, then give it back to me to light my candle. Relentlessly, the butane flame would go out again while I was trying to light it, without Steven's strength helping me.

We needed to get our own candles lit so we could then use our individual candles to light the main candle together, symbolizing unity. This ordeal took around five minutes, due to how long it took me to realize how much I needed Steven's strength in lighting that candle. I can now see how this symbolized 1 Peter 3:7. As a woman, my strength is weaker than my husband's strength. I see this fact constantly in our lives, in many different scenarios. God gave me this man of strength for many important reasons.

God built Steven just for me, as He knew I needed the strongest man out there. After learning firsthand how relentlessly stubborn Muslims are, I can see why they become the strongest in holding true to Christ when they convert to the truth of Jesus being their Lord and Savior. They have tremendous gratitude for their salvation. I now see how God saw all of this in advance and I am just discovering it. I am so excited to share this revelation with you.

Paz and his female friend from Calvary Chapel choir did a beautiful job singing "When God Made You" by *Newsong*. Looking at Steven, I sang it in my heart, mouthing the words to him while they were singing. The words of this song "When God made you, He must have been thinking about me" have come true more and more as our relationship blooms. I did the same, singing the words to God while looking up to the sky, when they sang, "I Am" by Nicole C. Mullen. The Spirit of God had clearly come over me as I sang. I still get moved with tingles every time I hear these two songs.

At the reception gathering in the back, Steven and I shared what we wrote to each other. Then, we danced to Christian songs that I had picked out in advance, for the most part. The food was gourmet food, better than any caterer could have made. When the thunderstorm arrived at the end of the wedding, we ended the day inside Nicole's house. It was a wonderful day, all in all. The Holy Spirit filled us to overflowing that day!

Love and Married Life

That night after the wedding, Steven and I experienced together the absolute divine and ideal will of God being fulfilled, in a perfect blending of two becoming one flesh. For the first time, I completely understood what Song of Solomon (2:7; 3:5; 8:4) meant: *"Swear to me, young women of Jerusalem… that you won't awaken or arouse love before its proper time!"* (ISV) It was clearly God's beautiful and perfect timing, as we followed His voice and now I knew 'true love waits'.

I discovered for the first time there is no shame or guilt inside the context of a covenant marriage as it was meant to be in Genesis 2:25 for Adam and Eve. The idea that true love is just the act of sex is a lie. True love is truly "love making" as God intended it to be. I recently heard something I feel is profound and true based on my own experience. A Christian counselor said that if you are only seeking self-pleasure in sex, rather than God's pleasure in intimacy, you are a danger to yourself and to the other person involved. I couldn't agree more from my own experience. God's plan is far beyond our human understanding, and nothing like our American culture or media projects it.

To keep the details sacred, as they are meant to be, I'd like to share a joke that I heard David Jeremiah tell. This joke describes it perfectly: There was a Christian family, the Jones, who inherited a parrot. The parrot embarrassed all the members of the family by continuously repeating the words "Let's kiss!" over and over, especially in front of visitors.

One day at church, a new family, the Martins, came. They shared with the Jones family that they had a parrot too, but it would not stop repeating the words "Let's pray!"

So, the Jones family thought it would be a great idea to invite the Martins over for dinner, as well as their parrot. They thought that maybe the Jones' parrot saying, "Let's pray!" would influence their own parrot, encouraging it to stop saying, "Let's kiss!" They hoped this would solve their problem.

Now, the day came for the Martins to come to the Jones' house for dinner. The parrots met each other. Sure enough, the Jones' parrot blurted out, "Let's kiss!" In an instant response, the Martins' parrot chirped with loud praise, "Glory! My prayers have been answered!"

Well, I praise God for answering the desires of my heart and Steven's prayers as well. God's perfect matchmaking abilities outdo all I could have imagined.

After our first night together, we left for our honeymoon. We went to Marco Island and then on to Clearwater, stopping at Naples to explore and have dinner. The outlet shops around us got me excited about going from men's shop to men's shop, to find new clothes for Steven. I had noticed that he needed a woman's touch in the wardrobe area, especially because he was in front of the public, speaking and teaching. After all, one of my gifts was having a fashion sense and now I could use it for God's glory.

For the first six months of married life, we would wake up every morning and question if maybe we were in Heaven instead of on earth. We kept pinching each other to see if it was all for real. It truly was hard for us both to believe that our dreams had come true and God had sent us true love. I had never before realized that God is such an incredible matchmaker. I have now found out how important it is to let Him do the job.

Steven had always worn clothes that were too big for him, so the "package" was never revealed to me in advance. Only after marriage did I realize he was more than I had ever imagined. His heart was so big, I never really thought about the physical aspects before marriage. We were definitely, perfectly, and literally "a match made in Heaven!" God certainly made us perfect for the other in every way you can think of and more. I felt so blessed and still do to this day.

Since that time, we have both learned about our temperaments. Only God would know that our area of affection was the same and made a perfect recipe. This divine God-ordained match in intimacy blows the whole concept of "two people must have chemistry" right out of the water! Trust me, God works intimacy out more perfectly than any human being can orchestrate.

It took us about a year or so to adjust to each other's cultural ways, our different temperaments, communication traits, accents and sayings. It also took time for Steven to learn more about women, and for me to learn that a man can be humble, selfless, and just love me for me. We were both so blessed to have the other to listen to our "God stories" – how God worked in all things in our lives. It was so freeing to just be able to share God's truths without the opposition we had both experienced in the past.

We would never run out of conversations in sharing what God would do daily in our lives. Our life together has been such a wonderful blessing! We just celebrated ten incredible years together at a Bed and Breakfast on the beach and it was such a perfect blessing! God sent three days of His sunshine on us while it had continuously rained before and after our tenth year anniversary celebration!

Best Bosom Friends!

While I praise God also for my dear female bosom friends today, including Tracy, Terry, Salwa, Laura, and Violetta, Steven has become my best bosom friend after Jesus Christ! He has made a lifetime commitment to be my best bosom friend, in spite of all my daily weaknesses. I still struggle occasionally with a temper and feeling offended – like Anne of Green Gables. My loving yet tender heart gets pricked when those I love dearly reject me and it instantly makes me shriek.

Steven, the love of my life, loves me just the way I am, with no expectations or judgment of my broken past, much like the way the prophet Hosea loved Gomer, with all of her junk. God's grace and Steven's patience have given me more and more wisdom to change for the better in growing to become more like Christ daily. My past living in promiscuity was a deep search for someone to love me just the way I was. While God forgave me and threw my sins as far as the East is from the West, the consequences would seep into some of our future.

For instance, while I came out of the worldly American sinful culture, having been redeemed by God, my family's sinful ways of using the Lord's name in vain, abusing the use of alcohol, and being surrounded with friends hostile to my new way of life and most certainly my husband's godly lifestyle, still affect us today. Therefore, no family I had, though fairly large in number, would make an effort to be around us. Even when Steven and I go to their hometowns, they rarely invite us to visit. That, added to Steven's family disowning him, leaves us deeply and forever grateful for our spiritual brothers and sisters who walk beside us on this earth, with more love than we sometimes know what to do with. God is so good in providing us exactly what we both need. We are eternally grateful to Him and bow down in devotion.

My own old ways of dealing with conflict would cause friction at times in our marriage. However, now I have my faith to dwell on. God had made His castle in my heart and I go there and talk with the King in difficult times. He is my Rock and my Salvation, my Refuge!

God created humans to be social, and He uses like-minded kindred spirits to remind me that I have the capacity to love others and stand in the face of controversy and danger. Yes, having true friendship after a poverty of loneliness is like a rare golden coin, a highly valued pearl, or your own version of manna from Heaven, given by the One Loving God who created you. Every time you are listened to, valued and accepted, it is like the greatest treasure, feeling richer than all the earth.

I'm so glad I was given the strength from my Lord to let go of past friends to embrace new ones in my maturity and growth in Christ. I needed to make room for the new. I did and I have been abundantly blessed. Only now looking back do I realize how desperately I needed to let go of past friends and places in order to learn and grow, so to be prepared for the abundantly blessed life I now truly value and thank God for daily. Best friends may be inseparable for a season before the road divides when we each take a separate road geographically, politically or spiritually but trusting our loving God in faith that He has a truly valuable and abundant blessing ahead – friends who will walk with us spiritually by default. We relish in the miracles God does and the incredible glorious future we have in Christ that is too beautiful to imagine!

The Importance of Listening to God!

The only regret Steven and I have is not having children together and enjoying more time together. We left the possibility of us having children up to God, and it has not happened. We feel that if we had met earlier in life, we would have had many children.

When I have prayed about it, I am reminded there are consequences to abortions. I then remembered a doctor I went to a few times who blurted out words that seemed to complain about a botched one, after which he made the comment: "Abortion is not a form of birth control!" Even if he turned the blame on me, it certainly was also my wrong choices that got me there. I thank God that Steven has not shown much regret, as God has certainly kept him busy being attentive to lost souls and that satisfies him.

As we reflect on our individual lives before we met, we both remember when we had been in the same general geographical area at the same time. We both remember God calling us to go in one direction and our own stubborn characters, listening to the taunting of Satan rather than to God, leading us each to our own demise of not being together earlier. We both regret our free choices that led us down the path of destruction in our love life and farther away from each other. Through our pasts, we both learned the hard way how to listen closer to the voice of the Lord when it comes to marriage. When it is God's doing, you have no doubts, but complete peace as you obey Him. God is so good and knows who will enhance your life so He can be glorified!

I have never looked back and wondered if my marriage to Steven was right, the way I did every time in my past when I let my flesh lead me to a man. God maintains the marriages He puts together. When we allow Him, He takes the weeds out along the way as we both grow closer to Christ, and to each other.

As a couple, we are a stronger unit. My husband and I have been together for over ten years, almost eleven and it feels as if we have known each other all our lives. We understand each other so well already, for we have the same Father who created us, whom we aim to emulate. We have complete transparency in communication. We both have a common goal to work toward: the purpose God has given us in life. He is our Director. We don't struggle with who is going to do what, because God has gifted me to do the things Steven doesn't do and has gifted Steven to do what I don't do. Together, we are like a well-greased machine that hums beautifully. God's true love is like a peaceful river that eases along, flowing gently through life with some curves and waterfalls, and rapids of ups and downs.

Through our marriage, we are being prepared as the Bride for our ultimate Bridegroom, Jesus. We do this in growing from glory to glory, in overcoming obstacles and learning to submit to our spouse through transparent communication and mutual understanding in our intimate relationship, while all along emulating and becoming more like Jesus every day. The Word of God is our guide and standard to live by and we are blessed every day!

Trust me; Satan does not want you to listen to what I have written in this book. He is miserable and knows his destiny is eternal destruction; he wants you there with him. The choice is yours; follow the holy manual, the Bible, or follow your own way, which is Satan's way. Heaven or Hell begins right here on earth and leads you to eternity in one or the other. It is your free choice.

12

Amidst trials the fruit of Service

When doors are slammed shut

The first trial we faced in our newly married life together was hurricane Wilma, which brought winds of 154 miles an hour to the Pompano, FL area. When Steven had asked me about previous hurricanes I faced and the importance of preparation, I was rather flippant about it. I had only seen up to 75 miles an hour winds before and hadn't put hurricane shutters on the windows while my neighbors all did. I had watched out the window and realized the shutters were not necessary in that experience.

In the meantime, my boss had given me his old galvanized shutters when he put in new electronic ones. These shutters required screwing tap cons into the cement blockhouse, which required proper tools, strength and some expertise. I had convinced Steven that shutters may not be necessary but should have recognized the thoughtful gift of shutters as a sign.

As the storm approached to the day, October 24, 2005, Steven convinced me they were necessary. With much prayer together, God sent a solution. Our friend from church, Bret, came to help Steven after finishing his own house nearby. With the proper tools and expertise, they put three quarters of them on before the storm hit hard. They had covered just the right sides of the house to give us maximum protection, but the shutters did not prevent a fourteen-year-old roof from peeling off. Steven and I were running around in the house with buckets and towels, catching the rainwater coming in through the roof.

No tarps were available in stores for months. There were lines for gas. We had to wait a considerable amount of time to put gas in our car so we could get out of town. The mold smell in our house forced us to go and stay at my parent's house for two weeks.

The ministry that supported Steven in his outreach did not continue. In addition, I also got fired on October 31, 2005, because of a personality conflict with a person at work. God graciously used the time after we both became *jobless* three months after our wedding. In spite of such a situation, very soon, we realized that the Lord called us out for the ministry He had for us together. As God would have it, within a year later, God used one of the board members of the ministry that supported Steven back in England, to be a spokesperson for Steven to make the board accountable by sending some funds for the ministry. They agreed by paying for several books and leaflets written by Steven to be printed in the USA and used in outreach. This allowed us to jump-start our new calling by equipping the body of Christ to reach Muslims through a discipleship ministry in America. We called it *Jesus to Muslims*.

God also gave us the added bonus of quality time to build the foundation of our marriage together as a couple and to know each other intimately. God miraculously provided for us day by day in various ways that strengthened our faith in Him. The Bible says a couple should spend at least their first year together. In Deuteronomy 24:5 it says, *"If a man has recently married, he must not be sent to war or have any other duty laid on him. For one year he is to be free to stay at home and bring happiness to the wife he has married."* I am sure most women reading this would applaud this wonderful idea.

For the first time in my whole life, I trusted God and my husband to provide for us every step of the way, regardless of the challenges we were facing. I was not in control. God was, and it was challenging at times to manage the pennies and wonder how God would bring the food to our table the next day. I received some unemployment eventually and we invested almost all I earned into the ministry we were beginning.

There were some adjustments that came into play in our first year due to past abuses causing low self-worth and Steven's bad dreams. God worked them out through our prayers, comfort of one another and with our consistent daily devotions and study in the Word. They were really only hiccups compared to our past and to

248

most marriages. Other than cultural differences—Eastern versus Western thinking—we have no major differences that have become a problem. Using God's Word as our standard, resolves problems so simply, since we both revere God, our Father and Creator, as our authority. Jesus is the mediator between us.

We praise God for those trials, as they have made us stronger and more dependent upon Him. *"Consider it pure joy, my brothers and sisters, whenever you face trials of many kinds because you know that the testing of your faith produces perseverance… so you may be mature and complete not lacking anything."* (James 1:2-4 NIV)

Ministry: A Journey of Faith

We prayed both together and individually over our life circumstances. In our humanness, it was hard to imagine how we would manage. I helped Steven send out resumes and did some follow-ups, but because of Steven's British way of doing things, he felt very uncomfortable with my persistence in following up. He first saw it as rude and felt we should just wait for someone to respond. I saw it as eagerness and being willing to do whatever it takes to go after what you want, as I had been taught in America and in my Mary Kay training.

God showed Himself by answering Steven's quiet patience. We got a phone call from someone who responded to receiving his resume in the mail; we had not followed up on it. I remember well; we got the phone call from a pastor on a Sunday morning at about 10:30 am before going to church. From that phone call, our initiation into this missionary organization became our first step in faith. The pastor offered us a place to live, with our little Pomeranian dog, in a four bedroom doublewide trailer in north central Florida. It sounded great.

In complete submission to my husband's calling and my calling as his helpmate, I laid down my whole life in south Florida, including my friends, my house which I rented to a tenant, all my 401K funds, and my car. I gave them all to the ministry calling and moved north when God opened the door there on March 1, 2006.

Soon, I took a full time job at the lowest salary I had made since age 22, at ten dollars an hour. I laid my whole life down for my Lord, for my husband and brother in Christ, and pressed forth toward the goal that lay ahead, which was mostly unknown. I felt a lot like

Abraham and his wife when God called them to leave everything behind and go to the unknown land where God would lead them.

It turned out the trailer needed renovations that took about two to three months to complete. Meanwhile, the three of us, along with our luggage, squeezed into a small dorm room usually rented out for one or two nights to missionary guests. Prior to this, I remember making a joke to my mother, that if she woke up one day and found Steven and me living in a box on her front lawn, to throw out her scraps and please don't kick us out.

Be careful what you say, for it just might come to be, as it did when we lived in a room about the size of a large box. This was our humble beginning of marriage and ministry together in God's plan. We were completely dependent on God for His provision and His opening doors to our first appointments. For the first time, Steven had to raise our ministry funds. The missionary way of life in depending on God to provide was totally new to me. However, God is always faithful and always right on time! I adored my husband and believed in him with all of my heart and still do. His unconditional love for me compelled me to submit to his leading me as God led him.

God was so merciful in connecting us with a precious gift He gave us—a young man in his twenties, named David. First, God used him to heal us from the pain in our hearts caused by the unwanted estrangement from each of our own sons. Secondly, this youth was a real Christ-like friend to us when no one else was in this new location. I had left about 150 friends in south Florida and a mega church. Now in horse and cow country and as a new member of a tiny church of barely fifty, I felt so lonely. David became an incredible blessing to us and still is dear to us to this day along with his entire family.

This church greatly needed spiritual healing. We had a very challenging time getting our ministry off the ground there but thank God for our growing friendship and all we learned from it. Within about a year, God directed us to a larger Bible-teaching church of about nine hundred in the same area, with a rapidly growing congregation. The senior pastor was humble and provided even more than he promised. He was compassionate and related to Steven personally from the start. Steven's testimony moved him so much that he continuously refers to Steven as "the real thing" – having been persecuted for his faith in Jesus Christ. Being physically persecuted for following Jesus Christ was and still is somewhat rare in America although there are some ominous signs of verbal and social persecution against Christians.

God led us to this new church through another Christian couple that we had known in south Florida. Remember the woman, Sharon, who discipled me at Calvary? They moved up after we moved here and she was still buying Mary Kay products from me. She reached out to me and invited us to visit their church when I expressed my frustrations with where we were.

Circumstances changed. God provided us with new living quarters through a compassionate real estate new friend I met, who had also left that first church. Sheila did all she could to not only help find us a house but to help us get financing, based on our own faith that God would provide the money by the time of the closing. When Steven and I were watching a Christian movie called *Facing the Giants* at church one night, upon its conclusion, Steven looked over at me and blurted out "We are going to buy that house!" I didn't know how it was possible based on my doing the accounting and never seeing that kind of money since we had married, actually, since I was a Mary Kay Director.

Without knowing how and scared as I could be, I supported my husband in his faith that God would provide somehow. We had never received the kind of financial provision needed to buy this house at this point. Sure enough, by the time we closed on the house, we had every dime required for the 5% down payment and all the closing costs without borrowing it anywhere. We have had God's provision for this house every single month since closing on it.

Now, for the first time in my lifetime, we were living in a brand new house. We walked through the process in complete faith. Then, God worked out all the details perfectly for us to obtain non-profit status for *'Jesus to Muslims'* as an independent ministry. Though that process was long and drawn out, our new home church supported us with the love we both needed from a church family, with financial support, as well as respecting and using the calling God gave us in their church. The *Jesus to Muslims* ministry has grown by leaps and bounds ever since God led us to this second church.

Unbeknownst to me at the time, in answering my lingering questions about 9/11 and fulfilling the deepest desire of my heart, to be loved, God was going to send me the whole encyclopedia on Islam and give me my true love and a new purpose, a new direction for my life. God in His perfect plan was going to begin a ministry, using us, to equip the body of Christ in America for telling Muslims about Jesus Christ. He established this ministry first through preparing each of our hearts toward His heart for the lost and then uniting Steven and me in marriage. God is intentional in everything He does.

My own experience has taught me that God is intentional. There are no coincidences. I had completely surrendered to God on 9/11/01 and asked Him to use me any way He desired for souls who might come to know their Lord and Savior as I did, and for the Holy Spirit to lead me to all truth where ever that would take me.

I have learned since then, that this story is not really all about me finding the love of my life, but about God's greater purpose to win souls to Christ. Ultimately, it is a story of how God used His plan of true love for His glory in retrieving souls from the devil's grip in order that they may receive eternal life. I feel that God's best for every woman's heart is for her to be loved for who she is. This is God's wedding preparation for eternity, birthed in His own heart—unconditional love.

God started our ministry to reach out to Muslims with the Good News, the Gospel of Jesus Christ, which is why we named it *"Jesus to Muslims."* This ministry is two-fold: we reach Muslims for Jesus and we equip Christians with the truth about Islam and teach them how to reach Muslims with the Gospel. We know and realize that the ministry that God called us to is a great challenge, as it is controversial in this nation, especially among such a large number of Christians who are weak in their faith.

God shows Himself mightily, however, as more and more Muslims are coming to have a relationship with Him, many of whom are drawn to Him by visions and dreams, as well as through our work and others. The persecution in other countries is one of many ways people are driven to Jesus. Some of Steven's books are translated into over thirty other languages. Today, he can receive up to 500 emails a day inquiring about Jesus, the ministry, or understanding Muslims.

Many of these emails are from Muslim seekers who are sincere in searching for truth.

Tragically, most former Muslims who make their faith in Jesus Christ known are persecuted, disowned, and in danger of losing their lives. Those who minister to them and to Muslims who are seeking are also in danger of being persecuted. However, as Steven has endured and overcome, the Lord has not only protected him, but has also bestowed abundant blessings upon him to this day. This has proved that obedience to follow Christ at all costs is worth it.

Even I have been mocked and avoided by my own biological family here in America. People who call themselves Christians, influenced by post-modernism and interfaith movements like "Coexist" and "Chrislam" as well as Christians who favor Politically Correct behavior, curse both Steven and me. This is really the hardest for both of us to bear. The hurt kicks up and gives me trouble from time to time. It is understandable when lost people curse us because they know not what they do, but when "Christians" do so, it hurts more.

Whenever I feel the lowest however, I think on how much Jesus suffered for us before He victoriously rose from the dead! We are taking up our cross and following Him faithfully in our calling (Matthew 16:24-25) until He returns or calls us Home.

We keep reminding ourselves that we work for an audience of one, Jesus, even if few may follow. We are not looking to become popular but to build up the body of Christ in the gift God gave us for the benefit of the body. This has certainly been a controversial ministry but we are blessed by those now reaching Muslims, both in the US as well as other nations, with what they have learned.

Jesus warned and advised us all in God's Word that people will hate us like they hated him (John 15:18). He also warned us not to be ashamed of the Gospel. He said, *"Whoever is ashamed of me and my words, the Son of Man will be ashamed of them when he comes in his glory and in the glory of the Father and of the holy angels."* (Luke 9:26). I am saddened that too many Christians are people pleasers instead of God pleasers.

In 2 Thessalonians 2:3, the Spirit tells us that in the end of times there will be a great falling away (rebellion, apostasy). In Matthew 24:24, Jesus Christ warns us that if it were possible, the elect will be deceived. We are seeing this falling away first hand when so many proclaimed "Christ followers" embrace *Interfaith,* meaning there are many paths to God. Muslims intimidate so many proclaimed "Christians" to give in to their demands in order to create "peace" through "coexisting" rather than sharing the one true Gospel (Good News of Jesus Christ). The Gospel is an exclusive message which Jesus' apostles shared and Jesus' faithful followers today share boldly and without fear, trusting in our Lord's protection.

Serving and Equipping

Since Islam is a missionary faith, as Christianity is also, Christians need to be prepared to share the hope we have in Christ with Muslims (1 Peter 3:15). Muslims love to talk about God and will talk to us about what they believe so to win us to Islam. We need to be wise as serpents yet gentle as doves (Matthew 10:16). We need not allow ourselves to be deceived by our enemy who is prowling around, looking to deceive and destroy people through Islam. Why would Satan use Muslims to tell us the truth about Islam? Satan is a liar! Yes, so many in America go to Muslims to seek truth rather than to God's called servants.

God knows the intention of everyone's heart and knows those who truly desire to know and love the true God. Sadly, Muslims have just been deceived into believing a different book, the Qur'an, which teaches them about a different god and a different Jesus - an "Islamicized" one that follows Muhammad. They are taught that the way to get to God is through the law Muhammad brought, through works. Many do not know that God has provided one and only one way: the truth and the life though Jesus!

I can see how God blended my gifts with Steven's and how two are better than one in this ministry. I learned that God's ways are much higher than my ways. I have peace with God and therefore peace with others. Steven and I began our marriage with no jobs and no money. However, contrary to the world's ways, God has blessed us in love, filling our needs and leading us in the ministry as we allow Him to lead us.

Old ways pass away and new life comes when we give Jesus our all. For example, I was an immaculate perfectionist in cleaning my house when Steven met me. Just as in the Cuthbert's' home in the *Anne of Green Cables* book, the house was so clean one could eat off the floor... until Anne would change everything.

Because ministry means making human souls my priority, I have dropped this perfectionism. While I still practice my God-given gift of hospitality and make sure the house is nice for guests, I no longer obsess over perfection daily.

Our combined income is still less than the average American income, yet God has blessed us with love and His peace and a happy home. I learned that money couldn't buy happiness. Being right with God brings me peace and all the desires of my heart above my own imagination, with more happiness and joy than in my entire lifetime. I praise His Holy name! I now see clearly God's ultimate purpose for calling Steven and me together in marriage, was to bring two separate units together for more strength, as one flesh, to do His work.

I promote my husband naturally. Steven says he would describe me with this saying: "Behind every successful man is a woman!" All I know is that I get excited about what I believe in. I watch Steven live and have learned how much knowledge he has of both the Bible and Islam. Yet, he remains the humblest man I know, even with his PhDs and years of study researching the Truth.

I am reminded how I used to promote Mary Kay products naturally also because I believed in them for myself, and went on to be a successful Pink Cadillac Mary Kay Sr. Sales Director. Now I see why God's Holy Spirit told me to step down because that was not who I was. God's plan was higher than my thoughts or imagination in His plan for me as Steven's partner in this ministry. He knew and I didn't but I just needed to be obedient and step down as He told me to do.

I sell more of Steven's books than his publishers. It's easy for me to promote Steven. I simply believe in the One he follows: Jesus Christ. God does the rest! You know how in those gang movies, the authorities say, "Take me to your leader"? Well, Jesus is his leader and the same Jesus is my leader too! So there you have it; it can't be any simpler than that. God has blessed us as we submit to Him. My advice to you is that you do the same, for your own good and for the good of the whole body of Christ, as well as the lost souls who still need to know where their hope lies.

Wives, Submit to Your Husbands as Unto the Lord

Ladies, it is easy to submit to a man when that man is willing to lay down his life for you, just as God intended it to be. Trust me, you don't want what the world has to offer. It is like living in hell on earth. The man whom God has for you is a great blessing, more than you can imagine. It's time to get obedient to God. Then watch how He'll bless your socks off!

First you need to live according to His Word, just as you would expect that a man who loves God should live. So, whatever you expect from him, you need to do also. Jesus led by example. You also need to lead other women by example. Then, God will send your Boaz in His perfect timing.

I have learned so much from my husband who "washes me in the Word" as God calls a husband to do. Steven is truly willing to lay his life down for me, just as Christ was willing to lay his life down for the church, and did.

Steven provides me the protection a husband should be providing for his wife. I've never felt so at peace and so safe, even while serving in a ministry where Muslims want to kill former Muslims who are apostates from Islam. I feel safe under God's hand and my husband's protection like never before in my life.

I have learned that Steven also lets his "yes be yes" and his "no be no." (Matthew 5:37) He actually lives God's Word. I have incredible trust that I can always count on him, since he is honest. God's blessing in sending Steven to me is more than I could ever have imagined in my heart, soul or mind. This is the abundant living I had only read about before. God has fulfilled His promises to me. Submission to Jesus first not only prepares you for your soul mate but also prepares you as that submissive Bride adorned for her Bridegroom for eternity.

God's Word Versus Islam

Did you know that out of 1.6 billion Muslims worldwide, only 1-2% is being reached with all Christian evangelistic efforts? Did you know that 40% of Non-Christians are Muslims and it is now being said to be the fastest growing religion in the world? Did you know that 55% of the whole world population is made up of Christians and Muslims?

256

It is often estimated that 12 to 20 million Muslims live in America today. Whatever the number may be, they all need Christ in order to receive the hope of eternal life. What are we doing about it? We pray daily that Christians will be awakened to these facts and wake up to do what will honor God's desire for all people to be saved. That does include Muslims, my friend. Reaching the lost, both Muslim and non-Muslim, will change this nation by saving one soul at a time.

After all, Jesus has given us authority to go and make disciples of all nations, baptizing them in the name of the Father and of the Son and of the Holy Spirit, and teaching them to obey everything He has commanded us. He reminds us, *"Surely I am with you always, to the very end of the age."* (Matthew 28:18-20)

At least Muslims are willing to talk about God, unlike atheists and self-centered people. They have just been taught lies about who God really is. It is Christians' responsibility to share the truth with them. If we don't, then how will they hear the Gospel? Isaiah 52:7 says, *"How beautiful on the mountains are the feet of those who bring good news, who proclaim peace, who bring good tidings, who proclaim salvation, who say to Zion, "Your God reigns!"*

The battle between Christianity and Islam is a spiritual one. How Muslims are won to the Lord is with love, not with hatred. Love overcomes hate. Life overcomes death, and light overcomes darkness. Jesus Christ commanded his followers to love their enemies (Matthew 5:43-48; Luke 6:27-37). As Christians, we need to learn how to love our enemies into the kingdom of God before Jesus returns to take us all home. Of course, loving your enemy requires the power of the Holy Spirit to do so fearlessly. If we really believe Christ like we say we do, we are willing to die for Christ's sake.

Perfect love casts out all fear. Loving one's enemy is supernatural, a miracle wrought through God's amazing power dwelling in His children. The Word promises us that we can do all things through Christ who strengthens us (Philippians 4:13). Steven and I have experienced all of this first hand. We give God all the glory for all He has done!

Islamic Assumptions

Islam accepts Jesus as a messenger from God but rejects his ultimate mission and his divine origin. The Qur'an, Islam's holy book, condemns those who believe that Jesus is the Son of God, that Jesus died for us and rose again, and that we are redeemed, adopted as children of God through what Jesus did once for all on the cross. Islam denies who Jesus is and His sacrifice for us:

> *That they said (in boast), "We killed Christ Jesus the son of Mary, the Messenger of Allah. - but they killed him not, nor crucified him, but so it was made to appear to them, and those who differ therein are full of doubts, with no (certain) knowledge, but only conjecture to follow, for of a surety they killed him not: - Qur'an, Surah 4:157 (Yusuf Ali)*

> *O People of the Book [Christians and Jews]! Commit no excesses in your religion: Nor say of Allah aught but the truth. Christ Jesus the son of Mary was (no more than) an apostle of Allah, and His Word, which He bestowed on Mary, and a spirit proceeding from Him: so believe in Allah and His apostles. Say not "Trinity": desist: it will be better for you: for Allah is one Allah. Glory be to Him: (far exalted is He) above having a son. To Him belong all things in the heavens and on earth. And enough is Allah as a Disposer of affairs. - Qur'an Sura 4:171 (Yusuf Ali)*

Christians must test the spirits (1 John 4:1) in order not to be deceived by false prophets who deny who Jesus is and what he did for us.

Islam focuses on following Muhammad as the "last messenger" and adhering to the *Sunnah*—Muhammad's way of life. Apart from religion, Islam is also a political system thus it is said: *al-Islam din wa dawla.* (Islam is religion and government). It aims to control every part of a person's life. It uses religious fervor to motivate its faithful. It is designed for conquering earthly kingdoms and peoples. Conquering is what Muhammad did once he had the power to do so.

Many Muslim leaders followed in his footsteps. They conquered many by the sword, killing and enslaving their opponents. This attacking mindset in the history of Islam and Muslims continues today, with different Islamic groups like ISIS and many others targeting each other, as well as Israel and the West. As long as the Islamic groups have a common enemy, they will unite to conquer through all means. Otherwise, they fight against each other for power. Isn't this just like the selfish greedy sin nature we were all born with? So what else would we really expect?

A Christian Approach

As I began to understand some of what motivated those Muslim men who killed so many American people on 9/11, as well as what Steven had gone through at the hands of his own father and other Muslims, my eyes opened to the bondage in which Satan has these people trapped. Since fighting and killing is part of the *Sunnah*, many of Muhammad's sincerest followers consider jihad to be Allah's greatest will. Allah actually implores them to go and kill for him to honor him and earn paradise. The Qur'an clearly states that 'Allah loves those who kill for Him' (Sura 61:4). Muslims are willing to die for a lie they believe is true, yet sadly most Christians today are not willing to die for the Truth. How big is your God anyway?

It is time to share the good news with our Muslim friends and neighbors that they do not have to hate, kill or be killed so to assure themselves of eternal life in paradise. God has already sent Jesus to die for the Muslims too and by believing in Jesus they too can receive eternal life (John 3:16)

Jesus said that people would persecute us (Matthew 5:9-12; 24:9-14). As they hated Him, so they will hate us who follow Him (John 15:18-25). Even though they mocked Jesus by their words, *"Come down from the cross, if you are the Son of God!"* (Matthew 27:40) Jesus prays to the Father to forgive them, *"for they know not what they do"* (Luke 23:34). Stephen followed Jesus' example and asked that the Lord *"lay not this sin to their charge"* about those who stoned him (Acts 7:60). We must not be afraid and draw back from Jesus. Rather, we are to live for an audience of One: the One and Only God. We are to please God, not man.

Although arrogant men ganged up in agreement to crucify Jesus, as well as curse, yell, and spit on Him, Jesus did not give in to their mocking and antagonizing. Yes, he was mocked, which fulfilled Scripture (Psalm 22:7-8; Isaiah 53:3), yet man did not intimidate Him in any way. Rather, he asked God the Father for forgiveness for them (Luke 23:34).

None can take our lives if God has not intended. Back in Pakistan one day Steven because of his faith in Christ was drugged and buried alive in a grave yard by Muslim students but God's hand washed him out of it by sending monsoon rains. That night 238 people died in the lower parts of Karachi, while Steven was saved.

Muslims are not taught by Muhammad to love their enemies, whereas Jesus focused on love: loving God (Matthew 22:37-38), loving one's neighbor as oneself (Matthew 22:39-40; Luke 10:25-37), loving each other (John 15:12), and loving one's enemies (Matthew 5:43-48; Luke 6:27-37). Jesus Christ did not establish a political system but rather provided, through His blood, access into the Eternal Kingdom of God for all people who truly believe and follow Him.

Both, the message and the work that Jesus accomplished is a threat to any ideology including that of Islam. While Jesus teaches to love all, Islam teaches about 'only a Muslim is a brother of a Muslim'. The Islamic law, *Shari'ah*, opposes Jesus' commands to love.

Jesus came to fulfill the law, not abolish it (Matthew 5:17). God knows no man can keep the law with the sin nature we have had since birth. Around six hundred years after Jesus, Muhammad told people that the angel Gabriel came from Allah to send him as the final prophet and *Shari'ah* as the final law. This totally rejects the Truth: that Jesus Christ fulfills the law. Why would a perfect unchanging God change His mind about what Jesus Christ did? He would not.

Paul says in Galatians 1:6-8, *"I am astonished that you are so quickly deserting the one who called you to live in the grace of Christ and are turning to a different gospel – which is really no gospel at all. Evidently some people are throwing you into confusion and are trying to pervert the gospel of Christ. But even if we or an angel from heaven should preach a gospel other than the one we preached to you, let them be under God's curse!"*

Today, after eleven years of training to understand the bondage of Islam, I can see clearly why Ephesians 6:10-20 teaches us about how to handle spiritual warfare by putting on the full armor of God—in order to protect ourselves from the trouble of the day. This armor does not consist of physical weapons in order to kill or hurt people. No! This armor consists of the following:

- Belt of Truth
- Breastplate of Righteousness
- Readiness that comes from the Gospel of Peace
- Shield of Faith
- Helmet of Salvation
- Sword of the Spirit, which is the Word of God
- Prayer in the Spirit on all occasions, with all kinds of prayers and requests

In John 16:33, Jesus says, *"I have told you these things, so that in me you may have peace. In this world you will have trouble. But take heart! I have overcome the world."*

When we understand that those on the side of God Almighty will ultimately win this spiritual battle, we comprehend that fear does not come from God but from the evil one. For God has given us a spirit of power, love and a sound mind (2 Timothy 1:7). If all Christ followers believed and received these truths, uniting together as one body with our Father through Jesus, that power would take the world victoriously!

The Role of Women in Islam

A few days ago a friend forwarded to me an advert with a few pictures of veil covered Muslim women against another picture showing six women from the Islamic world of prominent status. The statement on the top said: "When you think of women in the Muslim world, you probably imagine all the women sequestered in harems and draped in veils in public. The truth is, many of those countries are more progressive than you think; after all, many women have been chosen to lead their largely Islamic countries!"

The advert then mentions six prominent women as Benazir Bhutto, Pakistan; Sibel Siber, Northern Cyprus; Tansu Ciller, Turkey; Khaleda Zia and Sheikh Hasina of Bangladesh serving their countries as prime ministers. The advertiser seems to suggest this as proof that Islam gives women a prominent status. That is far from the truth. Have you seen in the media how many terrorists hide among children and even use them for atrocities? Well they use women too. To rescue themselves, they not only masquerade in women's veils but even use women or hide behind women so to hide their greater intentions and goals.

Let us check the cases above. Benazir came to power because of General Ziaul Haqq putting her father Zulfaqar Bhutto (elected prime minister) on the gallows. A decade later, Ziaul Haqq himself was killed in a plane crash. The country was in confusion. For cover up it was better to bring her to rule.

Similar circumstances took place in Bangladesh. The murder of Zia Rahman paved the way for his wife Khalida Zia to become the prime minister. In the case of Shaikh Hasina, her father Mujibur Rahman too was assassinated. This paved the way for her to become prime minister in a chaotic situation.

As for Sibel Siber in Northern Cyprus, she has been in the office for just a few months as an interim because of a no confidence vote in the elected prime minister, a man. Although she ran for the office, she was not elected.

As for Tansu Ciller being prime minister of Turkey during 1993-1996, we know this was a time when Turkey was trying its best to become part of the European Union. One of the tricks was to elect a woman so the West would be sympathetic. As for Pakistan and Bangladesh, similar tricks have played for sympathy and financial help from the West.

I really wish it was true that Islam as a religion and political entity honors women but it is not. Let's hear it from the Islamic sources. It concerns me greatly how women are treated in Islam. Women in the religious and political system of Islam are considered inferior to men:

- A woman is like a farmer's field (Sura 2:223).
- A woman is like a toy.[1]
- A woman should not say "no" when her husband calls her to bed. Refusal may earn her curses from the angels.[2]

---

[1] *Al-Musanaf* by Abu Bakr, Ahmad Ibn 'Abdullah, Vol. 1, Part 2, p. 263. Also *Ihy'a 'Ulum al-Din* by Ghazali, Vol. II, Kitab Adab al-Nikah, p.52.

[2] *Mishkat al-Masabih*, Hadith No. 54; also *al-Bukhari*, Vol. VII, Hadith 121.

- A man is allowed to beat his wife/wives (Sura 4:34).
- A man can lie to his wife/wives (Sura 2:225; 66:2).[3]
- "Had it not been for women, God would have truly, truly been worshipped."[4]

In Islam, a man can have up to four wives at the same time, whereas Jesus emphasized that one man and one woman are "one flesh" (Matthew 19:5). Islam is most definitely a belief system that caters to men's lusts while degrading and disrespecting women.

I had been in bondage to men's oppression all my life and finally came out of it to find the freedom and the grace of Jesus. Jesus rescued me from the miry pit of my own beliefs about my self-worth instilled in me from childhood and male domination in my life. I found that the answer to oppression is Jesus Christ. Jesus came to set the captives free. (Luke 4:18, Isaiah 61:1)

Tragically, here is a religion, Islam, which teaches women that oppression is their place in life. What is worse is that many are blind to how their gender is being oppressed. The tenets of this religion that promise many sex partners to Muslim males (Sura 2:25; 4:57; 44:54; 52:20; 55:72-75; 56:22-24) are used to brainwash many Muslim women into thinking this is fine and is God's ideal. My heart is just gripped with compassion for these women. The arrogance of these men who raise themselves above women in what they call a religion makes me angry, but then I remember it is Satan projecting his lies upon men and women through Islam, the ideology created by him.

I have seen over and over how women so easily believe the enticing words of men who so seductively lure their prey by promising love and protection. As I now understand, God perfectly designed woman that way for the right man. However, evil men can take advantage of this weakness. Through my own experience, I have seen

---

[3] Umm-Kulthum states that Muhammad allowed to lie in three things: war; settling disagreements, and a man talking with his wife or she with him (Ahmad Ibn Naqib al-Misri, *Umdatulsalik* (The Reliancee of the Traveller, A Classic Manual of Islamic Sacred Law), [tr. Noah Ha Mim Keller), Kitab al-Kadhb (Lying), pp. 745-747.

[4] *Kanz-el-'Ummal*, Vol. 21, Hadith# 825.

that just as I was easily lured by the words "I love you," "You're so beautiful," and so on, other girls and women are also led by lying lips because of their deep need to be loved and to love. We must remember that Satan was there when God created Eve and Adam; he imitates so to deceive.

Satan, the great deceiver and father of lies, wants to destroy every woman's testimony of Christ. Why? Remember, who was the first to tell everyone that Jesus was not in the tomb? Women! Why do you think God created women to be verbal and emotional? He did so to testify to the truth, as well as to discern the Holy Spirit, take care of and nurture her children, and care for her husband's needs. Watch how cunning Satan is in using this religion of Islam to suppress a women's value. Even the wording is so deceptive, as if women have never had value in any culture.

Muhammad's teachings, allegedly given to him by an "angel," were compiled into the Qur'an. But remember, God says in His Word that even if an angel comes from heaven to bring another gospel, do not believe in it! The Qur'an also values a woman's testimony as worth only half of a man's (Sura 2:282). In a *hadith*, writings about what Muhammad did and said, Abu Said Al-Khudri narrated the following dialogue between Muhammad and women:

> *Once Allah's Apostle went out to the Musalla (to offer) 'Id-al-Adha or Al-Fitr prayer. Then he passed by the women and said, "O women! Give alms, as I have seen that the majority of the dwellers of Hellfire were you (women)."*
>
> *They asked, "Why is it so, O Allah's Apostle?"*
>
> *He replied, "You curse frequently and are ungrateful to your husbands. I have not seen anyone more deficient in intelligence and religion than you. A cautious sensible man could be led astray by some of you."*
>
> *The women asked, "O Allah's Apostle! What is deficient in our intelligence and religion?"*
>
> *He said, "Is not the evidence of two women equal to the witness of one man?"*
>
> *They replied in the affirmative.*
>
> *He said, "This is the deficiency in her intelligence. Isn't it true that a woman can neither pray nor fast during her menses?"*

The women replied in the affirmative.
He said, "This is the deficiency in her religion."[5]

In the Qur'an, rape is not specifically mentioned. However, possessing captives "with one's right hand" is allowed, as well as practiced by Muhammad. This includes enslaving and having sexual relations with those captives (Sura 33:50). As for marriage, a Muslim is told in the Qur'an: "Your wives are as a tilth unto you; so approach your tilth when or how ye will . . . "(Sura 2:223).

Tilth is the process used by a farmer to break up the soil before planting seeds. Back to the Qur'an... does this include rape? For many Muslim girls and women, it sadly does. When a woman does not give her whole-hearted consent: this is rape. Islam's ideology puts women in bondage to men, just as Satan would have it, so to keep women from living out their God-given potential. I know how I felt used, demeaned and ashamed by men using me only for sex. I can clearly imagine how these Muslim women feel inside about themselves and their marriage. Remember, according to the Bible, the truth is Jesus came to set the captives free! That means everyone.

Many Muslim men who want to live out the *Sunnah* (the lifestyle of Muhammad) practice arranged marriages. This includes arranged marriages of little girls to old men. Just as Muhammad married and had sexual relations with Aisha when she was a young girl of nine, so many other young girls are faced with this tragedy. While some fight this, many young girls simply accept it as their fate, much like Aisha did, because her parents considered it a great honor for their child to be married to their prophet, Muhammad. Remember, without the Holy Spirit leading, received in salvation through Christ, man tends to please man over God and worship idols such as famous powerful people - even if they are evil and blind to the evil.[6]

---

[5] *Sahih Bukhari*, Volume 1, Book 6, Hadith #301

[6] For further details on, *The Role of Women in Islam* and *Marriage in Islam and Christianity* are online. See the website www.aishamydaughter.org. Then, click on the tab labeled "God's Guidance to My True Love"

The more I learned about the injustices of Islam, the more I wanted to help these children and women escape it. I know the freedom and the joy I found when escaping my past, and I know that every woman deserves freedom from bondage as well. What did Jesus die for, if not to set the captives free from Satan's lies and deception?

Join me to help set the captives free. Those innocent captive women of Islam need to know they have a choice to be set free, for the devil has them bound in a deceptive 'religious' ideology called Islam. So many women, like Soraya, are being innocently (like Jesus) led to the slaughter.

Unlike Jesus, they are ignorant to the truth. Jesus is the Truth they and the men in their lives so desperately need. God wants to use you and me to help them to know the truth so the truth can set them free. Together, we can do this with God's help and for His glory!

Islam's harsh penalties include amputation for stealing (Sura 5:38). If my parents had been Muslim, following *Shari'ah* as their law, can you imagine what would have happened to me if they had found out about the bracelet I stole as a teen? As for the abortions and sexual immorality, I would be charged with murder and adultery, facing execution or being stoned to death, according to *Shari'ah*.

Can you see how merciless the judgment of man is over God's mercy? He forgives us in our repentance and throws our sins as far as the east is to the west and remembers them no more (Psalm 103:8-13)! That is a cause for great celebration and thankfulness to God our compassionate Creator! God's love, mercy and grace for us, His creation, is much more compassionate than man's.

Be aware, my friend: unless the true body of Christ repents and humbles ourselves before our God and cries out for mercy, God will allow *Shari'ah* to come to this country fully! That's why prayer to our Creator and unity among believers are so important! I pray with a few nationwide prayer efforts to redeem this nation. Those who pray for our nation are so few.

Islam's Harsh Penalty for Apostates

When some of Jesus' disciples abandoned him, He continued to focus on the faith of His faithful followers (John 6:60-69). Unlike Jesus, Muhammad eventually ordered death for those who left the Islamic faith, as is evidenced in history. Steven's dad and other Muslims followed Muhammad's example when they were trying to kill Steven for his apostasy from Islam and his accepting Jesus as his Savior.

Even in the USA, Rifqa Bary merely wanted to follow her new-found faith in Jesus Christ and yes, nearly lost her life. If it hadn't been for her prayers to the real God who provided her escape to Pastor Blake's house in Florida, a family member could have killed her. We were so honored to go to the Orlando courtroom during her trials there in 2009, ready to stand up for her in explaining the apostasy law of Shari'a, since Steven could testify to that truth in our courts.

It never got to that real issue as Satan would have it but God gave her victory in His time. Her new book *Hiding in the Light, Why I Risked Everything to Leave Islam and Follow Jesus* is an amazing testimony. Rifqa testifies, as in Steven's life, how God rescues His own children from the hands of evil when they are obedient to His ways.

I feel great compassion for Steven because his own father oppressed him and even tried to murder him; I feel this same compassion for every former Muslim facing persecution for choosing to follow Jesus Christ. Even before I met him face to face, I could see Steven's incredible kind spirit. How could anyone, especially his own parents, want to kill him? Hatred and being deceived by Satan through the ideology of Islam is the sad answer.

God's Mercy Versus Islam and Human Judgments

As human beings, we tend to judge others' sins much more harshly than our own. We tend to measure sins according to what we believe is a bigger sin than another. While Islam and other religions may judge sin this way; that is not how the true God judges sin.

While Islam dictates harsh penalties for offenses, Jesus Christ came to save sinners, those who are lost. Jesus says, "*It is not the healthy who need a doctor, but the sick... For I have not come to call the righteous, but sinners*" (Matthew 9:12-13).

God said, "*I desire mercy, not sacrifice*" (Hosea 6:6a). I praise God for His mercy, which is so great! When we repent and accept the atonement of the blood of Jesus, the unblemished Lamb of God who is the only one that could pay the price for our transgressions, He forgives all of our past sins. When we repent, He throws all of our sins as far as the east is from the West (Psalm 103:12). He remembers them no more! What an amazing Father He is, full of mercy and grace!

As a redeemed child of God, I praise Him that I live today, in God's grace and in His perfect peace. I look forward to being with my Heavenly Father forever in Heaven when I leave this earth: whether it be through Jesus coming back for His bride (which is the church of true believers) or my death, which is separation from my earthly body.

I look forward to seeing all of those I so dearly love in Heaven, in celebration together, worshipping and singing praises to God. My sincere prayer for you is that you will also be healed and freed from your past sins, as well as any of Satan's strongholds in your life. I pray that you will get to know Jesus Christ as your Lord and your Savior and receive God's salvation. Jesus promises and gives assurance that those who believe in Him and live for Him will for eternity be in rela-tionship with our loving God Almighty, our Heavenly Father, Creator of the universe. Below are just a few of the promises God gives us through Jesus Christ our Lord.[7]

Christian Women and Witnessing to Muslim Men

In October 2004, on the Internet chat line where I met Steven; Muslim men had pursued me. When I say pursued, I mean they began asking me to marry them without having any prior conversation with me. I noticed that they all seemed to be from other countries, mostly of Middle Eastern descent. I decided to get off that site after my one-month free trial for that reason. That time I passed the test. I sought God's counsel by praying; I obeyed the Holy Spirit within me. God turned around what Satan meant for evil by connecting me with Ste-ven, a believer, instead of an unbeliever.

Through the conversations Steven was having on this chat line, I certainly understood enough about Islam to know that, since I am a Christian, marriage to any of these Muslims would be considered being "unequally yoked." I loved the Word and had learned a lot

---

[7] I encourage you to look them up for yourself: Matthew 5:2-12; Matthew 6:25-34; Matthew 7:7-11; John 4:10-14; John 10:27-30; John 14:1-27; John 16:7-33.

through my own school of hard knocks, so I knew God was protecting me. I finally learned to heed to 2 Corinthians 6:14: *"Do not be yoked together with unbelievers. For what do righteousness and wickedness have in common? Or what fellowship can light have with darkness?"*

Only now that I have obtained over a decade of education on Islam do I realize the deception of the motivation behind these men's quick pursuit. It has to do with these men wanting to get into the United States by pursuing American women for marriage. It is important for Christian women to put up a boundary against this tactic. I have counseled with and heard the tragic stories of so many Christian women who were lured to marry, live with and have babies with Muslims through various means: a foreign pen pal, a chat line buddy, an online college, and even in American Christian and secular colleges and universities.

The best protection to keep away from falling into the trap of marrying Muslim men is for Christian women to witness to Muslim women, and for Christian men to witness to Muslim men. While not a command, this cautionary boundary is designed to protect us from temptation. God, our loving Father, desires to guard women's hearts. It is crucial to know the Word of God.

Muslims are part of the mission field, as they follow Muhammad's teachings and example instead of following Jesus Christ.[8]

Most of these relationships happen because of the lie that Muslims and Christians worship the same God and believe in the same Jesus. That is a lie straight from the pit of hell, my friends! Recently, a Muslim man convinced one woman I encountered that Islam was just another denomination of Christianity. This is a price for the sin of man-made doctrines of church leadership created by Satan to divide the body rather than unite us in maturity to Christlikeness. Division will cost Christianity our witness to the lost.

---

[8] For further study, please see my husband's book, *Jesus or Muhammad: A Question of Assurance.* I highly recommend the small group study notebook that goes with this book. It would be a blessing to invite Steven to your church: to get to know him and learn from his testimony and studies personally.

Denominations are not from God and are clearly not in God's Word. Division has resulted in the body of Christ preventing the encouragement of the unity that Jesus prayed for in John 17:20-23. Ephesians 4:2-6 says:

> *"Be completely humble and gentle; be patient, bearing with one another in love. Make every effort to keep the unity of the Spirit through the bond of peace. There is one body and one Spirit, just as you were called to one hope when you were called; one Lord, one faith, one baptism; one God and Father of all, who is over all and through all and in all."*

If you are a true Christian, the Holy Spirit lives inside of you to guide you and to remind you of all that Jesus said. Jesus wants us all as believers to be workers for the harvest (Matthew 9:38, Luke 10:2). He gives us the Holy Spirit to help us witness and obey Him for He leads us into all Truth.

> *"... whenever anyone turns to the Lord, the veil is taken away. Now the Lord is the Spirit, and where the Spirit of the Lord is, there is freedom. And we all, who with unveiled faces contemplate the Lord's glory, are being transformed into his image with ever-increasing glory, which comes from the Lord, who is the Spirit."* - 2 Corinthians 3:17-18: (NLT).[9]

God's Holy Spirit leads and guides His children in following Jesus, including obeying Jesus' command to tell others the Gospel; the Good News of what Jesus said and did. This includes His death by crucifixion, His resurrection, and salvation through what he did for us, once for all.

---

[9] The following are some of the awesome verses about God's Holy Spirit. If you seek truth then meditate on them: Genesis 1:2; Numbers 11:29; Job 33:4; Psalm 51:11; 104:30; 139:1-18; 143:10; Isaiah 11:1-10; 42:1-7; 44:1-5; 59:20-21; 61:1-11; Joel 2:28-32; Zechariah 4:6; Matthew 3:16-17; 10:19-20; 28:18-20; Mark 1:6-11; 13:9-11; Luke 11:9-13, 12:11-12; John 14:16-17; 15:26-27; 16:7-15; Acts 1:8; 2:4-39; 5:32; 10:34-47; Romans 5:5, 8:14-16; 8:26-27; 14:17, 15:13; 1 Corinthians 6:19; Galatians 5:13-26; 6:1-10; Ephesians 1:13; 3:14-21; 4:30; 5:18-20; 6:10-18; Colossians 1:9-13; 3:15-17; 1 Peter 1:1-5; 4:14; 1 John 3:23-24; 4:1-21.

One way the Holy Spirit leads us is through giving us the words to say and when to say them (Matthew 10:19-20). While I tend to speak my mind, I have learned that the time is not always perfect to verbally express the particular knowledge on my heart. God has taught me to collect it in my mind for a later, more appropriate time – when the Holy Spirit would remind me of it and put it into my mouth to speak.

Christian Women: Witness to Muslim Women

Christian women: Muslim women need to hear about God's amazing, unconditional love through Christ Jesus. They are part of our mission field. Jesus said that the harvest is plentiful, yet the workers are few (Luke 10:2). Steven and I believe that Muslims are the other sheep Jesus must bring into His sheep pen (John 10:16). Sadly, many Christians are not participating in witnessing to them, but God is calling Muslims anyway – through visions and dreams. If Christians don't reach Muslims, God will one way or another. God knows who sincerely wants to choose Him.

Friends, the mission field is no longer a thousand miles away in another land. It is also here now on our doorsteps. Let me remind you again, twelve to twenty million Muslims live in North America today and the number is growing. Muslims make up forty percent of the non-Christians in the world, yet only one percent of the Christian evangelizing efforts are directed toward them. Therefore, evangelizing them needs to be greatly increased toward them. The harvest is ready but the laborers are few. Be willing to come forward and give a hand to those already in the field.

We pray daily for Christians to become equipped for the calling God has clearly given us here in America, so that more Christians will join us in reaching Muslims with the Truth of the Gospel. As Christians, we know the truth about how to get to paradise through Jesus, yet we aren't willing to lay down our own earthly lives for the sake of these deceived, lost people. The result is Muslims are dying daily to get to paradise the only way they know.

Sadly a great many American Christians are living for themselves, not for Christ to reach souls. What a waste of time! Consider what Jesus said: "Do not store up for yourselves treasures on earth, where moths and vermin destroy, and where thieves break in and steal. But store up for yourselves treasures in heaven, where moths and vermin do not destroy, and where thieves do not break in and steal. For where your treasure is, there your heart will be also." (Matthew 6:19-21) This life is temporary: not forever. We need to be storing up treasures in heaven, which is forever.

Just as God spoke to Ezekiel, He is speaking to each of us today in saying, "*Son of man, I have appointed you as a watchman for Israel* (the house of Israel is the whole body of Christ today). *Whenever you receive a message from me, warn people immediately. If I warn the wicked, saying, 'You are under the penalty of death,' but you fail to deliver the warning, they will die in their sins. And I will hold you responsible for their deaths. If you warn them and they refuse to repent and keep on sinning, they will die in their sins. But you will have saved yourself because you obeyed me.*" (Ezekiel 3:17-19)

Testimony of a Lovely Former Muslim Lady Who Accepted Christ
My greatest joys are in my relationship with God, then in my relationship with Steven, and then in the discipleship of women who have become Christians, escaping from Islam especially. Other women I disciple are those who have been deceived by Islam. Many of these lovely ladies live inside Muslim families and marriages. Recently, I witnessed and heard firsthand a powerful testimony of one young lady's mother finding Christ.

One day, I was in the presence of the power of the Holy Spirit while in the company of Sarah, a beautiful young lady of only 26 years of age, as well as her mother Mary, and Sarah's young son. Sarah had converted from Islam to Christianity, but Mary was still a Muslim. The last time I had seen Mary was about two or three months previously. She had been trying to persuade my husband and me, and a leader of a particular Christian church for Arabic people, to convince Sarah that she needs to stop saying "Jesus" so much around their Muslim family.

In other words, she wanted her daughter to stop giving Jesus so much glory. For if Sarah continued to do this, she would be in big trouble with them. She could even get herself killed by her male Muslim family members. This greatly concerned her mother, who loves her daughter very much and didn't want to lose her.

When Sarah had accepted Jesus Christ as her Lord and Savior, her mother had been furious and had done everything she could to change her daughter's mind. She begged, pleaded, debated, yelled, cajoled, threw her out of the house, although she later invited her back, mostly because she missed their mother/daughter relationship. Mary was at her wit's end in trying to rectify what she considered to be the effect of someone brainwashing her daughter. She even went to church with her, with the goal of proving Christians wrong.

When I met her for the first time, she had begged me with sincere concern to help her bring her wayward daughter back to Islam. My heart went out to this loving mother, but I told her that I couldn't help her do that. However, I could help *her* to know Jesus. I showed her God's love and how wonderful it is that her daughter is saved. I shared with her an example of how if she were to go to a really great restaurant, wouldn't she want to share it with all those closest to her? She said, "Yes." I said, "Well, that is how Sarah feels. She is so excited about finding the truth that she wants to share it with those closest to her."

Mary, however, was despondent, as she truly believed Islam was the truth. She then proceeded to talk to my husband in their native tongue: Urdu. She and her family are from Pakistan also. They talked for over two hours that night at fellowship time after church. Steven left her thinking about one thing. The real God is the God of the Christians, not the god of the Muslims.

Now back to this powerful day that was vastly different. This day, rather than grief and worry, I saw a joyful glow on Mary's face and shining light in her eyes. I could clearly see her soul through her eyes. Mary had accepted Jesus as her own Lord and Savior. She had found complete peace, and I could clearly see it!

There was so much love in her eyes; I could hardly keep from crying. Tears spilled from the corners of my eyes and rolled down my cheeks as inside my heart I thanked our Heavenly Father for this miracle of bringing Mary into His Kingdom.

Mary, in her joy, was explaining to me how she had desperately reached out for God during the days after seeing and talking with Masood. (She calls my husband by his Pakistani name, Masood.) She had seen the love of Jesus in him, as he so patiently listened to her and her dilemma with her daughter. He answered her questions and concerns about this Jesus her daughter so often talked about.

Mary had tried to convince Masood that all along she had been worshipping the right God, Allah. Because Sarah was her child, she felt she needed to stop this nonsense about Jesus and get her back to worshipping Allah for the sake of her own life. Mary pleaded for help: first to me, then the ministry leader, and then Masood. He, lovingly and kindly, explained the truth of Jesus to her in their language.

Mary had a sincere concern and desire to know what Masood had to say about it all. She had just listened to his full testimony at that service. Steven had a sincere heart to defend the truth that Sarah believed. He sincerely desired to reach Mary's eternal soul also with these truths, so that Mary may know and believe the truth.

Steven had said nothing to agree with Mary's Muslim beliefs; he just spoke the truth in sincere love. He had listened intently to Mary's sincere questions and concerns, so that he could answer those concerns, whether she decided to accept the truth or not. They had ended their conversation with Steven encouraging her to ask God directly about the truth.

This day, Mary was so excited to share with me how God answered her when she asked Him to reveal to her the real truth, no matter what it was. She explained that for four days after speaking with Masood, she would wake up thinking about what he had said about praying to the right God. She sincerely wanted to know that she was praying to the one true God! That was the Holy Spirit nudging her and God's Word not coming back void.

God then came to her in a dream. She woke up after seeing a finger draw a cross on her forehead and feeling a comforting hand on her shoulder. Out of sheer excitement, she ran to tell her husband what had so clearly happened to her. He, being a Muslim, just told her she was crazy! Her confidence that the Christian God was the real God overpowered her. Later she shared it with Sarah, who texted me about it. I confirmed with her that it was clearly God speaking.

However, Mary was now confused about how to pray to Him. She asked God again for further confirmation, as she only knew about praying in her old way, as she did to Allah on a mat after a cleansing ritual. She outwardly talked to God and told Him that she would pray the way she knew how the next morning. If this was wrong, He needed to stop her.

God gave her the perfect sign that stopped her from performing her prayers on that mat, as in the Muslim tradition. The next morning, after laying out her mat and completing her cleansing ritual, she got her menstrual cycle, which she had not had in about four years! According to Shari'a, it is "unclean" for women to pray during their menstrual cycle. This was a real sign for her, since she knew from her daughter that the Christian God never restricts a woman from praying to Him, at any time, including during one's menses.

As Masood also informed her, a Christian can pray continuously: everywhere and anywhere. Thus, she began to pray to God Almighty, the Christian God! God made it perfectly clear.

Mary felt real joy as she found herself praying and talking to Him constantly. Imagine the liberation from the "law: the perfect way to pray" here! When she told me about how often she catches herself talking to Him, I assured her, "Don't worry, He hears from me that way too! He can handle it!" as we laughed together. The power of the Holy Spirit to transform people and give us joy overwhelms me.

Mary asked God to reveal to her who this Jesus was that everyone was talking about to her. Jesus came to her in a dream that night, with a white robe and "some kind of jewels, mostly blue" on his chest. He was interceding for people to God and suddenly turned around and pointed his finger at her and said to her, "Got ya!" She saw Jesus and now knew, without a doubt, that the God of the Christians is the real God and that Jesus Christ is the Lord and Savior of us all, including her!

Mary and her daughter, now equally yoked as sisters in Christ, are very strong in standing for their faith in Jesus. We believe God will bring their precious male counterparts to Jesus, too. He may do so through their young son, who now goes to Christian school. Mary's testimony just cannot be argued with or contested, since God came directly to her and showed Himself to her. Her greatest testimony to family members is "Should I obey God or obey you? I can't help it that God came to me directly, but He did! What do you expect me to do? I must obey God, right?" I love it!

God is so personal. He shows Himself to be so real even today. He promises that He will be with us to the ends of the earth. Wow! What a relationship full of unconditional love. Who are we that God, the Creator of the universe, is mindful of us? He blows my mind.

Mary's journey to the truth reminds me of what Jesus said 2000 years ago: *"Seek and you shall find; ask and you shall receive. Knock and the door shall be opened to you."*(Matthew 7:7; Luke 11:9) I could hear the echo of this promise to her. Glory, Halleluiah! He hears the sincere hearts and answers them.

There is no greater joy than to feel and see the Holy Spirit working so powerfully among us. And my greatest joy in these times is when a Muslim comes to Christ. Thank You, God, for my new sister in Christ! Thank You, God, for the honor of serving You in this capacity. I am in awe of You, Father God!

Twila Paris' song "I Never Get Used to What You Do" comes to me now, as I remember this moment with such fond tenderness. Twila Paris speaks of the family life in the Spirit of God. As that was not the kind of family I knew in my growing up years, I am clearly one of those lonely children she speaks of in this beautiful song. I am so thankful for the family of God and all my brothers and sisters in Christ who love and know God, as well as love and understand me. Yes, God will bring us to Himself, as He did my friend Mary and so many others I now know. She asked God to reveal Himself to her by giving her the truth as to whom she should pray. She just wanted to pray to the right God and asked Him to show her. He made it perfectly, crystal clear that she was no longer to pray to Allah, but to the God of the Christians—the One and Only God, in the mighty name of Jesus.

Since Mary did not know Jesus, He revealed Himself to her when He came to her in a dream and told her it was Him. She saw Him in His priestly garment, which she knew nothing about. She had not read the Bible. This proves that God will do the work to draw sincere hearts to Himself, especially those looking for the truth no matter where it takes them, yes, even out of our comfort zones!

In the Great Commission, He has commanded us to go and share the Good News, disciple and baptize (Matthew 28:19-20). So, He is asking us to take part in drawing others to Jesus, showing God that we love Him. God is relational. He wants us to be part of His divine plan to draw souls to Him.

I see it the way my husband says it. Our "helping" is like a little boy who works with his daddy making a toy car. Daddy really does most of it but allows the boy to hold something or move something. When the car is complete, the boy tells everyone, "Look at the car that I made with daddy!"

Our Abba Father, our Heavenly Daddy, wants us to help Him with His divine plan. Is that not incredible? I get so excited about it and I so want to share this incredible excitement with you, too, my friend! Won't you join me?

What Is Your Role in the Body of Christ?

Like He has done with Steven and me, God has called you to do something in the body of Christ, to serve Him. Do you know what that is yet? Seek Him to discover your gifts. Start serving God with those gifts. If Jesus comes back while you are serving, He will say, *"Well done, good and faithful servant!"* (Matthew 25:21).

Go to God now. Pray to Him about the areas in which He has gifted you and called you for His glory. Do not be as the man who hid his talent that God gave him (Matthew 25:24-30) for on that great day, God will ask you what you did with the talent He gave you. He will call you accountable.

Ask Jesus into your heart to rule and reign over your whole life completely. Surrender yourself to Him. Be a "living sacrifice" unto Him (Romans 12:1). Our Bridegroom is coming for a pure and holy Bride, not one with secret and un-repented sins, which defile and blemish us. If your prayer was to receive Christ or to surrender revealed sin to God for forgiveness, then email me. I would love to hear from you, to hear what miracle God has done in your life to change you for His glory![10]

The aftermath of 9/11

The events of 9/11 temporarily changed and united many Americans. I remember how incredibly bonded everyone in New Jersey and New

---

[10] Karen@jesustomuslims.org

York became after 9/11/01. For the first time it seemed, people were so kind and polite. They allowed others to go first at intersections and in public places. The horn blowing was silenced! We all felt compelled to get American flags, if we didn't already have them, in order to display our patriotism for our free nation. God got our attention and we all felt undone before a holy God in true fear of Him. We were truly humbled.

If you know anything about the patience of people in New York City and the metropolitan area, including New Jersey, it was a miracle to see a line four hours long to get an American flag – with no one yelling, complaining, or getting agitated in any way. Everyone was making friends, no less! People were telling where they and their loved ones were at the time of the attack: who never went to work that morning that was supposed to have gone, who was stuck in traffic trying to get to work and ended up turning around when they heard the news on their radios, etc.

I would like to make it perfectly clear that almost every one of those people gave God the credit, without hesitation or blinking an eye! It just astonishes me that when life is good, no one wants to give God any acknowledgement, but as soon as there is trouble, everyone is crying out for God to rescue them. "Oh, God, help me!" goes the plea. Out of the heart, the mouth definitely speaks.

I was at an intersection and no one was tooting horns or racing their engines, I remember looking up and praying to God. I exclaimed, "God please let it always be like this! It is so beautiful to see the love and the harmony here that I never remember seeing in almost 24 years that I have been living in this metropolitan area."

Yes, we all saw a glimpse of what humbleness and unity were like right then, when people changed. The churches were packed. People came together as a nation with one common goal: to stand together united under God, as a nation against evil and for the truth!

I experienced firsthand the body of Christ united for at least a month, just as Jesus prayed for in John 17:22-23: *"I have given them the glory that you gave me, that they may be one as we are one – I in them and you in me – so that they may be brought to complete unity. Then the world will know that you sent me and have loved them even as you have loved me."*

I see these verses compelling God's true followers to open their eyes to the importance of unity as one body. It is that united oneness that can stand before our enemy with complete confidence, knowing the truth that when we are obedient to God, with Him on our side, who can be against us? Even Islam cannot withstand the truth.

Be aware though, for Satan imitates. He is at work by his deceiving many through *Interfaith* and *Chrislam* efforts. Did God say that people can come to him in their own way? No, he has drawn the line. It is through one name, Jesus they may come to Him (John 14:6; Acts 4:12; Hebrews 1:1-2).

What about you? Have you been awakened to the truth and turned back to Jesus? Have you made it all about Jesus as the song goes? Let us not waste one minute in bondage to Satan's lies. The truth will set you free. Who the Son sets free is free indeed! The only way the lost will see the light, love and life of Jesus Christ is if we are totally free from our sins, filled with joy and thanksgiving to Him! Then, others will want the freedom we have in Christ! Light, love and life is the beautiful dress of the Bride of Christ, a radiant picture of her joy and thanksgiving for her Bridegroom, Jesus.

Our Bridegroom is coming back for us soon! Are you prepared with your gorgeous dress on? I look forward to seeing you and being with you as we are taken up in the clouds that great Day: to take the hand of our perfectly pure and loving Bridegroom!

13

Reflections

Needs

For most of my life, I kept "putting the cart before the horse" as they say, thinking I needed to find a man to love me first and then I'd seek God again. Brought up to believe this way, I thought love came from a male relationship, without any consideration for how a loving God fit into my life. God showed me how detrimental this method is. He helped me see how my love for Him needed to come first.

The Sanguine temperament that God gave me particularly has a deep need for love, although every temperament has this need. God intended for that empty spot in my heart and soul to be filled first by Him, my Heavenly Father, who knew my husband before I did.

A human's second most important need is to have a purpose, which gives us hope. When my college career choice basically failed, I felt the need for another purpose. When my son came along, I had my next purpose. As he started pulling away in his teens, God gave me my next purpose in Mary Kay. I thought at the time that would be my final purpose. I could only go so far however before my deep-rooted sin needed to be weeded out. God knew that.

My anger issue, the weed, rose up less frequently with such a task before me. My Mary Kay female friends greatly encouraged me. It was still there though and needed to be pulled, and God knew it. Every time I would explode with temper, deep inside I knew I hated it. As Paul describes in Romans 7:15, I wanted for it to leave but did not have what it took to pull that weed myself.

Once God gave me a time to get away from all that was familiar by sending me to Florida, I became recklessly abandoned to Jesus, with Him as my main purpose. I could then hear His voice clearly.

God used a Biblical Counselor, one whom I never met nor saw again after that hour, to speak to me about the root issue. I obeyed Him one step at a time, going through all the Biblical healing courses recommended by these new servants He used to carry me through the most difficult 6-8 months of my life.

This cost me my Mary Kay career and it cost me my relationships with my old friends. It required my focused uninterrupted time, a one-year sabbatical from work, but God provided for me all I needed to survive in the wilderness.

The weed was pulled out by its root! Once I was delivered from that bondage, I could walk in the Spirit freely! Covered in God's love, with tremendous joy, I felt reborn, like a child.

God showed me a vision for understanding this through a literal "thorn in my flesh" years later on 9/10/11. This vision helps me teach others about the importance of weeding out our secret sins. The whole body of Christ, nationwide, is suffering from sin - this thorn in their flesh - secret sins that also need to be pulled out by the root.

What did I Learn?

The song that comes to me now about my past is "How Many Times Will You Pick Me Up?" by Laura Story, one of my favorite musicians today. God so gently answers me: "As long as you are seeking My face, My grace is sufficient." God was always waiting to rescue me when I reached out for Him in my heartfelt prayers. When I was willing to lay it all down before His throne in repentance, He forgave me, picked me up and brushed me off to begin again.

I learned my way never worked; God's way always worked and His rewards have been beyond my imagination! I have learned that seeking after TRUTH is the most important thing in life. Truth is not found in Hollywood or on our TV screens. Truth is not found in our circle of friends unless they are seeking God's Kingdom with all of their heart, soul and mind and can back it up with Biblical Scripture.

When the Bible as our point of reference, our righteous standard, is ignored and put aside, it becomes easier for people to follow what seems best to them. This makes Satan very happy. He makes sin fun and addicting, desirable to the flesh. It is the Bible which identifies Satan and warns us how he prowls around like a roaring lion looking to whom he can devour (1 Peter 5:8).

The truth often hurts but the old needs to be destroyed in order to build it back up on the proper foundation of truth. This means change is required. Unless the Spirit is drawing a person, they won't want the truth. Sitting on the fence between the truth and a lie cannot last long before a decision to choose is eminent. God blesses all those who choose the truth.

Our Disposition and the Solution

I learned that it wasn't only me who sinned but all have sinned and fallen short of God's glory and need a Savior in order to reconcile with God. We must humble ourselves and be honest about our sin, taking responsibly for our sin by confessing it with our mouth to our righteous God. We need to forgive all involved, including ourselves.

God is full of grace and mercy, ready to forgive us when we are sincere. Jesus asks us to go and sin no more. God hates habitual sin and will eventually turn us over to our own depraved minds when we are not sincere. Jesus is the Redeemer for all of us, not just for me or just for others who sinned less than or more than me.

There is no measure of sin to God but that is only with man in sin nature. God sees all sin the same so we cannot earn salvation through works. Our works are like filthy rags to God. God must punish sin and cannot let any sin into heaven. We must be constantly repenting of our sins so to be ready for our Bride Groom - Jesus.

To be a "Christian" is to submit in the light of the Scriptures and have a daily ongoing relationship with Jesus Christ, seeking His will to direct our path and teach us to walk in God's ways. This relationship needs to be completely transparent with God but we all need accountability to another Christ follower; to pray with us and encourage us, as well as call us out on sin.

We must be willing to grow and change old bad habits to godly discipline in order to become more like Christ. The Bible renews our minds to the truth. We will become more pure, holy, righteous humble, loving and other centered, willing to be led by the Holy Spirit over our selfishness. This is how we prepare ourselves to become the Bride.

Life's priorities – Jesus comes first

Because I believed on Jesus, God forgave me. He not only took on my punishment through being crucified and buried, he went to hell and back! He overcame death by being raised victoriously so I have eternal life through Him. I have freedom from sin through God's forgiveness. He gives me a peace I never had!

Jesus said, "If you love me, keep my commandments." (John 14:15) The heart's desire to obey the ways of Jesus is driven by God's perfect love for mankind through Jesus. He was the only man who fulfilled God's law perfectly. God's law is the only perfect standard that keeps man safe from evil and blessed by Him. Man cannot keep the law without the help of the Holy Spirit's power.

I learned that life lived abundantly is not about me but all about Jesus and living as He did, holy and set apart from the world. Living to please God through our obedience to His Holy Spirit leads us to use our gifts in order to help others and glorify Him. There will not necessarily be gratitude from people we help but God will bless our earthly life abundantly in ways we don't understand. He also promises a mansion and crowns in Heaven.

God's plan and my choice of Relationship

The Great Commission is a requirement by God from all Christians, not only for those gifted with evangelism. God has designed every human being uniquely with different gifts for his own specific tasks (ministry) on earth for the good of the whole kingdom of God.

God created every person in His image. We have been designed for worship and for His divine purpose. God has, through the grace offered by Jesus Christ, given us the choice to follow Him.

The ball is in our court to choose freely to love God with all of our heart, soul and mind, to consummate that intimate relationship with complete transparency to God. That is why it is a love relationship through Jesus, our Lord and Savior. It is not a methodical ritual of works religion.

This love relationship is likened to the husband and wife relationship, two people united as one who KNOW each other intimately.

God already knows you. We must choose to know Him by studying and applying God's Word to renew our minds. We need to allow the Holy Spirit to lead us through submission to Him.

More to the Wedding

I learned that God created women equal to men. He created male and female with different roles. God created marriage for man and woman to reproduce offspring and populate the earth. Marriage is an earthly example of the perfect Marriage, when Jesus comes for his pure and holy church.

God has designed the perfect mate for every person He has planned for marriage. As women, our heart's desire is for our earthly husband to show fruits of the Spirit, as well as be protective and lead spiritually. We want him to be brave and strong physically and emotionally in times of danger. We want him to be honest and willing to lay his life down for his bride. God knows this is what we need. He promises to prepare him but we need to trust Him with that. To have all such qualities, we need to look to God.

We need to wait upon our Lord to bring the groom and not chase him down or focus on seeking after a husband. We need to seek first the Kingdom of God and all these things will be added to us. Your part is to be recklessly abandoned over Jesus, seeking after Him first. Like He brought my husband to me and like He brought Boaz to Ruth, He will bring your husband to you in His time and will.

Wedding Preparation for Eternity

I also learned that after all this a great wedding celebration awaits us! God is getting ready to close the doors to the grace period. When He does He will send His Son, who is the Bridegroom of the remnant church known as the Bride. The Bride includes me. What about you? Jesus, our eternal Bride Groom will take you too if you believe in Him. It will be such a beautiful moment of bliss when we are taken up from earth suddenly!

Jesus' eminent return will be after the falling away, or apostasy (rebellion of the church) and the Antichrist is revealed, according to II Thessalonians 2:1-3. The falling away has already begun. Focusing on the Bridegroom, Jesus, He will return for a spotless Bride. That means the Bride includes truly born again Christ followers who go about the Father's business.

The Bride is set apart from the world, holy and righteous and full of peace, reflecting Jesus on earth. The Bride of Christ will be gathered together as one united body with one faith, one baptism, believing in the one Jesus, the Son of God sent from the one Father God as the only sinless man, the Lamb of God.

I have a picture on a wall at home that depicts the Bride of Christ. Her beautiful dress and train consists of millions of people gathered together who are Christ followers, known as the church, representing the one body of Christ. Jesus will come down from the clouds to take His Bride out of the earth and into the heavens with Him for the marriage supper of the Lamb.

We will celebrate together the marriage supper of the Lamb. What could be better than spending eternity with your Creator in an everlasting love relationship? We will rule and rein with Him over the new heaven and new earth.

Jesus promised in John 14:3, "And I go and prepare a place for you. I will come back and take you to be with me that you also may be where I am. You know the way to the place where I am going."

What will you choose?

Won't you begin today toward your own incredible journey of love by first choosing Jesus, your eternal Bride Groom? Only He knows who your earthly bridegroom is. Only He knows the plan for your purpose together on earth. Take His hand today and let Him lead you through His Word to get to KNOW Him. I promise it will be amazing!

Take the first step toward your eternity. Choose Jesus as your Lord and Savior and begin your daily relationship through praying to God, confessing your sins and repenting by turning around and sinning no more. Ask God for forgiveness and receive His forgiveness by forgiving yourself and others involved.

Resolve all conflicts with others and hold no grudges. Grudges only make you sick; they do nothing to the other involved. Begin reading, meditating on and applying the Word of God to your life so to renew your mind and replace your old self with the new. This will show God you love Him. He already loves you. He's waiting for you to freely choose Him to consummate the ongoing relationship with your Heavenly Bridegroom, Jesus.

Jesus knows who your earthly husband is so the closer you get to Jesus the closer you will get to knowing who your earthly husband is, or if you have the gift of singleness. God desires to lead you into His perfect plan, to bless you abundantly and use you for His glory.

God wants to mold you and shape you into His desired beautiful pot. Trust and obey His Holy Spirit, that still small voice guiding you into all truth and into God's purpose for you. Email me if you would like me to walk alongside you.

Get ready today:
1. Confess all sins to God through Jesus.
2. Repent. Turn and sin no more.
3. Develop a personal relationship with Jesus by daily communication through:
   a. Studying God's Word
   b. Prayer
   c. Getting an accountability partner (more mature Christian).
   d. Use fasting to seek difficult answers.
   e. Listen to God's voice and obey.
4. Purify your life by being set apart.
5. Love God with all your heart, soul and mind and love your neighbor as yourself.
6. Share your faith with others who are lost, as the Holy Spirit leads.
7. Disciple others less mature than you in their walk.
8. Use the gifts God gave you to glorify Him and build the body.
9. Get prepared for your Bridegroom, Jesus.

Maranatha! Jesus, come!
I come before You the King and lift my hands to praise You! There is nothing more worthy, nothing more precious than You Jesus! I yearn to know You more each day Lord, to be holy, pure, and set apart just for You. I pray that You would be proud of me for the way I live my life on earth and tell me one day "Well done, good and faithful servant." I desire to please You, God. I desire to be in Your presence, mighty King of kings and Lord of lords. I bow down to kiss Your feet,

for You are incredible, full of mercy and grace to accept me into Your presence and adopt me into your royal family!! Thank You my Lord! You are an amazing God! I am honored to serve You in Your calling, Your plan here on earth until You come to take me home with You forever! In Jesus name, Amen

Questions

I would love to dialogue with you over these questions:

- Was I really saved at age 13 by saying that prayer for salvation?
- Did I really abide in Christ while living according to my own agenda?
- Consider John 15:1-9. Was I producing fruit? Was I abiding in Christ?
- How does my life relate to the parable of the seed and the sower? (Matthew 13:1-23)
- Did I just get "stuck" in an infant stage of spiritual growth, needing to be discipled to maturity? Let's discuss this.

Somehow, I had the impression in my mind that "Once saved, always saved." Maybe I got this idea from that "dead" church after saying a prayer. I did believe I had done all it took to get to heaven and was "good enough" or at least as good as others I had met, and that prayer saved me. Allow me to reveal to you that I never really felt compelled to consult God or the Bible for any of my life's answers until life had taught me how badly I needed God's answers.

Was I really saved at all? Did the prayers of my Nana impact my life? What about God's Spirit who draws us? What about the Holy Spirit's help? Let us dialogue about this.[1]

Please ask yourself this question: Do you really love God with all your heart, soul and mind and love your neighbor as yourself (Matthew 22:37-40)? If you truly love yourself, you will bring your deep dark secret sins in your life to God, and repent, receiving forgiveness.

---

[1] E-mail me: karen@JesusToMuslims.org

You will ultimately be whole and free indeed. You will then be ready to joyfully serve God with your gifts.

God is refining you for your true love, as well as refining him for you. In His perfect time and perfect place and for His perfect work, He has a plan for you since the foundation of the earth. As part of the body of Christ, we are called to glorify God. It is all for His glory, not yours or mine. Are we humble enough to understand that everything we do is not about ourselves, but it is to glorify God?

God's heart is for the lost and He desires to use us to help Him save the lost. As a Christ follower, are you willing to lay your life down for the lost around you? Are you ready? Are those you love ready? Jesus will return to take us out of this sinful world so we can be with Him eternally in the new heaven and new earth! Get ready!

We Are Princesses of the King of kings!
Will you choose life or death? It is entirely up to you to choose freely. However, know this fact when choosing: The God of the universe and Creator of all mankind desires that you choose life. That truth is found in God's Word in Deuteronomy 30:19. Look for yourself and choose.

I am writing my story specifically to women who are looking for love from a man in a relationship. I warn you that there are many "wrong places" to look for love, and that includes looking in a church as well. Many men prey on innocent young vulnerable women. Their "love" is destructive; they thrive on controlling relationships.

God has created women to be man's helper, but helping the wrong man can be a living hell on earth. For many women, their quest for love has resulted in being abused, heartbroken, and lost. This has made it difficult for them to trust.

God is Love (1 John 4:8). God created you in His image. You are designed to love and to be loved. Divine love with God is the Perfect Love. God is your perfect Father and you are His child, His daughter, when you believe and trust in Him. As a matter of fact, He is the King of kings and Lord of lords; you are His princess!

The Bible is God's communication: His true, unchanging promises to you. The Bible is fully truth, from the first page of Genesis to the last page of Revelation, because God does not lie. God does not change. You must read the Holy Scripture (II Timothy 3:15-17) and meditate on it day and night to truly know God, your Father (Matthew 6:9) and to know who you are as His child (1 John 3:1). If you do not know your Father God and who you are as His child, you will never know His perfect love. Colossians 3 teaches us who we are in Christ. It is important we receive it and believe it to renew our minds.

Satan is bent on keeping you a sinner by keeping you from studying God's Word. If you prioritize your life by knowing your Father's true love first, you will then be ready for your earthly true love that your Father designed specifically for you. The closer your relationship with Him, the closer you will be to His perfect timing to connect you with your true love. God's perfect love desires the best for you.

God will ultimately use the divine union of two people who become one flesh for His glory. As you and your true love both continue to grow closer to God with Jesus as your solid foundation, you will also grow closer to each other. Your true love story centers on God instead of the flesh. The flesh is double minded in all its ways. We were all born sinners since Adam. The Spirit leads us to all truth.

God created a woman, Eve, out of Adam's side so that she would always be by his side. God created you specifically, dear sister, to be united with one man, the one He has created for you specifically, unless He shows you in this journey that you have the gift of singleness.

God is waiting for you to first choose to make Him #1 in your life. By doing so, He can refine you by the fire of the Holy Spirit, preparing you for the true love that He has prepared for you. The refining process can be difficult, as when gold is refined by fire. Hang in there my friend. I promise you it is worth it! He makes us purely golden.

Satan will tempt you more and more in your walk so keep your eyes fixed on the prize, Jesus. Once God unites you with your partner as one flesh, your future together has a purpose. He wants to use you both to bring more souls to the Kingdom, for He wants all to be saved (I Timothy 2:3-4). He wants you and your future true love to glorify Him. For this reason God made marriage a sacred covenant, symbolizing the marriage of Jesus to His bride, the church.

This is your wedding preparation for eternity. This is your Maker's instruction book for marriage; the equation is 1+1=1. Do not compromise God's principles and your Father's best wedding plan for you. You deserve the best, for you are heirs with Christ (Romans 8:17). You are a royal priesthood (1 Peter 2:9).

On the other hand, the culture is teaching you to go out and find the guy and try him out first. Then, legitimize your illicit sexual relationship through marriage. This is a dead end street and brings disasters, broken hearts, anger and pain that become baggage to take into another relationship. For some it can even end in suicide out of depression.

A man who says he wants a woman outside of marriage wants sex. He uses lies to lure women for what his selfish lust desires. These kinds of men treat women like a used cigarette. After smoking it, they discard what is all used up. That is exactly what Satan's plan looks like. He knows his destiny; he desires to take as many as possible to his miserable future of eternal death in hell.

Choose wisely, my friend. I am warning you, as I have already been down that road of destruction. Choosing God's plan is the victorious winner! The Holy Spirit promises to lead us to all truth so yield to His leading, that still small voice inside.

I know for a fact that every woman desires to be loved for who she is forever. Once a man touches her body, he touches her emotions. She naturally may begin dreaming of a wedding, with him as the groom. A perfect love life has already formed in her mind and heart. Men do not feel that for he is just visual. He easily files his emotions. Touch is not a big deal to a man who does not fear God.

Satan cunningly uses men to destroy women. That has always been Satan's agenda; his marriage equation is 1+1=2. Nothing is really new under the sun. I love my life today after choosing God's way but used to hate it while choosing Satan's ways.

A house divided will not stand. Removing sex from the context of marriage is devastating and less than what God intends for you. God, our Father, knows you and knows your human true love. Trust Him! Be still and know He is God (Psalm 46:10).

The two most important commandments are these: love God with all your heart, soul and mind, and love yourself so that you can love others as yourself (Matthew 22:37-40). Loving yourself is respecting yourself and understanding that you deserve God's best, as well as being willing to wait for it. In the meantime, Jesus is your husband!

For your Creator will be your husband; the Lord of Heaven's Armies is his name He is your Redeemer, the Holy One of Israel, the God of all the earth. (Isaiah 54:5 NLT)

The Divine Valentine

Each year millions of Americans send valentine greetings to each other. Here I share with you a reminder my dear husband gave me about God as our Divine Valentine:

A Valentine may play a love song for you but God sings you the sweetest love song in the universe. "The Lord your God ... will rejoice over you with singing" (Zephaniah 3:17).

A Valentine may give you flowers, but God sent you the most beautiful rose of all, Jesus. "I am the rose of Sharon and the lily of the valleys" (Song of Solomon 2:1).

A Valentine may take you out to dinner but God has invited you to the most amazing feast ever given. "Blessed are those who are called to the marriage supper for the Lamb!" (Revelation 19:9).

A Valentine may bring you chocolate, but God provides you with something even sweeter, His Word. "How sweet are your words to my taste, sweeter than honey to my mouth" (Psalm 119:103).

A Valentine may love you for a lifetime, but God loved you before you were born and will love you for all eternity! "Yes, I have loved you with an everlasting love" (Jeremiah 31:3).

A Letter to You

As the above became a reminder letter from my God-given fiancé (now husband) to me while waiting upon God's plan, here is a letter from your future husband to you (author and original title unknown):

Dear Beloved,

Everyone longs to give themselves completely to someone . . . to have a deep intimate relationship with another, to be loved thoroughly and exclusively. To a Christian, God says, "I cannot give you the person you were created for until you are satisfied, content, and fulfilled with being loved by Me alone."

Until we discover that only in God is our satisfaction found, we will not be capable of the human relationship God has planned for us. We will not be united with one another until we are united with Him . . . exclusive of anyone else, and exclusive of any other longings or desires.

I love you. I want us to stop planning, stop wishing, and allow God to give us the most thrilling plan in existence . . . one that we cannot imagine. I want you to have the best. Please allow Him to bring us together. Just keep watching Him, expecting the greatest things. Keep experiencing the satisfaction of knowing that He is enough. Keep listening to and learning the things that God tells you.

We have to wait. Don't be anxious. Don't worry. Don't look around at things others have gotten. Don't look at the things you think you want. We just have to keep looking up at Him, or we'll miss what He wants to show us.

And then, when we are both ready, He'll surprise us with a love far more wonderful than we could ever dream. You see, until we are both ready and we are both satisfied with Him and the life He has prepared for us, we won't be able to experience the love that exemplifies our relationship with Him . . . and that is perfect love.

My love, I do want you to have this most won-derful love. I want you to see in the flesh a picture of your relationship with God and to enjoy materially and concretely the everlasting union of beauty, per-fection, and love that He has offered us. Know I love you utterly. Believe and be satisfied.

Lovingly,
Your Husband

God, your perfect Heavenly Father, desires you to wait patiently for the earthly husband that He is preparing and planning for you.

Dear sister in Christ, Princess of the Living God and our King, don't deny Him the privilege. He has a divine purpose for your life here on earth that will glorify Him alone and bring you an abundant life, blessing many people around you.

"For no eye has seen, no ear has heard and no mind has imagined what God has prepared for those who love Him!" (I Corinthians 2:9) This is your wedding preparation for eternity!

"The Lord bless you and keep you; the Lord make his face shine on you and be gracious to you; the Lord turn his face toward you and give you peace." (Numbers 6:24-26).